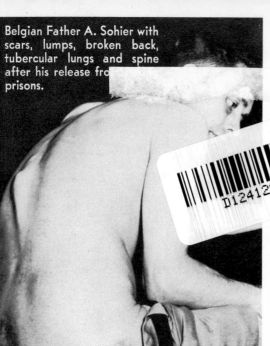

Belgian Father A. Sohier with scars, lumps, broken back, tubercular lungs and spine after his release fro[m] prisons.

(Courtesy, Mission Bulletin, Hong Kong)

Communist travel pass for train to Kioshan, Honan.

Some of the half million demonstrators at the First Anniversary celebration of the Chinese People's Republic.

(Sovfoto)

AUGSBURG PUBLISHING HOUSE

MINNEAPOLIS

BY HAROLD H. MARTINSON

red dragon over china

red dragon over china

Library of Congress Catalog Card No. 56-9461

Sketches by anonymous Chinese artist in Hong Kong
Maps and charts by Paul Konsterlie

Printed and manufactured in the United States of America
by Augsburg Publishing House, Minneapolis 15, Minnesota

dedicated

to my mother who this year in Hong Kong
celebrates her eighty-eighth birthday
and the fifty-fourth anniversary
of her coming to China;

to my wife without whose help this under-
taking would have been impossible;

to my sisters who have given unstinted encouragement and inspiration; and

to my children who have shown such vital
interest and have so freely helped.

foreword

THERE have been a great many books and articles written about Communism in China in recent years. Most of them follow one of three patterns. The first is biographical, wherein the author relates personal incidents concerning his own experience with members of the Communist party. The second is general, dealing with the entire problem on the basis of principle and theory. The third is reports of delegates of "peace missions," giving opinions often based on brief observation. The problem of Communism in China is too complex to be fully stated by any one method. Principle is involved, but the problem becomes acute when it reaches the individual. The individual is involved, but only because a principle is established in his country that affects all members of society as well as him personally. It is clear that "conducted tours" arranged by the Communist party are not a suitable basis for an objective study. We have had need of a book that could combine a study of the historical application of Communist principles in China with its effect upon the people of that nation. *Red Dragon Over China* is such a book. With a thorough knowledge of China, Mr. Martinson has produced an interesting story authenticated by factual accounts and enlivened by personal illustrations.

Casual observers have considered Chinese Communism to be of recent origin. The reader will be interested to note that it had a long and checkered history before it reached its present domination of the country. Mr. Martinson has lived in China through this period and traces its development in the first part of the book.

The second part of the book gives a series of case studies of Communism as it has affected the people. These studies present people of many ages, stages in life, occupations, and nationalities. The sum result of all these studies, each one an interesting story complete in itself, will do more to inform us as to the result of Communism than any theoretical dissertation.

Having spent most of his life in China, Mr. Martinson has studied Chinese Communism and its actual results in the country as well as its effect on the people. He has presented these matters to us in a concise and interesting form. We consider it an excellent contribution to present-day literature about Communist China.

R. A. SYRDAL

TABLE OF CONTENTS

part one : the cataclysm

part two : they saw it

author's preface

THIS book is presented to the public more from a sense of duty than from a sense of choice. Having witnessed at close hand the workings of Communism, I feel constrained as a Christian to inform, to warn, to arouse as many as possible against this terrifying blight.

In all my research I have not come across a single satisfactory survey of the rise of Communism in China. Hence in Part I of this book I have attempted to give a running account of Communism's take-over of that country. I have tried to avoid cluttering up the pages with a large number of footnotes. Rather, the documentation is contained in the bibliography.

In Part II, where I have presented case-histories under the new regime, I have followed a chronological order. For apparent reasons I have kept to anonymity, and my Chinese friends mentioned have been given fictitious names. I have made no attempt to "edit" the reports to eliminate repetitions. That would destroy the value of the source material. I have simply collected the reports as they were given from various sections of China separated by hundreds and thousands of miles. The repetitions emphasize the universally sinister character of this movement.

I wish to thank all who have in any way given a helping hand in this venture.

HAROLD H. MARTINSON

PART ONE

the cataclysm

And another portent appeared in heaven:
behold, a great red dragon—that ancient serpent,
who is called the Devil and Satan, the
deceiver of the whole world!

REVELATION 12:3, 9

CHAPTER ONE

a startling contrast

I WAS waiting at the station all set to go. It was exciting to be back in China after the exhausting war, and to see the new hope and expectancy and determination etched upon the faces of the people. Now there would be peace and reconstruction and a chance to pick up the threads of life where they had been rudely broken. There was an unmistakable lightheartedness to be seen, too, born of the realization that the war was over.

Suddenly there was the toot of a Dodge truck. The train was arriving. Yes, it was a Dodge truck pulling four or five old remodeled buses behind it—all rigged with train wheels and running on the railroad tracks! The old Peiping-Hankow trains had been destroyed by the war or moved elsewhere by the Japanese. This was one of their "little trains" which they had set up to keep communications going.

I was bewildered as I scanned the train. It looked more like a beehive than a means of transportation. The platforms were crowded and people were balancing precariously on the steps, clinging to the bars.

"How can I ever get on this thing?" I said to my friends.

Grabbing my bedding roll in one hand and my suitcase in the other, I hobbled the length of the train trying to wedge my way into each platform—but all in vain. There was not a square inch of free space where I might get a toe hold. I despaired of being able to make the trip into our field. The bright visions of seeing old friends and of having joyous fellowship with them once more began to fade from my mind. The train was ready to pull out. The flag man was about to give his signal. That I had bought a ticket meant nothing. Nobody was able to help me.

Suddenly, with the ingenuity born of necessity, my colleagues hoisted me up in the air and stuck me head first through an open window. I landed on a number of people but gradually worked my way to rock bottom. My bedding roll and suitcase tumbled in after me and the train was off.

I had noticed in the confusion that there were scowls on the faces of those who were already packed in the train tighter than sardines. But I also noticed that it was not long before those scowls gave way to pleasant smiles. Seeing that I was a foreigner—and a big one at that—the passengers nearest me struck up a conversation.

According to Chinese etiquette personal questions reveal personal interest. The inevitable questions came one after another.

"Your honorable name?"

"My unworthy name is Mr. Horse."

"And your eminent given name?"

"Born from Heaven."

"Oh, that is a good name, it smacks of real Chinese—Heavenly-born Horse. And may I ask you your honorable country?"

The eyes of all in the car were riveted on me. With a laugh I said, "Oh, I am Chinese."

With this remark a chain reaction was set up. Said one, "Yes, he must be Chinese, he talks just like one."

"No," said another, "can't you see his light hair and his eyes?"

Chimed in a third, "But if I didn't look at him I could swear from hearing him that he was Chinese."

"Indeed," said a little man in the corner, "he talks clearer than we do."

"But his face is white," added still another. "He must be Russian."

I sat there enjoying the debate and the pointed remarks about my long nose and special features. They were discussing me objectively with no intention of bringing insults. They seemed oblivious of the fact now that I could even understand all that they were saying about me. They were after the truth, much like a farmer who pokes around in the mouth of a horse, examining its teeth to find out its age.

"Come on," persisted the skeptic, "you aren't Chinese. Tell us what country you come from."

"Well, if you really want to know, I belong to the Kingdom of Heaven."

Puzzlement came over the faces of the hearers! "We have heard of the Warrior Kingdom (Great Britain) and of the Law Kingdom (France) and of the Rising Sun Kingdom (Japan), but never of the Heaven Kingdom. What country is that?"

Having come to China as a missionary to share with the people of that great land the glorious Gospel of our Lord Jesus Christ, I told my newly won friends about the grace and love of God which embraces *all* mankind. Even Confucius had said, "All within the four seas are brothers." The Bible says: "For God so loved the *world* that he gave his only Son, that whoever believes in him should not

perish but have eternal life." Christ died that we might
be loosed from our sins and all who believe on Him are
born into His Kingdom—the Kingdom of Heaven.

With eagerness my friends received the Christian tracts
which I distributed among them. Perhaps I would never
see them again. A prayer arose from my heart on their
behalf.

"If you wish to know," I said, "I am from the Beautiful
Kingdom (America)."

Immediately faces lit up and some of my fellow-travelers
extended their right thumbs in approval. "Good, good!
America and China are the best of friends. American flour
is wonderful, whiter than anything we have seen. America
sent us much flour during times of famine. Had not America helped us, we would never have won the war."

"Yes," I said. "China and America are the best of friends.
America has never coveted Chinese soil and her fondest
hope is that China may grow united and prosperous."

"You speak just like us!" said a man several seats from
me. "How long is it since you came to this country?"

"Oh," I answered, puckering my brow as though in
deep thought. "It is now some over forty years since I
first arrived here."

An "ah-h-h" of respect broke forth from my listeners,
as that was truly an honorable length of time.

"But," pursued a heavy-set gentleman who looked like
a merchant, "how old are you, then?"

All were listening intently, as we jerked along. "How
old do you guess me to be?"

Again there was a lively discussion.

"You must be eighty years old," replied a young phi-
losopher to my left.

"Never!" said the merchant. "You can see he doesn't
look that old. He must be only sixty."

The young thinker stood his ground. "He must have been over thirty when he came to this country and he has been here over forty years. What else could he be but eighty? Besides you see how he has lost his hair and what he has left of it has turned light."

I let them argue back and forth. Most of them agreed that I could not be eighty, that I must be around sixty. Finally I told them, "I will be forty-one next birthday." Seeing unbelief written on their faces, I added, "You see, I was born in China. That is why I told you that I was Chinese, because I am practically a Chinese." A burst of laughter broke out. Now they saw how it all hung together. With the puzzle solved they began to relax.

The day was wearing on. A couple of chickens tied together, belonging to a woman seated on her bedding roll in the aisle, objected to the cramped conditions and started to squawk and flop their wings violently. Dust and feathers flew in all directions. At station stops those nearest the windows leaned out and bought tea and delicacies. With typical Chinese generosity they offered me twisted doughnuts or salted duck eggs. Thanking them profusely I declined, saying that I had brought lunch along, but a drink of tea would be welcome.

In the late afternoon we neared Kikungshan (Rooster Mountain)—replete with memories for me. There I had been born. There I had spent most of my childhood years. There my father had died when I was only eight, and there my mother, with three small children, had courageously continued as an independent missionary, establishing new work among the sturdy mountain people.

In those days the hillside paths and winding roads had been peaceful and inviting. As children of missionaries, my two sisters and I had hiked by ourselves far into the heart of the mountains, following the meandering river whose white sands had always beckoned to us as we gazed westward from our mountain home. These all-day hikes had been full of interest, had struck a natural chord in our hearts. From the tall trees and the bushes birds called to us. Peasants were working in their fields. Wheelbarrows loaded with merchandise were squeaking along the rutted roads like so many cicadas in the summer time. We were happy and carefree. To supplement our picnic lunch we would buy sesame seed candy or glutinous-rice cakes—with never a question as to how many times these had been handled by unwashed hands. Laughingly and jokingly we visited with the curious crowds in their own tongue. Even at dusk of day or at nightfall, if we had not reached home, there had been no feeling of uncertainty or fear. These had been some of the experiences which had worked in our hearts an abiding love for the common people of China.

When in the thirties my wife and I had come out as missionaries and had been stationed in this very district, how different things had been! Added to warlordism, the far more sinister movement of Communism had been destroying the peace and freedom of the countryside. It had become highly dangerous, especially for foreigners, to venture among the mountains without first making thorough inquiry as to the whereabouts of the Red "bandits." Already several of our missionaries had been kidnapped and one had perished at the hands of the Communists. For a couple of seasons during the broiling heat we had not even dared to live at the missionary summer resort on Rooster Mountain. Then had come the Japanese war, and chaos had deepened.

A few jerks of the train and a halt brought my reveries up to date. "All hands out!" yelled the conductor. "Can't make the grade. Everybody out and push!"

It was not a bad idea. Most of us had been cramped all day in our positions on hard wooden benches, not daring to get out at the stations to stretch our limbs for fear of not being able to get in again. Tickled as children going out on a picnic, we got unraveled from the car. With hundreds of hands pushing the train, the Dodge engine came to life and sputtered forward. The spring breeze blowing into our faces was exhilarating. Flowers were blooming along the roadbed, and birds singing. Slowly we pushed the train over the hump until the wheels moved automatically. Though we had a hard time scrambling aboard again, this time everyone was accommodating and we fitted ourselves into our proper places like pieces of a Chinese puzzle. In another two hours we arrived at our destination.

Whether on this train trip, or in my contacts on our field, or in my travels to Chungking, the war time capital, where my assignment was to supervise the moving of the Lutheran Theological Seminary back to its old home in central China—everywhere I met with friendliness on the part of the Chinese. Except for a portion of the intellectuals who resented the blundering policies of the United States in the Far East, no matter whether the people were Christians or pagans, merchants or farmers, officials or ordinary folk, I sensed the existence of the "reservoir of goodwill." I was born in China and spent most of my life there, yet I may freely say that I had never experienced so much goodwill and such receptivity to the message which the missionary had to bring. The Chinese knew that the missionaries were their best friends. Scattered throughout the country—nearly ten thousand of them, Catholic and Protestant—they had stayed on during the Japanese war. Before Pearl Harbor they had, as neutrals, sheltered thousands of refugees, especially women and girls, in their compounds, risking their lives, experiencing bombings and invasions. After Pearl Harbor those in occupied territory had been interned and had suffered privations. The Chinese knew this and now they were willing to listen to what the missionary had to say. Reports were coming from missionaries on the vast plains of Honan. Never before had there been such crowds gathering to hear the Gospel. Never before had there been such receptivity to the preaching of the Word. Many of us looked forward to unprecedented opportunities, to an era of evangelism such as China had never seen before. At our Seminary we had the largest enrollment in the history of our institution.

But today in China—! All we hear is an outcry of anti-American hatred. Again and again and again the venomous words are spewed forth at international councils and over the radio and press. All missionaries (except those that have been killed and a few still in prison or under house arrest) have been expelled. Are the Chinese people so fickle? Those they esteem one day, do they despise the next? What is the explanation of this great change which has so suddenly come over this once friendly nation? In order to understand this problem we need to turn back a few pages in history and study an astounding phenomenon.

For centuries whenever there has been an eclipse, the Chinese have believed that the dragon is swallowing up the sun or the moon. With a great deal of noise and fanfare—the banging of drums and of tin pans—the people have tried to scare the dragon into disgorging what it has devoured. So far they have always been successful.

But today China herself has been swallowed by the *Great Red Dragon*—and there seems to be no prospect in sight that the dragon will be forced to disgorge its victim!

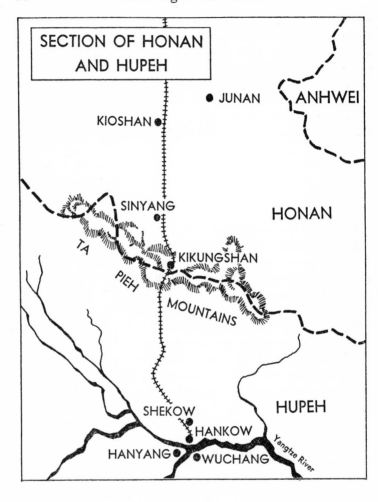

dragon egg hatches

"THE shortest way to Paris," said Lenin while scheming for world conquest—"the shortest way to Paris lies through Peking." Skeptical and unheedful of this fateful dictum the Western world has permitted a tiny nuclear disturbance, so to speak, to swell and mushroom into catastrophic, world-enveloping death clouds.

Who at the time of Lenin's statement would have guessed that a few decades later International Communism would actually have arrived at that way station of Peking? The general opinion was that China could never be Bolshevized because Communism ran counter to all that China's ancient culture stood for. Yet, today we see it as an accomplished fact.

Before the Russian Revolution of 1917 there was in China little interest in Marxism. In the *New Youth* magazine, founded in 1915 and used as a mouthpiece of the intelligentsia who ushered in the period known as the Chinese Renaissance, there was discussion of all types of Western philosophies and movements but little mention of Karl Marx. His outlook was considered irrelevant to

China's needs. But when the Russian Revolution transpired, the Chinese intellectuals, disgusted with the warlordism of their day and the failure of their own republic
modeled after France and the United States, showed
widespread interest in Russia's experimentation and
wondered if it might not be pertinent to their own problem. Dr. Sun Yat-sen, who was fighting an uphill battle
against China's internal chaos and getting little help from
the Western democracies, watched the Russian development hopefully. When Russia's Communism emerged
victorious, Dr. Sun, evading the censorship of the French
Concession in Shanghai, sent a telegram of congratula-
tions via America to Lenin whom he may have met previously during his travels in Europe. The young intellectuals of China, a considerable number of them returned
students from abroad, on hearing about this gesture of
their national hero applauded warmly, and many, including Mao Tse-tung and Chou En-lai, were being condi-
tioned to fall easy prey to the Communist world-wide
conspiracy.

From this time on a steady stream of Soviet agents and
propaganda (the latter coming largely through Japan to
begin with) invaded China and found a generation of
intelligentsia eager to be persuaded. In the National University in Peking, while Dr. Hu Shih and Ch'en Tu-hsiu
were heading the literary revolution, another outstanding
professor, Li Ta-chao, was leading a group of students in
the study of Marxism. Li Ta-chao on his return from Japan
had become librarian at the university, with student Mao
Tse-tung as his helper for a time. Later he became Professor of History. In the spring of 1918 he founded the
Society for the Study of Marxism comprised mainly of
students, including Chang Kuo-t'ao, his favorite, Mao Tse-
tung, Ch'ü Ch'iu-pai and others, who acquainted them-

selves with and critically examined the doctrines of Marxism.

After the success of the Russian Revolution the Communist Third International plotted the conquest of the world. Their agents were sent far and wide—even to Australia—to foment revolution. Being largely foiled in the more advanced countries of Europe and America they turned their attention chiefly toward Asia. In 1918 they established the Revolutionary Mongol People's Party to subvert Mongolia. By January, 1919, the Chinese Workingmen's Association had been organized in Russia with a membership of sixty thousand and with the avowed purpose of "carrying on revolutionary propaganda and establishing Soviets in China." Continuous appeals and offers of help were sent by Moscow to the Chinese. In March a message was sent to Dr. Sun in Canton praising him for his struggle against Peking the "puppet of foreign bankers" and against the "foreign imperialistic governments of oppression" and inviting the Chinese proletariat to join the Russian.

On May 4 a patriotic movement of intense heat burst forth among the students of Peking and spread throughout the nation. It was the fourth anniversary of Japan's humiliating Twenty-one Demands, violating China's sovereignty, and the news had just reached Peking of the betrayal of China by the West at Versailles where, in spite of the fact that China was one of the allies, the peace treaty transferred the German concessions in Shantung to Japan over the protest of the Chinese delegates. The two Peking University professors, Ch'en Tu-hsiu and Li Tachao, who had by this time come under the influence of Marxism, organized the movement. Ch'en Tu-hsiu addressed the five thousand students of Peking University and suggested that they elect committees to contact other institutions of learning throughout the city and environs and get each student body organized so all could act as one. A Peking Student Union was formed. Their purpose was to overthrow the government which had yielded to Japan's Demands. In the afternoon of the same day ten thousand students gathered at a mass meeting, then marched to the headquarters of the government, burned down the house of the minister of communications and through subsequent demonstrations, boycotts and strikes eventually forced the government to give way and the three pro-Japanese ministers—"national traitors"—to flee for their lives to Japan. The May Fourth movement was the father of the large student demonstrations which periodically arose from this time on throughout the country and of the organization of the students on a national basis.

One active youth at this time was Chou En-lai, the son of an official and grandson of a mandarin. He had attended an American-financed Middle School (high school) in Tientsin and was just back from a year of study in Japan. He now led student demonstrations and organized the Awaken Society for studying democracy, anarchism, nihilism and socialism as possible ways of saving the country. Years later he was to attain the Vice-chairmanship of Communist China as well as fill the positions of premier and foreign minister.

The great bulk of the students at this time knew little about Communism but they were intensely patriotic. However, World Communism was not slow to capitalize on the situation, and Mao Tse-tung even points to this movement as the beginning of Communism in China. In his *New Democracy* he writes:

"The 'May Fourth Movement' gave birth to a brand new culture of great vitality into which was breathed the Communist thought under the inspiration of Chinese Communists—that is, this phase of the Cultural rebirth owed its origin largely to the cosmic outlook of Communism and to the theory of the social revolution."

Again: "The 'May Fourth Movement' was thus responding, as it were, to the clarion call of the world revolution, of the Russian revolution led by Lenin, and became a component part of the proletarian world revolution. Although at this time the Chinese Communist party had not yet come into existence, a preponderant number of intellectuals were in active sympathy with the Russian Revolution. Like men possessed, the Chinese intellectuals were greatly stirred with the Communist thought."

From this time on Communist literature progressively increased. Secret presses printed an abundance of propaganda including translations of the writings and speeches of Marx and Lenin of which perhaps the most important was a speech by Lenin from the previous year urging the whole Orient to rise against imperialism. Students flocked to Russia for further enlightenment and the Soviets sent a secret agent, M. Popoff, to Shanghai to explore the possibilities and report back to Moscow.

Taking advantage of the bitter disappointment of the intelligentsia in the raw deal received at Versailles, Moscow made sweeping and flattering offers to win the Chinese. On July 25, L. M. Karakhan, Acting Commissar for Foreign Affairs, issued the famous Manifesto to the Chinese People with its high-sounding, deceptive phrases:

"All people, whether they are great or small, whether they have lived until now a free life, or whether they form against their own will a part of another country, shall be free in their inner life, and no power shall interfere with them within this limit. The Government of Workers and

Peasants has therefore declared null and void all the
secret treaties concluded with Japan, China and the ex-
Allies, the treaties which were to enable the Russian
Government of the Czar and his Allies to enslave the
people of the East. . . .

"We herewith address the Chinese people with the
object of making them thoroughly understand that the
Soviet Government has given up all the conquests made
by the Government of the Czar, which took away from
China Manchuria and other territories. . . ."

The Manifesto then promises to return to China the
Manchurian railway, the mining and other concessions,
the Boxer indemnities, and to cancel all extraterritorial
privileges. Innumerable copies of this manifesto were
printed in Shanghai and distributed throughout China.
This offer to treat China on a basis of absolute equality
was something never experienced by the Chinese before
in their dealings with the Powers, and it served, as intended, to make Soviet Russia tremendously popular, especially among the intelligentsia and revolutionaries.

It was at this time that Professor Ch'en Tu-hsiu made
contact with the Communist Third International, looking
forward to the establishment of the Communist Party in
China which took place less than two years later.

Toward the end of the year a young Russian named
Ivanov, who had been active in the Russian revolution,
was sent to the Peking University ostensibly to teach
French and Russian. Not long after that the President of
the All-China Students Association sent a letter to the
People's Commissioners at Moscow conveying to the Russian students (whom he called brothers), to the Soviets,
and to Lenin the admiration of all the students in China
for their splendid work in liberating Russia. Almost

simultaneously another letter using identical terms was dispatched to Moscow by the Kuomintang Party, of which Dr. Sun Yat-sen was leader. There could be little doubt as to who had dictated these letters.

In 1920 Lenin dispatched Marlin, his energetic and persuasive secretary, to China to confer with Sun Yat-sen and the northern factions and also to further the establishment of a Communist Party. In Shanghai Professor Ch'en Tu-hsiu with seven other persons who called themselves Communists started a proletarian newspaper and began organizing trade unions. Before long similar activities appeared in other major cities.

The same year the Third International convened a Congress of Oriental Nations in Baku where China was represented presumably by Li Ta-chao. The most important result of this Congress was the establishment of a Council for Propaganda and Action in the Countries of the Orient.

Another agent of the Third International, Grigori Voitinsky, was sent to China, and he together with Marlin were the active instruments for getting the Chinese Communist Party organized. Voitinsky contacted Li Ta-chao in Peking and Ch'en Tu-hsiu in Shanghai. Then Ch'en Tu-hsiu, with the Comintern agents as advisers, summoned a conference at Shanghai. There in July, 1921, at a girls' school in the French concession, the Chinese Communist Party was founded with about twelve original members, including Ch'en Tu-hsiu, the chairman (who was deposed from the Party leadership in 1927 for deviationism), Li Ta-chao (who was apprehended during the Peking government's raid on the Soviet embassy in 1927 and strangled), Chang Kuo-t'ao (who was expelled from the Party in 1938) and Mao Tse-tung. Before the secret meeting could be concluded the Concession police interfered, causing the members to flee to Shaohsing, Chekiang, where they concluded their deliberations in a boat on the sparkling waters of Lake Niehpu.

The following month, with financial help from Voitinsky, the Socialist Youth Corps was formed in Shanghai. After the founding of the Communist Party, branch organizations were established in Hunan (in October) and in other provinces and cities, while cells were formed in the government Kuomintang and in educational institutions throughout the country. The next year the Party became affiliated with the Third International. Activities were kept highly secret and membership slowly increased.

The Red Dragon had been hatched in China.

feeling its strength

WHILE the foregoing ominous events were transpiring in China, thousands of miles away other young Chinese had been infected with Communism and were banding together to further the cause in their homeland. Toward the close of World War I, because of the French manpower shortage, Mao Tse-tung had gone to Peking to further a scheme for getting thousands of Chinese students to go to France in the "work and learn" battalions, whereby they could work for the French part time and study in the schools part time, learning modern philosophies and techniques together with the methods of socialism, anarchism and revolution. By the end of 1920 about two thousand students had gone under this plan, among them Nieh Jung-chen from a wealthy farm home in West China; Li Li-san, a fiery nineteen-year-old youth; Ch'en Yi, a native of Szechwan; and Chou En-lai. The French Communists were out in front to welcome them and to subvert them. Chou En-lai kept in contact with the Communist leaders and in 1921, together with Li Li-san and others, organized the Chinese branch of the French

Communist Party. Continuing for several years to study
and work, he made use of his spare time delving into
Marxist literature and helping to found party branches in
Berlin, London and Marseille. In Berlin he came across
a former debauched Nationalist warlord, named Chu
Teh, who was anxious to reform and was studying military
science under a Prussian staff officer in hopes of returning
to China and being of some use. Chou En-lai recruited
him for the Party and eventually he became the commander-in-chief of the Red armies. During these years
Chou En-lai visited the Third International or Comintern
headquarters where he met Stalin and others of the
hierarchy. Deeply impressed with his abilities and suave
character, they marked him as a man of value.

While Russian agents were training future leaders for
the take-over of China, their armed forces were pressing
upon border states to hasten the process of subversion.
In March, 1921, a provisional Mongol government was
proclaimed in Russian territory. Previously Mongolia had
been considered as belonging to China. Following this
proclamation Soviet troops invaded Outer Mongolia in
the name of the newly created "republic" and captured
Urga the capital. On July 6 the Revolutionary Mongol
People's Government was established and, because of the
circumstances, it "petitioned" Moscow not to withdraw
her troops. These were then maintained in Outer Mongolia for some years, after which the territory was firmly
established in the Soviet sphere. This action created difficulty with the impotent warlord rulers of Peking, but
Russia had other methods for overcoming that. She sent
her agents, one after another, to propagandize the Chinese and placate the divided government.

In 1921 Yurin was sent to Peking but when his baggage
was found to be full of propaganda materials printed in

Chinese he could make no headway with the government. He was replaced with Paikes who did no better, though both these agents were able to get the ear of the intelligentsia. When the third envoy came in the summer of 1922—Mr. A. Joffe, a former ambassador at Berlin who had promoted Communist insurrection in Germany—he was warmly welcomed and feted by the head of the National University and by the students—but not so heartily by the skeptical government. This alien Red, more blatantly patriotic for China than the Chinese themselves, made splendid use of his stay by spreading propaganda, vilifying the "imperialist nations" and "capitalists" and furthering Communist activities in the capital. At the National University the lecture courses of Ivanov (mentioned previously) and other Russian helpers changed to political discussions. Coolies on the streets soon became familiar with slogans such as "Proletarians of the world, unite!" "Immediate recognition of Soviet Russia!" "Down with capitalism and imperialism!" Joffe also began organizing the sympathetic teachers and students in all the schools. In one school twenty groups of students were organized and assigned the task of preaching Bolshevism along the railways as far as Shanghai in one direction and Hankow in the other. When the authorities closed the school, student and labor demonstrations forced them to open it again. The Soviet news agency *Rosta,* established in Peking, filled the press with propaganda reflecting on the integrity of the West. Red articles were printed in magazines and Red magazines multiplied in number— and the authorities were powerless to control the situation.

When Joffe's negotiations with the government bogged down, a still more important personage was sent from Moscow—the foreign minister Mr. Karakhan himself. He was welcomed with open arms by the same group of intelligentsia and admirers who had received Joffe and he built upon the foundations laid by the latter. He filled the press with diatribes against the other Powers and pleaded for recognition of Moscow. Here is a sample of his style:

"The great Chinese nation, with her ancient culture, her profound love of peace, her wonderful industry, is the best ally that Russia could have in the Orient. China and Russia are in the same position internationally. We Russians have just won a bitter battle against the imperialist Powers who sought to make our country their colony. China is still fighting an identical battle to free herself from colonial dependence on those same Powers. She must keep up her fight until her liberation is complete."

Karakhan raised himself to the position of ambassador —all the other foreign envoys were ministers—and this automatically made him president of the diplomatic corps in Peking, greatly increasing his influence. With not the slightest intention of fulfilling the terms, he finally was able to conclude a treaty with the Peking government using such high-sounding phrases as the following:

"The Government of the Union of Soviet Socialist Republics recognizes that Outer Mongolia is an integral part of the Republic of China, and respects China's sovereignty therein."

"The Governments of the two Contracting Parties further pledge themselves not to engage in propaganda directed against the political and social systems of either Contracting Party."

In spite of repeated protests from China and corresponding assurances of unselfish intentions and noble purposes on the part of Moscow, Outer Mongolia, as stated before, slipped out of Chinese control and became one of the Union of Soviet Socialist Republics.

In May, 1922, the Communist-inspired First All-China Labor Congress and First Congress of the China Socialist Youth League were convened in Canton. The same year, the Third International summoned at Moscow the First Congress of the Toilers of the Far East in order to implement the decisions previously reached at the Baku conference. The University of the Toilers of the Far East, which Chu Teh attended, was established to give technical training to labor propagandists. Other universities were thrown open and special courses created to take care of the increasing flow of Chinese students whose traveling expenses were paid by Moscow.

At this time the Kremlin grand strategy had come around to emphasizing the policy of co-operation between Communists and "bourgeois nationalists." Since the Northern warlords of China were less co-operative, it was decided to form a "united front" with the Kuomintang government of Sun Yat-sen. Accordingly a Comintern agent, Dalin, was given the responsibility of negotiating with Dr. Sun for a Communist-Kuomintang alliance, and Marlin called a special meeting of the Central Committee of the Chinese Communist Party in August, 1922, at Hangchow where he imposed on the Chinese comrades the Kremlin decision that they join the Kuomintang and bore from within. At the Fourth Congress of the Comintern, held in Moscow three months later and attended by Ch'en Tu-hsiu who hesitated to join the Kuomintang, Radek came with a scathing rebuke for the Chinese delegates for harboring "too rosy expectations" and "overestimating" their strength in thinking they could work independently of the Kuomintang. Here the policy of collaboration with the Nationalist Party was underscored.

When Joffe's mission to the government in Peking had failed he had slipped away to Shanghai to hasten the process of persuading the southern faction led by Sun Yat-sen. Here, through a series of interviews, he impressed upon Dr. Sun the necessity of co-operation, but cleverly camouflaged the real intentions of the Comintern when, in January, 1923, he issued with Dr. Sun a joint statement setting forth their "most cordial and friendly" relations:

"Dr. Sun Yat-sen holds that the Communistic order or even the Soviet system cannot actually be introduced into China, because there do not exist here the conditions for the successful establishment of either Communism or Sovietism. This view is entirely shared by Mr. Joffe, who is further of the opinion that China's paramount and most pressing problem is to achieve national unification and attain full national independence, and regarding this task, he has assured Dr. Sun that China has the warmest sympathy of the Russian people, and can count on the support of Russia."

As a result of this accord the Kuomintang was thrown open to Communist Party members before the year was over.

After the issuing of the joint statement Joffe came in contact with a trusted friend and revolutionary co-worker of Dr. Sun who subsequently became the governor of Kwangtung. Quietly he indoctrinated him in the importance of peasant and labor movements in the revolutionary program and converted him into a staunch supporter of Russian policies which he later put into practice.

At this juncture a young man of iron will and rare capabilities was forging to the front. During Dr. Sun Yat-sen's political set-backs Chiang Kai-shek had faithfully stood by him and now had become his chief of staff. Chiang was rewarded with a six-month trip to Moscow to study firsthand the Soviet system and military organization.

As a result of the agreement between Sun Yat-sen and Joffe a group of advisers were sent from Russia headed by Michael Borodin, the political strategist and former jewel smuggler, who had worked as Communist agent in Turkey, Persia and Scotland, and General Galen, a military genius. These men arrived in Canton during the fall of 1923. With three million rubles financial aid from Russia they set about to establish the Whampoa Military Academy which they staffed with over thirty Russian military experts—the number shortly increasing to nearly fifty. Upon his return from Moscow Chiang Kai-shek was appointed principal. This Academy became the heart and center of the revolutionary movement, the power-house for the coming Northern expedition. Fiery young patriots and radicals from all over the country were chosen to attend this institution where they were given, besides concentrated military training, intensive political indoctrination, with special emphasis on Soviet principles and methods. Within a couple years several thousand young officers were turned out who were not only military men but trained political propagandists—who, filled with zeal for a revolutionary cause, transformed the army of the South into a fighting machine.

Shortly after Borodin's arrival ships loaded with rifles, ammunition, and even airplanes, steamed up the Pearl River and, at Canton, disgorged their cargoes—a gift from Soviet Russia which Dr. Sun had previously sought in vain from the West. Borodin's task was made easier after Dr. Sun had threatened to seize the customs—whose revenues, according to international agreements, were being sent to Peking—and the Western Powers and Japan sent gunboats to Canton to forestall the action. After this episode Sun Yat-sen publicly declared, "We no longer look to the West. Our faces are turned toward Russia."

The Russian advisers were busy and efficient. Before the end of the year they had mapped out the reorganization of the Kuomintang Party, streamlining it according to the Soviet model with definite principles, compact unity, strict discipline, and civilian control of the army. The Kuomintang (National People's Party) had been organized by Sun Yat-sen in 1912 and was a direct outgrowth of earlier organizations fostered by him for the salvation of China. Membership was now thrown open to Communists, both Russian and Chinese, and it wasn't long before they achieved a position of outstanding power. By January, 1924, all was in readiness for convoking the First National Congress of the Kuomintang Party in Canton, where the policy of collaboration with Communists was officially adopted with the understanding that the Communists accept the Kuomintang principles and not vice versa. The Communist Party, however, continued to function separately and Borodin, the heavy-set foreigner with the thick mustache, had the enviable position of dictating to both Parties. A fighting Manifesto was issued which became one of the basic documents of the Revolution. The new platform was built around: co-operation with Russia and the Chinese Communists; anti-imperialism; and a program for workers and peasants.

Li Ta-chao, one of the founders of the Communist Party and the leader of the movement in the Peking area, issued the following statement:

"In joining the Kuomintang, Communists of the Third International are to obey Kuomintang discipline and to participate in the national revolution. They have not the slightest intention of turning the Kuomintang into a Communist party. Those Communists who join the Kuomintang do so as individuals and not on a party basis."

In spite of these reassuring words, the Communists by

principle were dedicated to the conspiratorial overthrow of the government and of all other parties. Yet Sun Yat-sen was taking their promises at face value and trustfully believing that International Communism would make no claims on the Chinese Revolution.

The Communist leaders, Ch'en Tu-hsiu and Li Ta-chao, were, of course, included in the high councils. Mao Tse-tung, who had worked overtime in Hunan organizing the miners, printers, employees of the railway and of the government mint, into radical unions, was elected to the Central Committee as a delegate from Hunan and placed in the Peasant Bureau of the Kuomintang. Other Communists were placed in the Bureaus of Finance and of Supplies. Because of their cohesive unity the Communists had influence far in excess of their numbers. Chou En-lai, a favorite of Moscow, was appointed vice-chairman and political director of the Whampoa Academy. Making use of this excellent opportunity he organized the Red cadets into an inner circle of conspirators. From this group there later emerged such famous Red generals as Lin Piao, Liu Po-ch'eng, Nieh Jung-chen, Yeh Chien-ying, Hsü Hsiang-ch'ien and others. In the new government Eugene Chen, a flaming radical, became the Minister of Foreign Affairs.

After this time, words and expressions originating in Russia filled the Nationalist propaganda. On every hand one heard about "comrades," "Imperialist Powers," "economic exploitation," "the Capitalist Class," "the peasants and workers," "the organization of the masses," "the exploited workers," "Christianity, the opiate of the people," and so on.

Russia's subversion of China's youth was snowballing. In 1925 the Sun Yat-sen University for Chinese was established in Moscow with an initial enrollment of about six hundred. The overflow of students was accommodated in the educational institutions of Leningrad, Irkutsk and other Russian cities. Some years later two more universities for Chinese only were established in Russia. In China itself besides Ambassador Karakhan's propagandizing of the youth, there sprang up Communist colleges and universities in Shanghai and other cities. In a police raid on one of these schools an immense quantity of subversive literature was uncovered. The Russians and their henchmen were so enthusiastic that Dr. Ma Soo, one-time Chinese representative to America, charged openly that the Bolshevik Ambassador in Peking was subsidizing groups of professors and students in practically every Chinese school in the country. In Canton Borodin started another college, the Political Training Institute.

During this year two political events occurred which electrified the already tense atmosphere. A worker had been killed by police action in Shanghai when about two hundred employees had been attempting to destroy the property of a cotton mill. Students and strikers organized largely by Li Li-san, thereupon tried to appeal to public opinion by putting on a demonstration on May 30 in the International Settlement where such things were forbidden by law. In the ensuing riots, from which Li Li-san emerged as a "hero," the British police killed twelve and wounded seventeen—mostly students. The Communists immediately seized upon this affair as a rallying point against foreigners, the unequal treaties, and the like. Propaganda with startling distortions was spread throughout China resulting in such unrest as had not been seen since the Boxer Uprising.

Following upon the heels of this disturbance came the June 23 incident, when a great anti-foreign demonstration was planned in Canton as a protest against the Shanghai affair. Workers, students, soldiers, Whampoa cadets formed a huge parade opposite the foreign concession. Then shooting began. Fifty Chinese were killed and over a hundred wounded over against three foreign casualties. It was reported that a Russian from a second-story window started the firing. The preponderance of evidence suggests that something like this set off the explosion. It was all in line with the Soviet strategy.

The results of these incidents were manifold. With the addition of concrete examples, propaganda became more effective among the masses. The man in the street did not know much about the provisions of the unequal treaties— but he did understand when Chinese students had been shot down on British orders. An anti-British boycott and strike were organized which lasted over fifteen months. Borodin said at this time: "We mean to strike at England in China." The stronger the spirit of nationalism—the fiercer the anti-foreign, and especially anti-British, hatred —the nearer would be the goal of world revolution. One hundred thousand Chinese workers—about one-eighth of the population—withdrew from Hongkong to Canton, paralyzing trade in that center and causing the British to sustain losses into the millions of pounds. Li Li-san, the Moscow-trained labor agitator, stirred up passions and established a great strike fund in Shanghai. Under Borodin's inspiration the efforts at building peasants' and workers' unions were redoubled. From this time on Mao Tsetung shifted his emphasis from the laborers to the peasants and spent several months in Hunan organizing the poor farmers for revolt until he had to flee for his life. Back in Canton he supervised the collaboration work of the two parties and lectured at the Military Academy, laying stress on the importance of the peasants and training workers in the task of organizing them. Making skilful use of the wide ramifications of the Kuomintang apparatus, he arranged for the arming of the peasants; as Deputy Minister of Propaganda he fed them with a stream of subversive literature and drew the blueprints for their coming revolt.

Throughout the nation the Christian movement came under adverse scrutiny—especially the many mission schools which were of the best in China. Toward the end of the year an extensive anti-Christian demonstration was prepared for the whole country.

The Communist maneuverings were not entirely free from trouble. Splits and factions were created in both the government and the Kuomintang as opposition crystallized against this alien system. Nevertheless, with their indomitable methods, the Communists steadily gained control and showed their hand more boldly. The Central Executive Committee of the Kuomintang openly declared: "Leninism is Sun Yat-senism." When Dr. Sun passed away in March, 1925, during a visit to Peking to seek national unity, the radicals tried to ally his memory with that of Lenin. In a message to Moscow they said: "We, the heirs of Sun Yat-sen, greet you, the heirs of Lenin." By early July a Communist government was set up in Canton under the direction of the Central Executive Committee of the Kuomintang. An article in the *China Weekly Review* complained saying, "Every factory and large shop [in the Province of Kwangtung] has one or more paid agents of the Soviet Mission."

In the army set-up the Communists were achieving a closely-knit control. The appointment of high commanding officers and the decisions on important military matters were made by the Communist-packed Central Executive Committee of the Kuomintang. Each general was watched closely by the head of the political department attached to his army. The various army staffs each had a Russian military adviser responsible only to Borodin. Even the

Commandant of the Whampoa Military Academy, Chiang Kai-shek, was supervised by a left-wing radical, Wang Ching-wei, who years later was to become the renegade puppet of the Japanese armies of occupation. Chou En-lai was appointed political commissar of Chiang Kai-shek's crack First Nationalist Army.

While the trap was being set in the South, in the North the Russians had been trying to cultivate the friendship of one or another warlord to be used as their pawn in the conquest of China. They had settled on the "Christian General," Feng Yü-hsiang, and openly boasted that he was "their man." For over a year truck trains of ammunition and supplies snaked their way through the Gobi Desert to Feng's military base at Kalgan. In March, 1926, at Karakhan's instigation, General Feng tried to blockade the port of Tientsin in violation of the international treaties. This brought him into difficulties with the Foreign Powers, and, as the armies of the opposing coalition of Chang Tso-lin, the Manchurian warlord, and Wu Pei-fu, the scholar-poet general, were closing in on him, his troops retreated to their Kalgan stronghold and he himself fled via the trans-Siberian railway to Moscow.

Meanwhile in Canton, Chiang Kai-shek, a true patriot and no Communist—though he was willing to use the Communists as the Communists were willing to use him—became more and more restive under their controls. He saw through their machinations, and in March, 1926—retaliating for two attempts on his life and taking advantage of Borodin's temporary absence—he sprang an almost bloodless *coup d'etat,* forcing Wang Ching-wei, who headed the government and the Kuomintang, into exile in Paris, disarming hostile troops and arresting several Russian advisers. However, the time was premature for a clear-cut break with the Communists. General Chiang, on the one side, could not afford to lose the help he was receiving from Russia—now that the Northern expedition was about to begin—and Borodin, on the other, not wishing to have his plans ruined by a party split at this juncture, had to postpone any thought of prosecution. On Borodin's return differences were patched up, the advisers were reinstated, and the alliance with Russia was reaffirmed.

Early in July, 1926, with General Galen as his chief of staff and with fifteen Russian advisers distributed throughout the fifty thousand man army in strategic positions of military and political authority, General Chiang Kai-shek started the Northern campaign.

At the head of the Political Bureau or Propaganda Department was a veteran pro-Communist, Teng Yen-ta. He sent plain-clothes agents ahead of the army, scattering vast quantities of leaflets, handbills and posters. They preached to the farmers and villagers, promising them easy wealth through confiscation of the property of the rich and of foreigners, and holding out to them a rosy future with lower prices and general prosperity if the foreigners were expelled and the Nationalists permitted to rule. They infiltrated into the enemy lines and honeycombed enemy territory. The warlords were helpless against this type of onslaught which they had never seen before. The heart of resistance was destroyed before the Nationalists arrived, some armies folding up and surrendering without a fight.

The Communist slant to the propaganda whipped up nationalistic frenzy against the missionary movement. It is an unfortunate fact that the Protestant missionary movement did come riding into China on the back of the unequal treaties. The Communists were quick to seize upon this fact and blow it up out of all proportion to reality.

They identified Christianity with "imperialism" and "cultural aggression" and persecuted its Chinese adherents as the "running dogs of the imperialists." Everywhere the political workers of the Nationalist forces were anti-Christian, and as the troops marched through the land they occupied mission schools, churches and hospitals, sometimes destroying them and often driving the missionaries away.

As the Southerners advanced they enlisted the help of students who gave orations on street corners against foreigners and extraterritoriality, placarded the towns with slogans and posters, and helped indoctrinate the turncoat soldiers. Political agents organized the people, whether they liked it or not, into peasants' and workers' unions and established local Communistic governments. The Nationalist campaign developed into an avalanche, the armies swelled to twice their original number and by September 6 they had captured Hankow in Central China.

Explaining their phenomenal achievements the Kuomintang, now almost under the control of the Communists, issued a bulletin saying: "The secret of our successes lies in the fact that the soldiers are true to the Kuomintang principles. Ours is an army of Party men. It has received not only a military training, but also political instruction in the Kuomintang principles. Every soldier is, at the same time, a Party worker." This insight into organization and methods was the great contribution of the Russians.

With the prospects of success seeming bright, the Executive Committee of the Comintern, meeting in Moscow in December, decided that the Chinese Communist Party should continue to collaborate with the Kuomintang and should redouble its efforts to gain control of that organization.

an abortive lunge

THE young Red Dragon was feeling its strength in China. One desperate lunge—and perhaps the whole country would be devoured! But it was not to be *yet*. The Red Dragon was to be foiled in its attempt and to come inches away from being beheaded.

In some over five years the Communist Party had grown from fifty in 1921 to nearly sixty thousand adults and thirty-five thousand junior members in 1927 besides an estimated two million eight hundred thousand trade-union workers and nine million seven hundred and twenty thousand organized peasants directly under their control. They occupied many positions of importance in the Kuomintang and the government. Stalin, through the Comintern, but with the violent opposition of Trotsky, was directing the Chinese Communists to "squeeze out the Right like lemons" and then seize control of the Kuomintang.

There had been indications that a showdown was building up. After the Nationalist armies had reached Hankow in the fall of 1926, Borodin had requested that an extraordinary session of the Central Executive Committee be held at Canton while Chiang Kai-shek was away leading the armies in the field. Since Borodin's aim was to establish a radical government based on the peasant and labor unions and in close touch with Moscow, it had been decided at this meeting to move the capital to Hankow and recall Wang Ching-wei from Paris to head it. Thereupon Borodin and the left-wing leaders had left for Hankow to put the plan into effect. Meanwhile Chiang Kai-shek had captured and set up his headquarters at Nanchang away from Communist control. Thither the remaining and more moderate members of the Central Executive Committee had gathered from Canton. Now Chiang called on the Hankow branch to come down and join him. This they refused to do and mutual recriminations followed. The rift was widening.

Chiang Kai-shek was becoming alarmed at the radical trend of the Communist-controlled left. The peasant unions in several provinces, especially in Hunan, were taking things into their own hands, immersing themselves in an orgy of blood, driving away or torturing and killing the landlords, destroying the land registers and dividing the land among the peasants. In the towns and villages open courts were held where victims were summarily tried and executed without defense. These acts of mob violence were done independently without any reference to the authorities in the government. Before long an All China Peasants' Union was organized with Mao Tse-tung as its first president. Early in 1927 Mao reported to the Central Committee on the peasant movement, deeply impressing Sydor Stoler, the new Comintern delegate from Russia, but failing to get from his comrades the arms for which he pleaded.

During January, 1927, through mob violence directed by the Communists, the British were forced to give up their concession in Hankow. From the countryside streams of missionaries were converging on the city and evacuating from China. An eyewitness of the moving events of those days wrote:

"It was a wonderful drama, there at the center of the world's interest, in the heart of the Chinese Revolution. But while we watched act and scene following each other, often with kaleidoscopic suddenness, as the purpose and trend of events began to take shape and stood out more clearly, and above all as I saw the attitude of my Chinese friends and acquaintances change from eager hope and patriotic enthusiasm to perplexity, misgiving, and in some cases finally to resentful antagonism and despair for the immediate future, a vague feeling of foreboding and apprehension began to hang over me in spite of myself— it oppressed us all. It was a sense of a purposeful force, planning, directing and driving on the movement, which steadily became more and more convincing. And the ideal which inspired this sinister activity, the methods employed, the origin, and the ultimate purpose were none of them Chinese."*

In March, 1927, the breaking point between Chiang and Borodin was reached. At Nanchang Chiang called a meeting of the Central Executive Committee without the Russian advisers while at Hankow Borodin called the same meeting for the Communists and Kuomintang radicals. At the Hankow gathering Chiang Kai-shek was relieved of his post as commander in chief. He was also dismissed from being chairman of the Standing Committee of the Central Executive Committee and Wang Ching-wei was chosen to take his place.

With the strongly organized proletariat under Com-

---

*Chapman's *The Chinese Revolution 1926-27*, p. 37, courtesy of Constable & Co., Ltd., London.

munist control and with sixty-five thousand troops under
the Hankow command as compared to the thirty-five
thousand under General Chiang, it seemed as though the
Communists might win the day. Yet Chiang Kai-shek defied them. Realizing that he stood no chance against Borodin and the highly organized laborers of Hankow and
feeling his need of support for his armies, Chiang, contrary to the strategic plans of the Party, turned East to
Shanghai where he planned to ally himself with the mer-
chant-banker class and receive loans for his campaign.

The Hankow faction condemned Chiang as a feudal
militarist and plotted his downfall. In a race for Nanking
the radicals won, arriving there March 24. They forthwith
proceeded to attack the foreigners expecting that the
Powers, with their gunboats anchored in the river, would
retaliate with a general bombardment of Nanking, killing
many Chinese and so angering them that the radicals
could easily seize permanent control. No time was wasted
in finding the foreign residences and property, both business and mission, as the maneuver had been carefully
planned. Houses were entered at bayonet point, money
was demanded, foreigners were shot at the least pretense,
property was looted and the populace was called in from
the streets to finish the job. When the soldiers were summoned to retire, with the precision of a military movement they were called off by bugles sounding all over
the city. Much property had been destroyed and six foreigners had been killed. This incident set off a second
wave of evacuation of foreigners from China. The consulates of whatever country ordered their nationals out,
and within a few days the stream of refugees which had
dwindled to a trickle swelled once more into a tide.

Nevertheless, the Communist strategy backfired. Far
from unseating Chiang, the atrocities and excesses shocked

the Chinese public opinion and strengthened his position. Immediately he sent all available troops to Nanking where they overpowered the radicals and disarmed them. Disassociating himself from the violence, Chiang ordered the execution of a number of the soldiers involved in the outrages.

The Communists had planned a similar attack on foreigners to be pulled off in Shanghai on Sunday, March 27, and Chou En-lai had been sent to organize the six hundred thousand workers into terrorist bands, but a few days before the deadline Chiang's troops took over the city. Thoroughly aroused by the Communist menace, he acted quickly. Learning that Moscow had ordered the Labor Unions to bury their rifles and munitions and not wanting any possibility of armed insurrection in his rear, Chiang Kai-shek determined to deal ruthlessly with the danger. When the Communist-trained Labor Unions flaunted his authority and by means of armed pickets maintained a government within a government, he cracked down on them and, at a considerable cost in casualties, disarmed the pickets. A general strike was called but Chiang dealt with it firmly, closing all the Labor Union headquarters and arresting and executing the ringleaders. Chou En-lai was thrown into prison and sentenced to death but managed to escape. In the purge during the first half of April much blood was shed. Besides Shanghai and Nanking, concerted attacks were carried out in Soochow, Foochow, Changchow and Canton. In the last named city during an all-night raid two thousand arrests were made, including all the Russian advisers, and subsequently some were executed. All the Communists were ordered to report in ten days or be shot.

On April 15, when the Shanghai-Nanking area had come effectively under his control, Chiang Kai-shek convened a meeting of the Central Executive Committee at Nanking for the purpose of "purifying" the Party of its Communist and left wing elements. A policy of moderation was adopted. The Shanghai Chinese Bankers Association made a loan of thirty million silver dollars to be used in setting up an anti-Red, anti-Hankow government, which was established at Nanking on April 18. Not long afterward the foreign Powers began withdrawing their representatives from Hankow and recognizing the new government.

At the Fifth Congress of the Chinese Communist Party, meeting in May, the strange medley of international agents—Borodin, Mif (both from Russia), Earl Browder (from the U.S.), Jacques Doriot (from France) and Roy (from India)—were at a loss what to do. Reacting convulsively to developments, the Hankow regime dismissed Chiang from all Government positions, expelled him from the Party and frantically through the press and in meetings branded him as a traitor and counter-revolutionary. But it was too late. A series of events had already begun to transpire which were to expose Russia's perfidy, catapult Chiang Kai-shek into the hero's seat, boot the Russians out of the country and cause the Communists to go underground.

At the end of February a Russian steamer on the Yangtze opposite Nanking, the *Pamiat Lenina,* had been searched, incriminating documents seized and Mrs. Borodin taken into custody.

On April 6, Chang Tso-lin, the Manchurian warlord now in charge of Peking, sprang a sudden raid on the Soviet Russian Embassy (which according to international law was supposed to be immune) and an astounding quantity of illegal materials was taken over. An eyewitness account by a news correspondent is given in *The China Weekly Review* for April 23, 1927:

"Leaving Legation Street and its throng of foreign and Chinese onlookers your correspondent hurried along to a three-storied building adjacent to the invaded premises, and having obtained permission to occupy the balcony of the top floor he was enabled to watch through a pair of field glasses practically the whole of the proceedings in both the raid and the struggle with the flames. Judging from the smell the documents which it was thought well to destroy had been drenched with oil, and a thick cloud of smoke was pouring from all the windows of the building concerned as well as from the chimney. . . . Half an hour after the alarm was given the fire was conquered, and the police began to crawl in through the windows of the house and pass out masses of papers, some smouldering and some undamaged.

"Treasure troves now began to emerge in bundles, first a machine gun, then a boxful of papers in Chinese, then a Cantonese flag and a number of smaller banners followed by fifteen or twenty rifles and a number of revolvers together with ammunition for same.

"Altogether some fifteen carloads of pamphlets and suchlike were removed, some in Russian and some in Chinese. . . . It was very interesting to watch the expression on the faces of the crowd as the material accumulated and was taken away. . . ."

The Peking Communist leader, Li Ta-chao, who had become Karakhan's right hand man, was found in the embassy and arrested together with other Communists. Not long thereafter he and about twenty-five others were put to death.

The huge mass of documents seized contained thousands of papers in several languages. They revealed the intricate workings of the Communist system and the all-pervasive machinery of Moscow in China. They showed that Russia was not interested in the Chinese Revolution as an end in itself but only as a step to World Revolution, that the Chinese Communist Party was merely a tool of the Comintern, and that Borodin had been getting his orders directly from Moscow. One of the documents seized contained a resolution just recently passed at the seventh plenary session of the Executive Committee of the Comintern in Moscow giving detailed plans for the communization of China. When a number of these papers were published with photographs of the originals, the overwhelming nature of the case struck the public. In spite of the solemn promises in the treaty of 1924 to refrain from propaganda work—here the Russians were using their Embassy as the nerve center for the subversion of China! Diplomatic relations with Moscow were forthwith broken by the Peking government.

In Moscow the raid hurt. The Kremlin let loose with volcanic blasts against the imperialists and reactionaries who had showed such cunning in forging these documents to defame and malign her!

Close upon the heels of this raid there followed another one on the Russian-controlled institutions in Tientsin—as had previously been done in Shanghai—and much subversive literature was unearthed.

As though to underscore the world-wide ramifications of the Communist Movement, on May 12 the London police raided the Arcos (Association of Russian Co-operative Societies), ostensibly the headquarters of the Russian trade delegation but actually an arm of espionage and subversion. Here were brought to light documents revealing anti-British intrigue and schemes to undermine Britain in the Far East together with abundant evidence of Soviet activities in China.

As these disclosures were rocking the diplomatic world

and the responsible people in China, giving rise to an anti-Communist outcry which greatly strengthened the forces rallying around Chiang Kai-shek and correspondingly weakened the position of the Hankow regime, a capital blunder by the chief Comintern delegate, Mr. Roy, a Hindu Communist working with the Hankow group, rang out the doom of the radicals. Stalin had sent instructions to Borodin and Roy, without the knowledge, of course, of the left-wing Kuomintang members, that the Communist Party should start land reform without consulting the government; that they should obtain the leadership, then overthrow the Kuomintang Party; that they should liquidate the counter-revolutionaries; and that they should raise a large army outside the control of the Kuomintang. Through some whim or fancy Roy showed these instructions to Wang Ching-wei, now back in China as the chairman of the leftist Party and Government, and thereby alienated him and his followers and aroused them to the danger.

In June as Borodin was negotiating with Feng Yü-hsiang who was back in China and in control of Honan Province, the "Christian General" turned on him, in spite of the help he had received from Russia, and allied himself with Chiang Kai-shek. Thereupon the two Generals—in secret understanding with Wang Ching-wei and his followers—sent ultimatums to Hankow demanding the expulsion of the Russians, the suppression of the Communists, the disbanding of the Labor Unions and a reconciliation with Nanking. On July 18 troops from Changsha loyal to Chiang occupied Hankow and fulfilled the ultimatums. Borodin, who wept like a child, was banished together with Galen and the other Russians; the Communist Party was outlawed; the laborers were disarmed, their leaders arrested, and a bloody suppression of the radicals was effected. Anti-Communism became the rallying cry for a rejuvenated Kuomintang. As many Communists as could scurried from the scene. Madame Sun Yat-sen retired to Moscow (where she studied Communist doctrines for three years in the World Anti-Imperialist League) bewailing the fact that the Revolution had been "betrayed." From Moscow came the ominous pronouncement from the Executive Committee of the Comintern:

"The revolutionary role of the Government at Hankow is finished. It is now counter-revolutionary and must be thwarted. Therefore Communists must spread an agrarian revolution and arm workers and peasants."

Instructions to Party members were to "lie low," to "bore from within," and to "work underground."

And so ended the abortive lunge of the Red Dragon in its first attempt to swallow the great country of China.

burrowing underground

ACCORDING to ancient Chinese belief the dragon inhabits the earth as well as the air and the waters. It is therefore dangerous to dig in certain places and to mine coal, as the unnatural activity may disturb the dragon. Aroused to anger it will shake itself and cause a violent earthquake.

In China, to be sure, the baby Red Dragon, after its defeat in the open, bored underground and there developed to full proportions. Later, when the National Government tried to dig it out, it emerged in great wrath and convulsed not only China but the whole world. For the present let us trace the underground movements of this Red Conspiracy.

After the Communist debacle of 1927 Galen returned to Russia and, under the name of General Blücher, took command of the Siberian Far Eastern Forces. Borodin returned to his own country but, being an Old Guard Bolshevik, fell under the consuming suspicion and jealousy of Stalin, was banished to a Siberian slave labor camp and died there at the age of 68, a short while before Stalin himself. The other Russian advisers fled to their homeland together with a number of their Chinese henchmen. Chou En-lai, who, with a price of eighty thousand silver dollars on his head, managed to escape detection by growing a beard and living at expensive hotels, followed some months later. Other Chinese Communists disappeared into the countryside or were lost in the cities.

The militant Communist unions had been crushed by a fearful counterterror and the workers were reorganized into Nationalist-controlled unions. So effective was this work that the laborers themselves turned against the Communists, accusing the latter of only making trouble for them and never bettering their lot. This attitude persisted until the final Communist victory.

Radically inclined students operated quietly in the universities where Communism had been banned. They had, however, a fertile field in which to work. The *Chinese Recorder* estimated that in 1927 among the quarter million students in China 75 per cent were atheists or agnostics and only 10 per cent had any personal religious convictions. It was from the intelligentsia and the student class—not the laborers—that the Communists in China had received their original impetus and it was from this same class that they received their most effective recruits for leadership as the movement developed.

After the break with the Kuomintang and the expulsion of Russian agents from China the Comintern did not by any means relinquish its hold upon the affairs of its daughter movement. Delegates appointed by the Comintern were yearly sent to attend the meetings and to advise and work with the personnel of the Chinese Communist Party and the latter sent representatives to the meetings and deliberations of the mother organization.

Following the Comintern's shift of line which sanc-

tioned the formation of military forces directly under
Communist control, a number of insurrections were staged
in armies already infiltrated by the Communists. In Nanchang Chou En-lai brought an order to Chu Teh, whom
he had befriended in Germany, to rise up against his
superiors. Chu Teh, who headed the military school and
commanded the Kuomintang garrison in the city, had,
unbeknown to Chiang Kai-shek, been a secret Communist
for years. On August 1, 1927, he, together with Generals
Yeh T'ing, Nieh Jung-chen, Lin Piao, and Ho Lung (under
the instigation and guidance of Chou En-lai, Chang Kuo-
t'ao, Li Li-san, P'eng Pai and others who had constituted
themselves into a "revolutionary committee") staged a
revolt in the Kuomintang's best army corps called the
"Ironsides" and broke away with about twenty thousand
seasoned troops which became the nucleus of the future
Workers' and Peasants' Red Army. This move marked the
beginning of separate military power for the Communists
and, ever since, August 1 has been commemorated as
"Chinese Red Army Day."

From Nanchang the rebels drove on Swatow, with the
hope of founding a Soviet (or Communist government)
along the coast. Their occupation of the city, however,
was shortlived as they were expelled after only one week
and driven into eastern Kwangtung.

With the unfavorable turn of events in China which had
led to the break with the Kuomintang and to the supres-
sion of Communism, Stalin, who was well-versed in shift-
ing responsibility for failures to the shoulders of others,
put the blame for the deteriorating situation on the
Chinese leaders. Even though Ch'en Tu-hsiu, the founder
of the Chinese party, had time and again bowed to the
superior wisdom of Moscow, he was now made the scape-
goat for past errors. Mandalian, the Comintern delegate,

time and again attacked his leadership. As early as May 1 at the Fifth Party Congress Ch'en had been forced to make a confession of his mistakes and on July 14 Bukharin himself attacked him as an opportunist. The outcome was inevitable. On August 7, 1927, an emergency meeting of the Central Committee of the Chinese Communist Party was called in Hankow and presided over by Lominadze, the new Comintern delegate. In attendance were Mao Tsetung, Chang Kuo-t'ao, Li Li-san, Chou En-Lai (fresh from the Nanchang uprising), Ch'ü Ch'iu-pai and others. They ganged up on Ch'en Tu-hsiu, accused him of "rightist opportunism" and "Trotskyist deviation," deposed him from the leadership and drew up an elaborate account of his errors for circularizing the absent members. The Comintern and Party were whitewashed as always having been correct, and failures were blamed to the sabotaging of their policy by opportunist leaders. Great stress was layed on the peasants as constituting the crux of the revolution in China, though the proletariat were still expected to furnish the leadership. Being in hostile surroundings the Communists emphasized secrecy for their future movements. They also called for "armed uprisings on every hand." Their new leader, Chü Ch'iu-pai, was a well-indoctrinated Stalinist, educated in Russia.

The alliance with Feng Yü-hsiang and the defeat of the Communists did not place Chiang Kai-shek in as fortunate a position as one might think. In Shantung the Japanese blocked the passage of his troops through the railway center of Tsinan as he sought to drive northward to unify China. In the Kuomintang, leaders fell to fighting and quarreling among themselves. In an attempt to bring about unity Chiang, on August 12, suddenly resigned and retired to Japan. This led to political confusion and business stagnation which threatened to end in chaos. Again the country was about to fall to pieces at the seams and revert to sectional warlordism. Chiang Kai-shek was the only man big enough to hold things together. Once more he was offered the position of generalissimo and in December he accepted the far from easy responsibility.

Meanwhile the Communists had not been idle. After the Hankow emergency meeting of August 7 the headquarters of the Party were moved to Shanghai where the Communists could do their secret work more conveniently under the shelter of the foreign Concessions. Secret agents were trained and dispatched to various localities to stage uprisings. It was planned that peasant revolts should later be co-ordinated with city strikes.

Mao Tse-tung had already been sent to Hunan with Ch'ü Ch'iu-pai's blessings, albeit with certain reservations because of his all-out bias on behalf of the peasants. Working in late August and into September with remarkable speed he gathered a makeshift army of peasants, Kuomintang deserters and fierce, radical Hengyang miners. These became the spearhead for the subsequently famous First Army. By September 12 he was ready and with the help of Hsiang Ying sparked the revolt which became known as the "autumn harvest uprisings."

Perhaps the leadership assumed that this timing was particularly propitious as the landlords and tax collectors would be coming around for their levies. However, the uprisings were a dismal failure, the peasants were mowed down and Mao himself was captured. Making his escape, he led some hundred of the remnant warriors in a precarious retreat to the south. His adventures earned him a dismissal from the Politburo and also from the Front Committee of the Party. In spite of his disgrace Mao remained unbowed and held to the conviction that he was following the right track. With his followers he invaded the Hunan-Kiangsi border region, making the pine-covered, temple-dotted mountain of Chingkanshan his headquarters. The Buddhist monks were driven out, their buildings taken over. Only one week after their arrival the Communists were printing a newspaper on the backs of Buddhist scrolls. The following months were occupied with digging in, foraging for supplies, absorbing bandit troops, putting down mutinies and expanding their position. This policy of concentration of military power at almost inaccessible bases became a keystone to later Communist success.

Elsewhere also the Communists were busy causing trouble. P'eng Pai, a recently returned graduate of Moscow's Sun Yat-sen University, the son of a wealthy family, fleeing from Nanchang and Swatow with the remnant troops of Yeh T'ing, Ho Lung and Chu Teh, arrived at his former stamping grounds in the Hailofeng area of Kwangtung. Here in the early twenties, long before Mao had caught on to the potentialities of peasant organization, he had achieved success among the farmers far outshining Mao's accomplishments to date. Now, in harmony with the new line adopted by the Comintern on September 19 of authorizing the establishment of separate Soviets in China, P'eng Pai set up in November the first Chinese Soviet Government—a state within a state—which continued for some months before being wiped out by the Kuomintang. Land was redistributed, title deeds burned, a local militia formed and some thirty thousand landlords and peasants slaughtered as class enemies.

In other provinces—Shensi, Kiangsu, Chekiang—sporadic uprisings were engineered by the Communists, but all of them collapsed. Not to ignore the cities, Ch'ü Ch'iu-pai tried to force strikes in Shanghai, Changsha and elsewhere, but they came to nothing.

WUHAN

HUPEH

KIUKIANG

ANHWEI

CHINGKANSHAN

NANCHANG

HUNAN

KIANGSI

KIAN

FUTJEN

TUNGKU

HENGYANG

HSINGKUO

FUKIEN

JUICHIN

MAP OF

KIANGSI

KWANGTUNG

HAILOFENG

The situation looked bleak indeed for the Communists. In Russia Stalin's fight with Trotsky was deeply involved with the development of the China Revolution. With every setback, charges and countercharges flew back and forth. (Eventually Trotsky was ousted and had to flee for his life.) Stalin, who was in the ascendancy, needed a victory to justify his theorizing regarding a "rising revolutionary wave" in China. At its November 9 meeting the Chinese Communist Party echoed the Comintern line and emphasized the fact that the work in the cities had been neglected. Li Ang, the corresponding secretary of the Chinese Party at this time, wrote later: "The Comintern sent telegrams daily urging the Chinese Communist Party to bring about uprisings in Canton and other large cities. These telegrams were all extremely emphatic in tone and allowed no room for argument."[*]

Laying the groundwork for the Canton uprising was the German Communist leader, Heinz Neuman, in conjunction with P'eng Pai (who was apprehended and executed in Shanghai some years later), Yeh T'ing, Yeh Chien-ying (who is today Commander of one of China's seven major military districts and a member of her highest politico-military organ of twenty-two members, the "People's Revolutionary Military Council"), Nieh Jung-chen (who was educated in France, Belgium and the USSR, had taught at the Whampoa Academy and is today Deputy Chief of Staff of the Red Army, Commander of one of China's seven major military districts and a member of her highest council), and Hsü Hsiang-ch'ien.

---

[*]Reprinted by permission of the publishers from Benjamin I. Schwartz, *Chinese Communism and the Rise of Mao*, pp. 105-6, Cambridge, Mass., Harvard University Press, Copyright 1951 by The President and Fellows of Harvard College.

On December 11 the local garrison composed of two regiments well infiltrated by the Communists and swelled by a horde of vagabonds and coolies, seized Canton, burned down ten thousand houses, slaughtered up to fifteen thousand people and set up a Soviet form of government with Yeh T'ing appointed as Commander-in-Chief of the troops. But the Canton Commune, as it is called, was short-lived. Workers of the Mechanics' Union and other laborers attacked the new government with "dare-to-die corps" and were joined by loyal Kuomintang troops from the outside. After three days the city was recaptured and a counterterror was instituted to clean out the Communists both Chinese and Russian. The Soviet vice-consul was executed and the remaining Russians expelled. According to a *New York Times* dispatch, firing squads continued to "mow down as many as a hundred suspected Communists daily." As a result of this episode, on December 15 in a sweeping gesture the National Government closed all the Soviet consulates in its territories and broke off relations with Russia. Thus Soviet official power was cut off—but by no means its influence.

Mao with his followers continued at Chingkanshan through the winter and the whole of the following year. In May he was joined by Chu Teh (today's Commander-in-Chief), Chen Yi (who after the Red takeover of China became mayor of Shanghai, Commander of the Third Field Army, Commander of one of China's seven major military districts, and a member of her highest council), Lin Piao (who later was to direct a million troops in their sweep through the country and today is Commander of the Fourth Field Army and a member of the highest council) and their battered remnants. Later P'eng Teh-huai (who was to become Commander of the Chinese troops fighting in Korea and is today Deputy Commander-

in-Chief under Chu teh, Commander of the First Field
Army, Commander of one of China's seven major military
districts, and a vice-chairman of the highest council) with
his forces gathered at the mountain retreat, then Ho
Lung (who is at present Commander of one of China's
seven major military districts and a member of the highest
council). From this time on a most remarkable team-
work was struck up between Mao and Chu which has
lasted to the present day. It was decided that Mao
should be the civilian leader and Chu the military chief,
thus subordinating the military to the civilian.

It was during these months that Mao Tse-tung worked
out the outlines of a strategy which was to lead him to
ultimate victory. In a report to the Central Committee in
1928 he listed the following conditions for maintaining
armed Soviets:

1. A strong mass base—the peasants—to be won by a
   program of land reform.
2. A strong party organized according to Lenin's
   principles.
3. A strong Red Army.
4. Control over a defensible, nearly inaccessible area.
5. Self-sufficiency.

He also worked out a technique of guerrilla warfare based
upon the advice of Sun Tzu, a military genius who lived
about the time of Confucius—five centuries before Christ:
"When the enemy advances, we retreat. When he escapes,
we harass. When he retreats, we pursue. When he is tired,
we attack." These he formulated into catchy slogans which
his followers chanted.

With regard to choice of strategic bases Mao's prefer-
ence was for "border areas." These had definite ad-
vantages. First, reports of the prowess of the Communists

would spread in both directions and thus influence both provinces. Second, at such a base far from the Government's seat of administration, the authority of the decentralized state would be weakest. Third, if attacked by the troops of one province the guerrillas could step across the line into the other where, due to lack of co-ordination between the provinces, they would be safe.

At this time, although Chiang Kai-shek's forces had been hindered by the Japanese from reaching the North, his ally Feng Yü-hsiang joined by Yen Hsi-shan of Shansi pressed upon Peking and forced Chang Tso-lin to retire to Manchuria (where he was killed by the Japanese in a bomb explosion). On June 8, 1928 their troops entered the old city, its name was shortly changed from Peking (Northern Capital) to Peiping (Northern Peace), and the archives were moved to Nanking, where the National Government was established in October with Chiang Kai-shek as President. Thus all of China south of the Great Wall was at last nominally unified and some over a month later the young Manchurian warlord, Chang Hsüeh-liang, eldest son of Chang Tso-lin, also declared his allegiance to Chiang.

With the Chinese Comrades living as fugitives, there was no longer a safe place in China for convening the Sixth Congress of the Chinese Communist Party. It was therefore held in July, 1928, in a suburb of Moscow under the close supervision of the Kremlin. For this reason it holds a place of special sanctity in the orthodox writings regarding Chinese Communism. There were 170 delegates in attendance and the Comintern was represented by Bukharin.

Ch'ü Ch'iu-pai, who after the Canton failure and subsequent adverses had tried to use the Communist trick of blaming local leaders for their "subjective mistakes," was unable to throw off the consequences, was forced as a result to confess his sins and was easily unseated by Li Li-san, Hsiang Chung-fa, Chou En-lai and others. Ch'ü Ch'iu-pai and Chang Kuo-t'ao were designated to remain in Russia as delegates to the Comintern. Elected as leader or General Secretary was Hsiang Chung-fa, an uneducated boatman, who was actually a figure-head with Li Li-san as the real power. The latter was made Minister of Propaganda and Chou En-lai the Minister of Military Affairs. Mao Tse-tung was once more brought into the good graces of the Party and for the first time his guerrilla activities were given limited approval as the Party could not afford to reject any encouraging sign from whatever quarter. Mao himself claimed later that from this time all disharmonies between the Central Committee and the guerrilla areas were resolved. However, the Congress still insisted that the peasant movement, though basic, must be under proletarian leadership and therefore the city bases must be recaptured. Li Li-san returned to China with instructions to prepare for armed uprisings and to achieve victory in one or several provinces—a difficult task indeed!

With the increase of Mao's followers to about eleven thousand men, surrounded by a ring of government troops, Chingkanshan became untenable. Hardships and lack of food gave rise to mutinies and defections. Late on January 1, 1929, Mao and Chu with about four thousand men made their way down the mountain into the gathering dusk below, leaving P'eng Teh-huai in charge of the mountain fortress. For weeks they roamed through the mountains capturing cities and replenishing their supplies, but before arriving at Tungku and Hsingkuo where they planned to establish their new base, they were engaged in a fierce battle in which half their troops were wiped out. It was a staggering blow, but doggedly they kept on.

In the hinterland other groups were forming Soviets in widely scattered areas. Hsü Hsiang-ch'ien, a former teacher, arrived in the neighborhood of Hankow in the border region of Honan, Hupeh and Anhwei—not far from our Mission Field—to direct the Red Bandits and form a Soviet. Ho Lung founded another in the Hunan-Hupeh border region, and Kao Kang still another in northern Shensi. Other Soviets were formed in Kwangtung, Kwangsi, western Fukien, northeastern Kiangsi and elsewhere.

In the early part of 1929 Chou En-lai, after having spent a year in Moscow, returned to China to join his old friend from Paris days, Li Li-san, who was now the Red boss. The Chinese Revolution was not developing in accordance with Leninist theory. Chou En-lai reported in April that since the previous year the percentage of proletariat party membership had dropped in favor of the peasants from ten to three per cent and the Communists had not been able to gain control of the workers. Nor were Li and Chou permitted to be alone with their troubles. A stream of letters from the Comintern was subjecting the Chinese Party to unremitting pressure, calling for action in the cities and proclaiming (as evidenced by the political instability and civil wars) the start of a new revolutionary tide of which the dynamic development in the Soviet areas was a side-current.

In his frantic efforts to do something, Li Li-san was constantly criticized by his deposed predecessor, Ch'en Tu-hsiu. It was not before the very end of 1929, however, that he was able to rid himself of this plague. In the spring Chang Hsüeh-liang, the young Manchurian warlord, had tried to seize the Chinese Eastern Railway from the Russians. The latter had then called upon all world Communists to protect the Soviet Union! Without hesitation Li Li-san rallied against his own country to the defense of Russia. "Protect the Soviet Union" became the slogan of the Communist Party under his leadership. This gave the National Government good ammunition for use against the Communists. It was not the first time the imperialistic Russians had tried to encroach on the interests of China! Ch'en Tu-hsiu justly criticized the slogan for not being subtle enough and a spirited altercation followed which could have but one ending. The veteran founder of the Chinese Communist Party was accused of Trotskyism and disloyalty and was expelled from the Party.

By 1930 Mao Tse-tung's development of power in the Soviet areas was something to be reckoned with. On February 7 a Provincial Soviet Government was established in Kiangsi. Similar regimes on a smaller scale were set up shortly thereafter in Fukien and Kwangsi.

Isolated in the interior of an undeveloped country, in difficult, mountainous terrain, far removed from railroads and lines of communication, connections with Moscow were necessarily loose and the Chinese Soviet area leaders were left largely to their own initiative and resources. The difficulty of contact is illustrated by the fact that an article was printed about this time in the Russian *Inprecorr* giving an obituary for Mao Tse-tung who was said to have died of tuberculosis! Nevertheless, indissoluble ties were there. The Chinese offshoot owed its origin to Moscow. Mao himself was deeply committed to Marxist-Leninist teachings and considered himself a true Stalinist. Even when his practices diverged from the official line because of peculiar circumstances which it was impossible for the Kremlin to understand thousands of miles away, he still tried to rationalize the contradictions away to show that his course was simply a further development of Stalinism. Being thoroughly imbued with the Communist viewpoint regarding party hierarchy, he did not dare to flout openly the Central Committee which was more directly under Moscow's control. He made regular reports to the Committee and entertained their inspectors in his area, though he was not always happy about their criticisms. In one report Mao petitioned the Central Committee: "Henceforth, in issuing directives, we earnestly request that you study our reports and not simply rely on the one-sided reports of your inspectors. . . . In issuing directives concerning military actions we beg you, by all means, not to be too dogmatic. The letters of the Central Committee must consider the conditions in which we are operating. It must leave us some room to maneuver."[*]

Another factor to be considered is that Chou En-lai, who was Li Li-san's faithful colleague at this time, headed the department of military affairs and had direct influence on many of the generals in the Soviet areas, such as Chu Teh himself and those who had served under Chou at the Whampoa Academy.

In spite of the above, the Central Committee was dissatisfied with its hold on the Soviet areas. The latter with an autonomous army, independent territorial bases, and a peasant population producing revenues, were acquiring an authority all their own. Within the Party they became known as the Real Power Faction. Hoping to gain a firmer control over them so that he could help them to develop the way he and the Comintern thought they should—that is, with a more positive proletarian leadership—Li Li-san called a Conference of Delegates from Soviet Areas which met in Shanghai on May 30. Plans were laid for setting up an over-all Soviet Government and laws were enacted, but the achievements were of little significance and were a disappointment to Li.

---

[*]*Op. Cit.*, p. 179.

In the spring of 1930 the delegate appointed to China by the Comintern was Pavel Mif, director of Moscow's Sun Yat-sen University and Russia's acknowledged "expert" on China. With him came a group of admiring Chinese students who had spent the last four years at his feet being indoctrinated. They were noted for their ardent defense of Stalinism against every type of heresy and for their doglike devotion to their master, Pavel Mif. They earned for themselves the nickname of "The Twenty-eight Bolsheviks." Their leader, Wang Ming, encountering difficulty, was smuggled into China in Pavel Mif's baggage. He was to displace Li Li-san as the next leader of China's Communist Party.

Another interesting personage of this group was Liu Shao-chi, a great writer and lecturer who was to become party theoretician, chief author of the Red constitution promulgated in 1945, and Chou En-lai's rival for second place in the Communist hierarchy. His work *On the Education of a Communist* has become a standard handbook for party members old and young. He has become today one of the chief liaison officers between Moscow and Peking and is one of the vice-chairmen of China's highest politico-military council. The degree of his orthodoxy is evidenced by his constant reference to Americans as "swine" rather than simply as "imperialists."

Under Comintern pressure Li Li-san worked out a plan envisaging a whole series of attacks by the Red Army on large cities including Changsha, Nanchang, Wuhan (the tri-cities of Wuchang, Hankow and Hanyang) and even Nanking. Mao Tse-tung vehemently opposed the plan but was overruled. When civil war broke out again between Feng Yü-hsiang and the Government, and troops were siphoned off from Changsha to help Chiang Kai-shek, the time seemed opportune for action. On July 28 P'eng

Teh-huai led his Fifth Red Army with about ten thousand men armed with spears, mattocks and rifles against the depleted garrison. By sheer ferocity they captured the city. When news of the exploit reached Moscow, the *Inprecorr* proclaimed triumphantly: "With the capture of Changsha there has commenced a new chapter in the history of the Chinese revolution. It is the first time since the Canton Soviet revolt in December, 1927, that a great industrial city is in the hands of the revolutionary workers . . . . The leadership of the city proletariat in the whole revolutionary movement is strengthened by this victory."*

In another quarter the Red Army captured Kian and marched on Nanchang and Kiukiang but were thrown back. Changsha itself was held for only ten days when overwhelming government forces retook the city. Retiring with large stores of supplies and munitions and with three thousand workers recruited for the Red Army, P'eng Teh-huai joined forces with Chu Teh in Kiangsi. Li Li-san pressed for an attack on Wuhan but this time, following the failure of Changsha, Mao Tse-tung's counsel prevailed.

The failure of Changsha was the doom of Li Li-san—though Moscow was reluctant to recognize the error which she had initiated and supported. Yet the repercussions in the world press were of such magnitude that the event could not be ignored. The catastrophe could not be blamed to Moscow's infallible judgment, but only to those who had tried to carry out her will.

The roving Communist bands which were beginning to fill many parts of the country were hard to distinguish from ordinary bandits. They plundered and killed and held for ransom, but always "promised" help for the poor and oppressed. Their cruelty was terrifying and

*Op. Cit., pp. 144-145.

part of their official program. Their savagery was beginning to have international involvements.

In September two English women missionaries held
captive in Fukien for two and a half months were executed after horrible tortures. On October 5 Kwangshan,
one of our Mission Stations, was captured by the troops of
Hsü Hsiang-ch'ien (today about the 8th ranking Communist in China), and the Reverend Bert Nelson was
taken for ransom. A few days later two more of our missionaries, Miss Bergliot Evenson and the Reverend K. N.
Tvedt, were seized. The ransom agreed upon for the last
two was paid, but only the lady was released. Nelson and
Tvedt were kept as prisoners in Hsü Hsiang-ch'ien's Soviet
area. Eventually when arrangements had been made for
their release, again the Communists broke their promises,
allowed Tvedt alone to leave but detained Bert Nelson
who, after almost two years of captivity, died at their
hands.

Toward the end of 1930 the ax began to fall on Li Li-
san. The "returned student clique," because of their intimate connection with Pavel Mif, won high positions in
the Party councils. Considering themselves more capable
of handling the situation than Li because of their recent
return from the center of World Communism, and re-
senting his determination to hold the reins of power in
his own hands, they set about to undermine his influence.
At a meeting of the Central Committee in September, because of Li Li-san's powerful, personal machine of loyal
followers and Chou En-lai's support, they failed to un-
seat him. Infuriated over the setback, Mif redoubled his
efforts to discredit Li, reporting the latter's incompetency
to Moscow. His task was made easier because of the Kremlin's desire at this time to reorient its strategic policy in
China from that of capturing large cities to that of allow-

ing the Soviet peasant bases to develop along the lines
that had proved so successful to date. Henceforth the
uneven development between town and country, between workers and peasants, was to be remedied, not by
dissipating the strength of the Red Army through attacks
on the cities, but by bringing the level of the proletariat
up to that of the peasants. This was a real triumph for
Mao's strategy. As a result Chou En-lai was summoned
to Moscow for consultations. On November 16 the Comintern sent a stern letter to the Chinese Communist Party
condemning the Li Li-san line and on November 25 the
Chinese Politburo was convened confirming its complete
agreement with the Comintern, forcing Li Li-san to make
an abject confession of his past mistakes and causing him
to resign because of his "adventurism." He was succeeded
by Mif's protégé, Wang Ming. After this Li Li-san soon
left for Moscow where he humbly submitted to the Kremlin and made his recantations. After fifteen years of further
training and indoctrination in Russia he was finally to
emerge with the Soviet Army in Manchuria, becoming
General Lin Piao's political adviser, and is today in high
position as the head of all Chinese labor organizations.

Not only in the Central Committee were there power
struggles, but also in the Soviet areas. Mao did not reach
the pinnacle of recognition without his hands stained with
the blood of his comrades. In the beginning of December
a revolt broke out in Futien, a "people's conference" was
called to overthrow Mao Tse-tung's arbitrary rule, and
a rival Soviet was set up in a neighboring county. Acting
swiftly in a harsh and bloody campaign, Mao struck at
the rebels, arresting and liquidating their leaders. To
consolidate his power the Mao machine during this period
eliminated long lists of commanders, burying many of
them alive, and replaced them with loyal personnel.

writhing in fury

WITH the Communist bands becoming so strong that they could attack large cities like Changsha (according to figures given the Lytton Commission, the Communists in 1930 administered 181 counties in the interior of China) the National Government began to take notice. Preparations were brought under way to rid the country of the menace through military force. From 1930 to 1934 five "annihilation campaigns" were directed against the Communists; but, due to the general situation as well as to the extraordinary stamina of the Reds, the movement ended in failure except for the overrunning of some of the smaller Soviets.

In the first campaign which started in the latter part of December, 1930, with close to one hundred thousand government troops surrounding the Communists, the Red Army scattered and hid, dissipating the strength of the pursuers and enticing them to advance deeply into prepared traps, then suddenly concentrated their forces at predetermined points to launch devastating attacks. One government division, wandering in the unfamiliar mountains, was "pleasantly" surprised to find aid arriving in the form of Red Troops wearing Kuomintang uniforms and carrying Kuomintang banners. Before they knew what had happened, half the division had been liquidated and the others routed. During the campaign the Communists lost seven thousand men, but they completely defeated the government, captured thousands of soldiers and conscripted others to bring their army back to strength, seized over four thousand rifles and huge quantities of ammunition and supplies, including two radio sets. A top National General, Chang Hui-tsan, was taken prisoner and after awesome tortures put to death. Immediately after the victory the Central Committee of the Communist Party sent Hsiang Ying from Shanghai to the Soviet area to organize a Military Commission with himself as chairman and Chu Teh and Mao Tse-tung as vice-chairmen.

On Chou En-lai's return from Moscow the Central Committee held a meeting in Shanghai on January 7, 1931, reaffirming its rejection of the Li Li-san line. The spirit of Mif dominated the sessions. Chou En-lai, as well as others, was forced to make an abject confession of past mistakes; but, being extremely pliable, he was still able to win a high position in the new Central Committee. With Moscow's switch toward Mao Tse-tung's strategy, Chou En-lai gracefully switched, also.

No sooner had the first "annihilation campaign" subsided than preparations were afoot for the second campaign which came off in February. This time two hundred thousand government troops under Ho Ying-chin closed in upon the Kiangsi Soviet. Using lightning tactics the main group of Reds traveled 235 miles in fifteen days and fought five battles. In the main action, after ascertaining the enemy's weak point, they squeezed in between two major forces to defeat a weaker division, then struck the

side troops in quick succession bringing surprise and confusion. This time they made good use of their captured
radio sets for diversionary actions in the enemy rear. They
completely routed the government troops, gaining another
twenty thousand rifles. Once again their losses were made
up with the prisoners taken and their territory was expanded with the acquisition of almost a dozen new cities.
Of Kiangsi's eighty-five counties seventy had now come
under the control of the Communists.

Considering the root of the Red menace to lie in Shanghai, the government began to comb that city for Communist agents. The head of the dreaded secret police
(equivalent of the Russian GPU, now called NKVD) of
the Communist Party was arrested on a mission to Wuhan.
He turned informer and gave up the addresses of the
prominent members of the Central Committee leading
to the seizure and execution in June of Hsiang Chung-fa,
the puppet chairman. Being warned in time, most of
the other leaders escaped, but an active "white terror"
had been initiated, which eventually resulted in the arrest or defection of 162 members of the Central Committee and 12,900 Party members.

In July the third anti-Communist campaign was waged
with an imposing array of three hundred thousand troops
equipped with two hundred cannon and one hundred airplanes. Chiang Kai-shek himself with a staff of German
advisers came to Nanchang to direct the operations. Much
had been learned from the past experiences of defeat. In
the beginning the Reds lost heavily as the planes spotted
and bombed their concentrations and the torrid heat cut
down on their mobility; but with the coming of heavy
rains the tide was turned. Again the Reds achieved a startling victory through excellent intelligence, through a complete familiarity with the terrain, through mobility and

forced marches, through extending the enemy lines, through leading the enemy into traps, through weaving among the enemy columns—as though performing a dragon dance—through withdrawal and swift return and, above all, through a will to conquer. The government troops on the other hand were inferior in training for endurance, lacked accurate knowledge of Red strength, did not have proper co-ordination, and each division hoped some other division would bear the brunt of battle. In their withdrawals the Communists had removed all food supplies or buried them, so the Kuomintang were unable to get enough provisions over the rugged country-side to support their troops. By the end of September the Communists had retaken all the territory lost in July and had been joined by thirty-five thousand deserters (won largely through propaganda) who brought their rifles and machine guns with them.

A contributing cause to the National defeat at this time was the growing pressure from without of Japanese aggression. On September 18 occurred the "Mukden Incident" which led to Japan's occupation of Manchuria. National troops had to be largely withdrawn from the anti-Communist campaign in order to deal with the new menace from the northeast. Taking advantage of the lessening pressure on themselves, the Red troops redoubled their efforts to expand their own position. U.S. Secretary of State, Stimson, urged united economic sanctions against Japan in order to force her to give up her agression in China, but the other leading Western nations were not so far-sighted. The result of this appeasement was a chain reaction which we know only too well: Italy, seeing Japan's immunity to punishment, started off on Empire-building of her own, seizing Ethiopia. Shortly Hitler started on his rampage to be met with more appeasement which lit the fuse to World War II. And since the war Empire-building on such a scale as the world has never seen before has been fed by appeasement after appeasement until the Red Menace threatens to envelope the whole globe. What is not done cheaply and according to principle at the right time must be paid for later at a fantastic price of material wastage and human suffering.

On November 7, 1931, the First All-China Congress of Soviets was convened in Kiangsi, at Juichin, and the Chinese Soviet Republic was established. Mao Tse-tung was elected president and Hsiang Ying and Chang Kuo-t'ao, vice-presidents. A blueprint, which has changed little through the years, was outlined for the Communist government, envisaging the ultimate aim of the "dictatorship of the proletariat." The crying need of Mao's growing power was to bring his peasant movement into rational alignment with Leninist-Stalinist theory. Nowhere in all his writings does Lenin ever hint that the Communist Party can exist except on a *proletarian* base, whereas Mao was achieving success through the imposition of Leninist organizational principles—together with most of the Marxist doctrines—upon a *peasant* base. Stalin had worked for the sovietization of China through the establishment of city bases. Mao was applying the "heretical" strategy of the "encirclement of the cities" through organization of the peasants. To cover up the discrepancy an elaborate labor code was drawn up dealing more with the problems of laborers than of peasants, although the labor class in the Chinese Communist movement was conspicuously absent. The spiritual loyalty to Russia and World Communism was written into the constitution by proclaiming the Soviet Union to be the true ally of Soviet China and by establishing national holidays on the anniversaries of Lenin's death, the Paris Commune, and the inauguration of the Soviet Union.

The Chinese Communists rose to power largely because of favorable international circumstances. Had it not been for Japanese aggression, the Red menace would likely have been stamped out of China, but in troubled situations Communism thrives. Beginning on January 28, 1932, three months of fierce fighting broke out in the Shanghai area between the 19th route army under Tsai Ting-kai and the Japanese. More Government troops had to be withdrawn from the forces guarding against the Reds in Kiangsi in order to cope with the Japanese. The Communists, on the other hand, instead of fighting the Japanese actually worked with them. For propaganda purposes they declared war on the Japanese but in reality they availed themselves of the opportunity to fight against the Government. They called for strikes in Shanghai. On April 20 they took Changchow in Fukien and held it six weeks. They also occupied other cities. The city of Sinyang, where I was working at the time, had become, with Peng-pu, a center of military transportation. The Communists handicapped the Government in its struggle by constantly tearing up the railway tracks and derailing the trains. They planned an attack on Sinyang—and even on Wuhan and Nanchang—but were not successful. In the end in Shanghai the Government troops were defeated by the land, sea and air offensive of the Japanese and forced to sign a truce which strengthened Japan's position in East China.

After these bitter experiences Chiang Kai-shek realized more than ever that before he could successfully withstand the Japanese he must clean house in his own domain. As a result a fourth "annihilation campaign" was put into operation. Some Far Eastern "experts" have criticized the policy of Chiang for wanting to clean up the internal situation before taking on Japan. They naively suppose that the Japanese could not have progressed so far had the National government concentrated on resisting them instead of dissipating its energy in futile drives against the Red armies. This viewpoint shows a complete ignorance of the danger of Communism. It would lead to the swift destruction of the Government itself and the certain ascendancy of Communism—and no one knows this better than the Reds themselves. The policy would be suicidal—as it would be for a prize fighter to take on his opponent before he had recovered from an attack of pneumonia!

By June the campaign was launched in our area with Sinyang as an important base of operations. The Honan-Hupeh-Anhwei border region, where Hsü Hsiang-ch'ien had his Soviet, was overrun. Before evacuating this territory General Hsü instituted a severe purge in which two thousand of his followers—considered unreliables—were liquidated in the Ta Pieh Mountains. One of his followers, T'sao Ming-tao, thoroughly disillusioned, escaped and later, after his conversion, became one of our leading pastors.

After the Red evacuation one of our own veteran missionaries, Mrs. Anna Lee Wold, went into the area to work. This is what she told me later: "In village after village it seemed to be the same story; two out of every three people had been killed during the Red occupation. The Communists had a special form of torture they used on fat people—cutting slits in their flesh and pouring in salt. In one place at an evangelistic meeting, one man came under a deep conviction of sin and cried out in his agony:

'Can there be any forgiveness for me? With my own hands I have killed a hundred people!' The Lord, however, had mercy on him and I believe he was saved."

Fleeing with his troops Hsü Hsiang-ch'ien made his way to Szechwan province where he and Chang Kuo-t'ao established a new Soviet, next in size to Mao Tse-tung's. Hsü's Fourth Front Red army grew to contain some forty thousand troops. Today Hsü Hsiang-ch'ien is Chief of Staff of the Chinese People's Liberation Army.

As has been pointed out, in the power struggle within the Chinese Communist Party, Mao Tse-tung, because of his real strength—with armies and territories and revenues at his disposal—was forging to the head. Moscow, it would seem, had originally no intention of handing over supreme authority to the Mao faction but had hoped for the "twenty-eight Bolsheviks" to hold control. Their grasp of power, however, was slipping in favor of the Front areas.

Being President of the Chinese Soviet Republic and having succeeded in his strategy of peasant organization, Mao Tse-tung felt he was now strong enough to assume control of the whole Communist movement in China. He therefore wrote to the Central Committee to escape the "white terror" in Shanghai and transfer its headquarters to Juichin where he was. As the Soviet Union during this period was so deeply distraught with internal problems that she could allot only $15,000 to all her work of subversion in the Orient, the Shanghai Committee was becoming more and more dependent upon the Soviet areas for funds to carry on. As a result, when Mao suggested that funds might not be able to get through, the Committee transferred its headquarters without argument. After its transference it was completely subordinated to the authority of Mao Tse-tung. Whoever might be the General Sec-

retary elected to office, it was Mao Tse-tung who succeeded Wang Ming at the end of 1932 as the head of the
Chinese Communist Movement to the present day.

Being shrewd realists the Kremlin accepted the leadership of Mao Tse-tung and ever since has tried to rationalize the unorthodox advancement to success of the
Chinese Communist movement. In the new set-up some
of the "twenty-eight Bolsheviks" won high positions and
Chou En-lai with his amazing elasticity became Commissar of Military Affairs and co-Commander-in-Chief with
Chu Teh. Wang Ming was elected delegate to the Comintern in Moscow where he won an outstanding reputation
as the interpreter of Chinese affairs and champion of the
"United Front" policy.

Meanwhile the fourth annihilation campaign of the
government dragged on into 1933. The National forces
besides having overrun the Honan-Hupeh-Anhwei border
area, overran the Red Lake Soviet and the Hunan-Hupeh-
Kiangsi border region, but were not so fortunate in their
invasion of Mao Tse-tung's stronghold. Marching deep into the territory they were unable to get reports of the
enemy, got lost in the maze of unfamiliar roads and passes,
and had their divisions chopped up and defeated one by
one. A large number of troops fell into Communist hands
only to be indoctrinated and added to their forces. The
Red Army had now achieved a total strength of five Army
Corps with approximately three hundred thousand men.
Tanks and airplanes also were captured but had to be
destroyed for lack of gasoline and pilots. From this time
on a thorough study of these campaigns became an integral part of Red Army training and contributed in no small
degree to the final defeat of the National Government.

Immediately after the failure of the fourth campaign
a fifth one of still greater dimensions was planned. This

time a careful strategy was mapped out in which political considerations were given twice the importance of military maneuvers. All officers were required to take a course in anti-Communist ideology and technique. The *pao-chia* system (the pyramidal organization of families into tens and hundreds, etc.) was emphasized. A strict embargo was placed upon all trade with the Soviet areas, thus cutting them off from such daily necessities as edible oils and salt. Highways for transporting military supplies were constructed. With the help of German General von Falkenhausen, Chiang Kai-shek introduced the strategy of the "fiery wall." A steadily advancing line of blockhouses was built and all the area covered was put to the torch—a modified "scorched-earth policy" borrowed from the Communists.

Operations were officially launched in October, 1933. Against the new maneuver of slow blockade and compression of territory the Communist tactics of guerrilla warfare were of little avail. Already the economic situation had become critical as, according to Chu Teh, the Reds having dispossessed the landlords had no further sources of revenue. The peasants under Communist rule were gripped with hysteria. Thousands perished in the fighting and other thousands died of starvation. The German Communist General, whose name in Chinese was Li Teh, issued the military directives for the Red Army but only brought ruin the closer. When it became clear that they could no longer hold out—their forces had now been cut down to less than one hundred thousand troops—Mao Tse-tung, Chu Teh, Chou En-lai and the other leaders after much discussion decided to break out of the iron encirclement and make a dash for some remote region of China where they could set up once more. To facilitate this maneuver Hsiang Ying and Chen Yi were left behind

with the difficult task of performing rear guard action.
(They did not rejoin the main group until they showed
up in Yenan three years later.) Thus was born on October
16, 1934, the famous "long march" of the Chinese Communists.

By many this phenomenon has been idolized as the
"epic long march" which took the Communists through
nine provinces covering six thousand miles of territory
within a period of fourteen months. Actually it was a huge
sickleshaped swath of deviltry cut in a large arc through
China, leaving a trail of blood and devastation and human
wreckage in its wake. I spoke with one missionary, the
Reverend R. A. Bosshardt of the China Inland Mission,
author of *The Restraining Hand,* who had been dragged
along for ransom and had spent many months with this
army of "heroes." Their mouth was full of cursing and
their hands full of blood. At the least pretense they would
bayonet a poor wayfarer who might be too nervous to
answer their questions satisfactorily.

Formed into a number of columns, joined by fleeing
comrades from other Soviets, fighting battles and dodg-
ing government concentrations, they harassed the countryside in their crazy march through the land. They seized
people for ransom (including many missionaries), tortured the rich, violated their women. One group captured
a missionary couple. The young mother was raped to
death in the presence of her bound husband who was
himself thereupon gruesomely killed. All this was done
to achieve Communist "justice." One need not be shocked
—it is all in the book of standard methods used by the
Communists against landlord families and "reactionaries."
Any form of torture is permissible—often demanded—
against the "class enemies" of Communism.

After the Communist and the National troops were

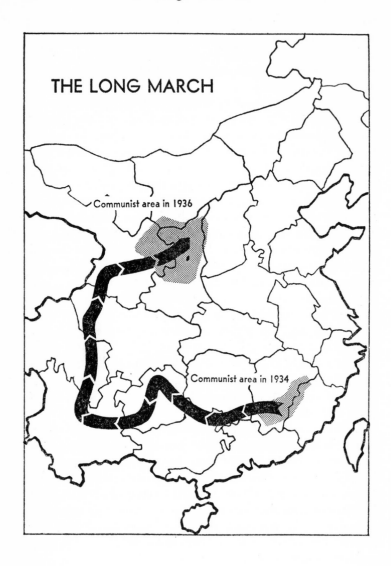

done with Kiangsi, the population of the province had been decimated. Millions of people were demoralized and without homes. A terrific problem of rehabilitation faced the Government. This was solved in co-operation with missionaries by setting up centers of self-help through the Kiangsi Christian Rural Service Union.

In January, 1935, the Red columns from Kiangsi had arrived at Kweichow Province. Here in the city of Tsunyi the Politburo convened a conference in which Mao Tse-tung officially took over the chairmanship of both the Central Committee and the Politburo. During the sessions Chang Kuo-t'ao, who had come from Szechwan to attend the Conference, had stormy disagreements with Mao. He advocated settling in Szechwan, where his personal influence had already been established, or pulling still farther west. Mao insisted on moving north and opening an international line. The latter counsel prevailed.

By summer Mao's troops had joined those of Chang Kuo-t'ao and Hsü Hsiang-ch'ien in Szechwan. The heated discussions from the Tsunyi Conference persisted, but in the end the course already decided upon was followed. The main forces under Mao Tse-tung, P'eng Teh-huai, Lin Piao and Chou En-lai set out for Northern Shensi while Chu Teh stayed with Chang Kuo-t'ao and Hsü Hsiang-ch'ien to follow later.

By December, 1935, the vanguard of the survivors from Kiangsi had arrived at another "border region"—this time not of provinces but of China herself. At Pao An and Yenan in Shensi, close to the USSR sphere of influence, where Kao Kang had years earlier established a Soviet, the Chinese Communists set up their new regime to which gradually other straggling columns gravitated. Of the original almost one hundred thousand who left Kiangsi, less than twenty thousand survived the Long March.

After the flight of the Reds from our Honan-Hupeh area we enjoyed comparative peace in our mission work for a time. However, remnants of the Communist forces had been left behind and others infiltrated back into the region, forcing us to make careful inquiries as to the whereabouts of the Communist bands before we dared to venture into the mountains to certain of our outstations. I think of one place in particular where neither the Chinese pastor nor I had been to administer Communion for over a year. When I heard reports that the situation had eased, I made preparations for a quick visit. Early one Sunday morning rolling my *p'ao tzu* (cotton wadded garment) into a bundle containing my Bible, hymnbook and the elements, and securely fastening it to the carrier in the rear, I hopped on my bicycle and slowly pumped my way over narrow, rocky pathways—now winding along the bank of a stream, now following a range of low-lying mountains. I arrived at the humble village, nestled among the hills, in good time for a cup of tea and some visiting before services. The Christians and friends were most happy for the occasion.

It was a great joy to preach the Word of God to the hard-working peasants and petty merchants who composed the congregation. Before I was finished, however, I noticed a disturbance at the door, but paid little attention. When I was through speaking the elder of the congregation came up to me and said that reports had just been received that the Communists were headed this way and perhaps I had better leave. We had planned the Communion Services for the afternoon, so I was loath to leave without having accomplished my purpose. We then decided to urge the Christians to have lunch immediately and return for an early afternoon meeting. When the time arrived the elder arranged for someone to keep posted on the situation while we met in the church. What an inspiration it was to administer the Bread of Life to these hungry souls—the rich, the poor, the landlords, the farmers, the traders—all kneeling in the bond of love before one Lord, one Master! Nothing untoward developed and after affectionate farewells I jumped on my bicycle and arrived home without incident.

That night the Communists arrived at the village. For two weeks the inhabitants did not dare to sleep in their homes—except for the poorest of them—but slept under the trees in the surrounding hills and valleys. Passing on their way the Red band came unawares upon one of our preaching places. There they seized one of our inquirers and for no other reason than that he was working in a government post office stoned him to death. They captured one of our Christians and sawed through his head. When they were gone his son, who worked in our Sinyang Union Hospital, found needle and thread and, after recovering the corpse of his father, with tears repaired his remains and gave him a decent burial. These were only a couple of cases among hundreds—but they concerned us directly and left their impression.

By 1936 the Communists were becoming a serious menace again in our locality. They waylaid buses and executed the occupants. They derailed trains. In June they captured the Reverend Knut Samseth of our sister organization, the Norwegian Lutheran Mission. By fall they were once more at one of our outstations displaying the missionary from a platform to impress the crowds. That was the last ever heard of our friend.

During these years of underground existence, bruised and tormented, the Red Dragon had been writhing in fury. It was soon to emerge with deceit and cunning, then in great wrath devour the whole land.

red dragon emerges

G LOOM settled over the land of China. The baleful news spread—news that seemed fantastic, unreal. "The Generalissimo has been kidnaped!" That was on December 12, 1936.

Pessimism took possession of officialdom, of the man in the street. Never before had we realized so clearly what Chiang Kai-shek meant to the Chinese people. With aggression looming without, with Red insurrection tearing the nation within, the people had hooked their star of hope to this one great leader.

In spite of Japanese encroachment and Communist harassment, it is amazing what progress Chiang Kai-shek had brought to the country in the few years since his coming to power. This period has been named the "Golden Decade." We lived in the midst of it and were impressed by the enormous strides being made toward modernization.

The variety of piece goods sold in the inland shops, the local brand thermos bottles, the utensils, all testified to the expansion of China's industrialization as well as to the volume of foreign trade. Bananas and other perishables from the South were sold on small street stalls in the far interior. Merchants and small traders were flourishing in their business, and the farmers on the whole seemed satisfied. The poor as well as the rich were thriving.

In Shanghai—one of the busiest marts in the world—Chinese and foreign importers worked in harmonious co-operation. Tourists flocked to the port. China's economy reached such a stability that, for a time, the silver dollar was almost on a par with U.S. currency.

Power plants were built and electricity introduced to many inland cities. Even the radio made its appearance. Telephone lines connected out-of-the way villages with main centers. These were used for government administration but were accessible to the public. China's post office system never functioned any better. Education was forging ahead, no longer primarily dependent upon mission institutions. Mass education movements were afoot. Government experimental stations for agriculture and forestry were scattered throughout the country.

Perhaps the most noticeable achievement was in the line of transportation. Modern comfortable river liners, British and Chinese, plied the waters of the Yangtze. Broad highways were being constructed, radiating into the country from communication centers, so that now—with good springs—one could drive a car from Shanghai to almost every province in China. This was something unheard of before. To the far-flung Southwest one could drive to Indo-China, Siam and Singapore. New railways were constructed and others projected. It was now possible to travel by rail from Hongkong through China to Great Britain or to any large city in Europe. The "blue express" and other specials were punctual, fast, clean, and not overcrowded. For short distances we did not hesitate to have our children ride in them third class. Air lines connected most of the large cities of the country so that where one formerly consumed weeks in travel now he could almost do it in as many hours.

All these things are forgotten by many people who remember only the dilapidated conditions existing in China after eight long years of debilitating warfare followed by renewed civil strife brought on by the Communists.

Aside from the strife-ridden areas, Chiang Kai-shek had brought prosperity to the country and was forging China into a modern state. He alone had been big enough to dominate the remnants of warlordism. What would happen to the Nation now if harm should befall its leader?

Eager to rid his country of organized treason, to stamp out a movement which owed allegiance to Russia above the motherland, to abolish the state within a State which coined its own money, made its own laws and had its own army (let those who criticize Chiang for the civil war ask themselves: what modern state would ever countenance such a situation? What did Lincoln do to preserve our own union? What head of State being a patriot would surrender his country to stooges of a foreign regime?)— eager to do all these things so that he could face Japan without being hamstrung from the rear or stabbed in the back, Chiang Kai-shek had flown to Sian to galvanize the forces there into action against the Reds. He had heard of vacillation among the troops of Chang Hsüeh-liang— now deputy commander-in-chief of all National forces— who had been entrusted with the chief part in a renewed attempt to exterminate Communism. Disregarding his own personal safety, Chiang had flown to the Northwest to encourage his colleague. He was not aware of the extent of Communist infiltration, fell into a trap and was kidnaped by his own subordinate. It was hard to realize that this "Young Marshall," as Chang Hsüeh-liang was called, a reformed opium smoker, a sportsman whom I had met not so long before on the tennis courts of Kikungshan, had turned traitor and arrested his superior!

There was a reason for the *coup:* it was Communist intrigue and infiltration at work again. The whole case was tied up to the international situation and World Communism.

In their brazen aggression in China the Japanese had been creating an escape hatch for the Chinese Communists. After annexing Manchuria they had expanded their holdings through the "battle of the Great Wall," adding Jehol, northern Chahar, and eastern Hopei to their control. They forced the Kuomintang to remove its headquarters from Peiping and Tientsin and threatened to take over North China. Much of the nation was in a frenzy of frustration. It was this situation, then, of which the Communists tried to take advantage. They realized that under peaceful conditions their program would have little chance of prevailing; but, if they could get China into an open war with Japan, they would ease the pressure on themselves and be able to capitalize on the ensuing chaos to spread their influence.

In the dark days of Mao's struggle for survival before he was forced into the Long March, to save his movement from total annihilation he had appealed to the Kuomintang and the nation for a united front against Japan. Little heed was paid to this suggestion. The Communists, however, are a race not easily discouraged. They kept playing on the theme in their propaganda—while dragon-dancing across the country, later while digging their lair in the caves of Shensi. Oft-repeated words have strange effectiveness and the Communist refrain was beginning to be sung by China's intellectuals.

On the international front Hitler had come to power and, with Italy and Japan, loudly threatened anti-Comintern action. To forestall a war on the "Socialist Fatherland" and to break up unity among capitalist nations, the Seventh Congress of the Comintern in Moscow had, during the summer of 1935, called for an "Anti-Fascist United Front of all Peoples of the World." It had also ordered the Chinese Communist Party to form a United Front against Japan.

It was therefore only natural for the Chinese Communist Party, after settling down in Shensi, to repeat its call time and again for a united national front against Japan. But the Kuomintang after its experiences had been in no mood to accept Communist co-operation. Chiang Kai-shek had stationed Marshal Chang Hsüeh-liang and his formidable army, together with other units, in the Northwest to cordon off the Red troops at Yenan. Government forces had been squeezing the Communists into a tight pocket so that at their lowest ebb in 1936 they occupied only Yenan and two other counties. These barren mountains and wastelands were not able to support them. A foraging raid into western Shansi ended in failure. In their desperate need for self-preservation, therefore, they concentrated their attention on subverting the troops that surrounded them and in this they were successful.

Since Japan's take-over of Manchuria, Marshal Chang Hsüeh-liang and his army of well dressed, well equipped troops had been exiles from their home provinces. Chou En-lai—today vice-chairman of the Chinese Soviet Republic—with his "smooth talk and persuasive manner" directed the psychological offensive. Victory was a matter of life or death with the Communists. Taking advantage of the traditional love of home among the Chinese, Chou sent his agents to persuade the soldiers that they ought not fight against their countrymen but rather join with the Communists to expel the Japanese so that the "North-eastern Army" could return to its home provinces. "Fight the outsider!" became their slogan. "Don't shoot fellow-Chinese!" Women agitators were used to shout across the trenches seductive phrases of disaffection. Sabotage began to appear on the front lines. In one surprise maneuver the Reds captured several generals with whom Chou En-lai eloquently pleaded that they ought not fight Chinese but regain Manchuria from the Japanese. It is understandable what a terrific appeal this would make. After good treatment and indoctrination the captives were released and given the mission to arrange a secret meeting between Chang Hsüeh-liang and Chou En-lai. The Young Marshal was completely won over to the Communist viewpoint. There were strange goings-on between the two opposing forces and fighting came to a standstill. By the time Chiang Kai-shek had received reports of possible sedition and had flown to Sian to deal with the situation in person, the city was already seething with Communist agitation. Agents had infiltrated into Chang Hsüeh-liang's headquarters and those of his associates. Communist front organizations had mushroomed into being all over town.

Chiang Kai-shek arrived at Sian on December 7, 1936. On the twelfth while he was at a hot-spring resort outside the city the place was surrounded, most of his body-guard were killed in defending him and Chiang Kai-shek—though injured in falling—was taken captive. Outraged over the insult he refused to negotiate with his captor but, instead, castigated him for his insubordination and demanded death rather than agreement made under duress.

Meanwhile, according to information from high Communist authorities, the Reds at Yenan were engaged in heated discussions, the majority of the military leaders favoring the outright killing of Chiang Kai-shek for sheer revenge. Suddenly overruling orders came from Moscow. Wang Ching-wei, who later became Japan's puppet, was returning to China from a German sanatorium with the blessings of Hitler upon him. To forestall his getting into power the Comintern directed that Chiang be released at once and brought safely to Nanking to lead a coalition against Japan. When these instructions had been received, all differences were resolved at Yenan and Chou En-lai (with Yeh Chien-ying and Po Ku) proceeded to Sian to "mediate" between the Government and the rebels in a situation which they themselves had created!

The Young Marshal was deadlocked in his efforts to wring concessions from the Generalissimo. He had outlined eight points, but each time he tried to present them the Generalissimo scolded him for rebellion and demanded to be released or shot without delay. He could get nowhere.

Chou En-lai then stepped in and had several conferences with the prisoner. Only one thing mattered for the Communists: that the war against them be called off. If this were agreed to, the captive might go free. Others had joined the negotiations, including Madame Chiang Kai-shek. In the end the Generalissimo was prevailed upon to discontinue operations against the Reds and consider a united front against Japan.

I was at the time at an outstation deep in the interior of China. We had celebrated Christmas with special meetings and I was about to retire. Suddenly shooting broke out all over town. Things had seemed peaceful enough during the last few days—but perhaps it had been only the calm before a storm. My first thought was that the bandits had opened a surprise attack. Now the whole town was in an uproar. I stepped outside to learn what was happening.

"The Generalissimo is free," someone shouted, "the best Christmas gift we could receive!" The whole town was in jubilation! By this time the fire-crackers were going off not singly, but in strings.

When Chiang Kai-shek and his party had left Sian by plane, Chang Hsüeh-liang had accompanied them to Nanking in order to confess and plead for leniency. Later he was court-martialed and sentenced to the loss of his freedom. When I visited Formosa in 1953, a friend of mine who was driving me through the country pointed out a spacious establishment behind the walls of which the impulsive Young Marshal was living out his sentence.

After the release of Chiang Kai-shek the Communists gained enormously in reputation. They took to themselves the whole credit for obtaining Chiang's freedom and put out highsounding propaganda about their own magnanimity and patriotism. They also took credit for putting an end to the civil war in order that China might be united in facing Japan.

On February 10, 1937, the Communists sent a telegram to Nanking offering: (1) to give up all attempts at overthrowing the Government by force; (2) to change the name of the "Soviet Government" to "Special Area Government"; (3) to put the Communist army under the direct control of the Central Government; (4) to practice universal suffrage in the Special Area; and (5) to abandon the revolutionary confiscation and redistribution of land.

As news of the generous offer "leaked" out public esteem for the Communist Party skyrocketed. The intellectuals were taken in by the unselfishness of a party which put national welfare above partisan politics.

While negotiations with the government were progressing (Chou En-lai was in Nanking representing the Communists), on July 7, 1937, a shooting incident at the Marco Polo Bridge near Peiping furnished Japan with the excuse for starting her war of aggression for which she had been preparing for years. This hastened the formal establishment of the Chinese United Front. An agreement was reached including fundamentally the propositions earlier submitted by the Communists. Chiang Kai-shek was acknowledged the head of the Government. The Red Army was "incorporated" into the National forces as the Eighth Route Army and the Communists were given the right to govern their own areas within the National framework. Anti-Government propaganda would cease, agrarian revolution be abolished. Democratic reforms were to be instituted at once by the Government with Sun Yat-sen's Three Principles as the basic code of the land.

Thus we see the Communists—whatever their guileful reservations—emerging from underground existence and in the eyes of the people *appearing* to be a respectable, patriotic, reasonable party of the United Front. The ordinary Chinese wondered at such high-principled politics and rejoiced that the Communists had abandoned their peculiar views regarding the class struggle. The Reds had made really big concessions—even though only on paper—and they seemed so earnest! The educated classes were fascinated. Enterprising students from all over the country flocked to the Communist university in the caves of Yenan where they were given more indoctrination than education, thus being fitted for future leadership in the reviving Communist movement.

Once more in the open, the Red Dragon licked its wounds, regained its bearings and prepared for mortal strife.

growing fat

FOR the next decade or so after the Sian Incident, with the invaluable breathing spell furnished under the formula of a United Front, the Communists in China made astounding progress. To begin with they outwardly worked with the government, even praising Chiang Kai-shek and the Kuomintang—as Mao did in his report *The New Stage* delivered in October 1938—to cover up their own intentions. Secretly, they worked for the expansion of their system in flagrant violation of their pledges.

The months following the Sian Incident may be designated as the period in which the Communists were courting the Kuomintang—not out of love, to be sure, but out of ulterior motives. The year following the outbreak of the Japanese war was the period of their honeymoon. After that the unfaithfulness of the one party was more and more coming to light leading to mutual suspicions, tensions and violent encounters which continued until their final divorce in 1947.

During the first months of the war in 1937 Chou En-lai was in Nanking mobilizing the Red forces. From the scattered groups in Central China which operated around our field and clear down to Nanking, he formed the New Fourth Army which was put under the command of Yeh T'ing. Their tentacles stretched into the district where I was working and their method of inflating their size was observable. From a nucleus of two thousand the forces had grown to five thousand when recognized by the Government and "incorporated" into the National Army in the Third War Area for carrying on guerrilla warfare against the Japanese. As they later admitted, the officers had no intention of abiding by the agreements made with the Government but were determined to enlarge the territory under their control. In another six months they nearly tripled their numbers, largely by nibbling away at isolated Government units and local militia and impressing the captives into their ranks. This was a standard trick with the Communists—to conscript or capture young men, give them thorough indoctrination and assimilate them into their strait-jacket system. Once in, it was next to impossible to get out again. Thus step by step the Communists enlarged their borders and swelled their illegal man power. The Kuomintang, preoccupied with its life-and-death struggle with Japan, was more or less helpless in the face of these tactics.

As Mao Tse-tung told Edgar Snow, the chief tasks of the Red Army were to recruit new troops and to thoroughly sovietize the new areas they acquired. They were never idle; they performed their task with admirable energy. Another cardinal principle of Mao Tse-tung was that the soldiers, as vanguards of the Communists, must win the favor of the people.

In order to understand how this policy worked out, let us review a specific instance of Communist expansion under war conditions.

In the Second War Area during the latter part of 1937 when the Japanese were beginning to penetrate into Shansi, the Communist Eighth Route Army was ordered by the Government to march against them. Its vanguard of five thousand men under Nieh Jung-chen crossed the Yellow River, surprised the Japanese in a mountain pass and worked its way to the enemy rear, infiltrating into Chahar (part of Inner Mongolia) and Hopei Provinces.

Whereas the National troops were meeting the frontal attacks of the Japanese and being beaten back, the Communist troops seldom engaged the enemy face to face. They were more interested in increasing their own power than in sacrificing themselves for the nation. When convenient they attacked the Japanese to replenish their own stocks of weapons and supplies, but it was more convenient, as a rule, to prey upon the retreating and scattered Government troops.

In their rapid advance the Japanese occupied 80 per cent of China's railroads, but left large pockets of territory insufficiently garrisoned. Thus in Central Hopei they left a huge vacuum containing twenty million inhabitants and miscellaneous groups of bandits, guerrillas and defeated soldiers. Government authority had broken down and the people were at the mercy of whoever could force his authority on them. Into various parts of this fertile field came small detachments of the Red Army.

One of the defeated generals of the National Northeastern Army, a regimental commander, Lü Cheng-t'sao, whose forces had been crushed by the superior firepower of the Japanese, was floating around in this area with some of his remnant troops. The Eighth Route Army persuaded him to join them, thus considerably augmenting their own forces. After thorough indoctrination he and his men came to An Kuo to set up headquarters.

At An Kuo, according to an eyewitness account, they set to work on the people immediately. The military aspect was one of the least of their worries. They attacked their assignment *simultaneously* from the psychological, educational, social, economic, political and military angles. With the precision of clockwork they got their complicated machinery going.

The ordinary soldiers had their place in the scheme of things; they were the first to arrive. Their foremost duty was to win the goodwill of the people. They were generally polite and well-behaved, courteous to women, calling them "sister-in-law" and "grandmother"; they refrained from looting and brought back things they borrowed. Whenever there was a breach of discipline, it was followed with swift punishment in public. The soldiers were on the lookout for opportunities of being helpful; they offered to sweep floors, carry water, work in the fields. They were the "People's Army" and they let it be known, often ridiculing the Kuomintang soldiers in comparison. The inhabitants were completely swept off their feet by such conduct. What a contrast to the behavior of the undisciplined National troops! This was surely a new ideal for the future China!

Unaccustomed to lying propaganda and fraudulent actions on such a scale, the people, rich and poor, were easily taken in by this play acting. Those who had heard tales of horror regarding the Communists began to doubt their information—believed that the Communists must have been victims of malicious slander.

Besides creating a good impression, the troops also performed the essential function of spying on the people. Having won their confidence they were able to talk to them freely, like one of the family. From their casual conversation they would find out who possessed rifles, who were rich or poor, who were decent, respected people and who were cunning and unscrupulous. Later the authorities made use of this information to liquidate the influential and put the scoundrels into positions of power where they could use them. Gradually they got their stooges into key positions in the village structure. By the time the people woke up to the meaning of the Communist farce, it was already too late. Through deception they had been thrown off their guard while the straitjacket had been fitted on.

The psychological and political offensive was launched from the moment the Communists arrived. They ground out propaganda—books and leaflets for the literate, lectures for the unlearned. They kept pounding on the central theme: "The People's Army will save you from the Japanese." World news with a Communist slant was read from the roof-tops in the cool of the evening as people gathered to hear. They were delighted with the innovation. Every center had a newspaper condensed from the big papers which were all alike in Communist territory.

The cultural program launched by the Communists had the greatest appeal, promising to add entertainment and pleasure to the humdrum existence of the people. This was used as a strong arm of propaganda. The reading of poetry and the plays performed in the open-air theater of the village were all injected with Communist ideology.

Under the pretext of having to guard against traitors and spies the Communists told the people they would have to register and obtain travel passes, even for neighboring villages. The people submitted to this innocent-looking restriction for the sake of their country; but through it the Communists subtly got control of the movements of the people. From the detailed information submitted they also obtained material for use later in the wholesale liquidation of the upper classes.

Under the slogan "total mobilization of the people" for the salvation of the country, the Communists tightly organized the whole population. The new setup was put into effect quickly. The Communist workers knew exactly what to do and how to do it. Their blueprint for action was precise, their work methodical.

The people were organized into groups. The pottery makers, workers in brick kilns, and others were formed into labor unions; the peasants into farmers' associations; the homemakers into women's guilds; and the young people and children into youth corps. Communist workers—efficient, well trained—moved into each group. Depending on their size, the groups were subdivided—the youth corps, for example, according to age beginning with four-year-olds. Meetings were called continually for long periods of indoctrination. Besides being drilled in the Communist teachings, the peasants were promised things which they wanted—improved farming, less taxation, better prices. The youth—even the girls—were given military training with special indoctrination.

Every group was combed for the most promising and progressive individuals who were given more training and used in positions of leadership. These were then watched with special care in order to spot the calculating and heartless members for possible party membership and training. In these indoctrination schools the most ruthless and vindictive students achieved the highest Marx!

Everyone was required to do some work for the Party. *Hsi nao chin* (wash the brain) was a phrase used over and over again to break down old conceptions and instill the new. Whoever did not learn properly was "against the revolution" and subject to suppression. Each individual was compelled to accept the Communist view of life and of society.

Soon the people were surprised to find that in their zeal for national salvation their personal initiative and freedom had slipped away and been replaced with group action under strict Communist control. No longer could one spend a quiet evening at home, if he so desired; he would be considered a traitor and a spy. However tiring the organized activities, however boring the indoctrination classes, he could not absent himself. He had become a cog in the machinery.

There were drives for voluntary contributions to the war chest, great appeals to patriotism. The wealthy, to gain favor, would come forward and give generously, only to have the authorities turn on them saying they could afford much more in comparison to the poor. As the Communists were eager to get hold of all the local rifles, they would set a date, issue official orders and ask the large contributors to bring so and so many rifles to headquarters at the specified time—if they were truly patriotic people. As their life depended on it they would scurry around trying to buy rifles until the price of weapons skyrocketed and the rich broke themselves in trying to keep out of the hands of the rulers. Others were arrested and fined rifles instead of money. Nor was there any end to the process; no sooner had a fellow payed up for one fine than he was arrested for something else—usually trumped-up charges— and had to go through the whole nightmare again until he sank deeply in debt. By then he realized that he had been marked for ultimate destruction. As for the Communists, the more rifles they obtained the more powerfully they applied their methods.

When the Communists first came to An Kuo they were few in number. Guerrillas and bandits were roaming the countryside at will. The Red leaders acted warily, avoiding any clashes, yet keeping an eye on the groups. As soon as they were strong enough to take over villages and counties, they cracked down.

About this time one guerrilla leader with a hundred men happened into An Kuo. General Lü invited the patriot to tea. There he was told it was either capitulation or annihilation. After choosing to live and join the Communists, the guerrilla chief and his men were sent off for special indoctrination. Inside a year this man had recruited ten thousand followers and became a prominent Red general.

When the Communists were ready for bandit suppression they launched a concentrated propaganda drive. Great stress was laid on the idea that it was "for the benefit of the people." Most of the population were co-operative and enthusiastic for that kind of thing. There were plenty of informers to tell where the bandits were hiding out and the latter were handled unit by unit. There was always the choice: incorporation or annihilation.

The guerrillas were given the same choice. One famous group composed of university students from Peiping under the leadership of Chao Tung rejected the "friendly" advice to be reorganized. The whole detachment was forthwith annihilated and Chao Tung tortured and killed.

By the early part of 1938 the Communists controlled 24 counties in this area. By the end of the year all banditry had been suppressed and General Lü had increased the number of his troops from one thousand to one hundred thousand. By applying their rigid ideological measures the Communists had completely enslaved the peasants and all other people. The first illicit regime of this period was set up and known as the "Shansi-Chahar-Hopei Border Region Government." This example of Communist expansion is typical of their work in all the areas.

Some "experts" suppose that the Chinese Communist movement was a *spontaneous* uprising of the peasants against unbearable sufferings and oppression. To be sure, there was plenty of suffering for all the Chinese, and for the poor peasants in particular, and there was a nucleus of unprincipled ruffians about whom the Communists could build—but if the majority of the peasants, rich or poor, had known what they were getting into, or had a free choice in the matter, they would not have joined the movement in a thousand years. As anyone who has been intimately acquainted with Chinese life knows, Communism cuts straight across the whole background and tradition of Chinese peasant society and runs counter to their love of freedom and individualism. For that reason "old China hands" almost unanimously predicted that China could never go Communist—but they had never dreamed of the devilish cunning of the Bolshevik terror.

The Communists needed no majority in order to operate; all they needed was to throw the wool over the eyes of the majority. Then like a mighty steamroller they pressured the peasants into line. To a society in flux they came with a definite program and through *deceiving*, first of all, then organizing, dividing man against man and class against class, threatening, bullying and terrorizing, they forced the peasants and populace to follow their way and become integrated in their movement. When the people were once entangled in that system—where personal survival became a paramount issue—the mob spirit took over, masterminded by the trained Communist agitators. Like a giant rolling snowball the movement increased in size until it was next to impossible to stop it.

For any society not to be on its guard against the subtle workings of Communism is fatal. The only time to stop it is *before* it infiltrates into a community. Once it has gained a strangle hold, the people are powerless to throw it off.

In April, 1938, the Eighth Route Army in the Second War Area was reorganized into three divisions of the Eighteenth Army Corps of the National Government. (However, the name of "Eighth Route Army" continued in common usage.) Chu Teh was commander and P'eng Teh-huai vice-commander of the Communist troops with Lin Piao, Ho Lung and Liu Po-ch'eng as divisional commanders. By previous agreement, of course, the number of Communist troops was to remain fixed.

While Chu Teh and his top commanders kept their legal divisions in the open at the places assigned by the Government, they used other troops secretly for expanding their territory. Thus Ho Lung infiltrated into Northwestern Shansi and before long was commanding seven full divisions, though officially he had only one. Thereupon the "Northwestern Shansi Administration" was established.

In July, 1938, a branch of the army belonging to Nieh Jung-chen, deputy-commander under Lin Piao, penetrated into Eastern Hopei. There the "Eastern Hopei Administration" was founded.

The third divisional commander of the Eighth Route Army, General Liu Po-ch'eng, was quite a character. An out-and-out Communist, having been converted in his early twenties, he was the first of his comrades to get thorough military training in Moscow where he attended the Red Army Academy for three years. When he fought with the Russians in 1929 against the troops of Chang Hsüeh-liang in Manchuria, he won the notable honor of being the first Communist general to fight with a foreign power against his own people. He was said to have been wounded in almost every engagement he entered. His very name—the Chinese call him "One-eyed Dragon" because in one battle he lost an eye—was enough to instill fear into the hearts of his enemies. He is today Commander of Red China's 2nd Field Army and is a member of the highest politico-military council of the land.

This outstanding general was entrusted by Mao Tse-tung with advancing into Southeastern Shansi for guerrilla warfare in the Tai Hang Mountains. His exploits were many and his area became the headquarters of the Eighth Route Army.

One exploit of the "One-eyed Dragon" was the incorporation into his forces, almost intact, of the New Shansi Army which he had been sent to bolster against the Japanese. But the story goes back several years to the successful infiltration of the army by Communist agents.

Back in 1928 a young man, good-looking, eloquent, by the name of Po I-po, with six of his fellow students at the Taiyuan* Normal School joined the Communist Party. (By 1952 Po had risen to the position of Finance Minister. In 1953 he was arrested for some mistake or other while on a mission to Moscow and dismissed. His subsequent fate is unknown.) After their graduation these seven engaged in underground activities but were caught in 1932 and placed in a Government school for thought reformation. Here Yen Hsi-shan, the "model governor," was deeply impressed with their ability and sincerity. Yen Hsi-shan—who is today in Taiwan (Formosa)—was one of the first to co-operate with the Reds even before the outbreak of the Japanese War. Soon after the release of the students upon their "renunciation" of Communism, he appointed Po I-po as his secretary.

Then came the Japanese who captured Taiyuan. Po I-po and his comrades were left behind the enemy lines to organize guerrillas. They hammered together four "dare-

---

*Taiyuan was formerly the name of the capital city of Shansi. Now called Yangku.

to-die" corps which operated with great efficiency. Impressed with their success, Yen Hsi-shan incorporated the guerrillas into his New Shansi Army which was whipped into shape largely by these seven former Communists who were given positions of command or advice. This New Army was Yen Hsi-shan's great pride and joy, and soon it was expanded into fifty regiments. Now, having obtained the governor's implicit trust, Po I-po and the others made every new officer appointed by Yen join their organization —or he was secretly murdered.

In the Second War Area was a Russian adviser by the name of Ivanov. Through him in 1939 Mao Tse-tung appealed to Po I-po and his comrades to desert with the New Shansi Army to swell the ranks of the Communists. As they were secretly plotting with Liu Po-ch'eng ("One-eyed Dragon"), their plan was detected by an Old Army general who reported to Yen, suggesting that the young officers be arrested at once. As the governor still trusted the young men, he hesitated to take such drastic action.

Sensing danger in the air, Po I-po appealed directly to Yen Hsi-shan against the Old Army faction who, he said, were jealous because of their achievements. Pretending to be most concerned for Yen Hsi-shan's welfare, he even offered to resign in order to preserve the unity of the army. Because of such honest and self-sacrificing solicitude, the governor's suspicions were dispelled. Before anything further could be done, however, the revolt was perfected and the young officers at their posts ordered their troops to join the Eighth Route Army. The governor had been betrayed. So well had the New Shansi Army been infiltrated by the Reds that of its fifty regiments forty-eight left to unite with the forces of Liu Po-ch'eng and Ho Lung, most of the Province thus falling into the hands of the Communists.

Another exploit of the "One-eyed Dragon" was the wiping out of three crack National armies, almost sixty thousand Chinese troops, in the Tai Hang mountains in 1940, instead of taking the offensive against a strategic force of twenty thousand Japanese idling in the sun fifty miles away.

We have all read about the praying mantis (can it possibly belong to the *Dragon Family?*); the fierce, voracious female, after mating, eats up its partner. That is the kind of union the Communists believe in.

We shall examine this Tai Hang incident more in detail.

Along the Peiping-Hankow Railway the militiamen of General Chang Ying-wu had successfully harassed the Japanese for almost two years; but he needed communication lines with the rest of the Government forces. Consequently, National troops had come up from the south to open a road across the Tai Hang mountains making it possible for the armies behind them to pour out on to the Hopei plains for an all-out attack on the Japanese to cut their supply line near the railway city of Changteh. The Eighth Route Army, however, was not too happy to have the Government troops work their way to the rear and join up with Chang Ying-wu's guerrilla forces; they preferred to control the mountain pass themselves and gradually absorb the guerrillas into the Red Army.

As a result, while the Government forces were massing along the Tai Hang pass, the "One-eyed Dragon" sent his wiliest emissaries to negotiate for a part in the "common effort" against the enemy. They wangled a place high in the mountains between two of the National Armies. In that rugged terrain communications were slow. The exemplary behavior of their troops disarmed any suspicions that might have existed. Then suddenly at an opportune moment they struck a one-two punch which sent the

National troops reeling. On March 7 they wiped out the 97th Army to their right; the next day they turned on the Provincial troops to their left and virtually annihilated them. Then early on March 9, in a swift maneuver for which they were famous, they surprised the New Fifth Army of Sun Tien-ying to the South and all but wiped it out. After accomplishing these lightning strokes for which they had carefully prepared, they shrieked out their most abusive vituperations, vilifying the Kuomintang troops for their base attack on their brothers and beclouding the issues with their propaganda. The Communists were always out first with their dispatches and the network of their news service both to foreigners and Chinese was excellent. The Kuomintang was deficient in all these ways.

Thus ended another exploit of Liu Po-ch'eng and his troops. They were, however, only obeying the directive of their master, Mao Tse-tung, who had ordered the Red Army: "Fight ninety per cent against the Kuomintang, ten per cent against the Japanese."

After this it was comparatively easy to force the guerrillas of Chang Ying-wu in Hopei and of Chin Chi-yung in Shantung, as well as others, into submission to the Communists. Soon there emerged in Liu Po-ch'eng's sphere of influence a new administrative area which was designated as the "Shansi-Hopei-Shantung-Honan Border Region Government"—an extensive field, indeed!

In their official *History of the Revolution* the Chinese Communists later boasted about the "areas of liberation" which they had established during this period. And according to their own testimony, in the first three years of war they had increased their forces about eightfold—the Eighth Route Army from forty-five thousand to four hundred thousand and the New Fourth Army from fifteen thousand to one hundred thousand.

CHAPTER NINE

stalking its prey

I N THE spring of 1939 I made a trip across the Japanese lines from Free China into occupied territory. The purpose of my trip was to visit my mother who had been cut off from some of the rest of us by the war. She was doing missionary work which she had started many years earlier on Kikungshan and vicinity.

Passing through no man's land was uneventful except for the occasional booming of guns in the distance and the anxiety to get across while the going was good. But once on the Japanese side, there followed weeks of tiresome negotiations before I was able to travel the remaining thirty miles. Only through the help of a Christian Japanese Captain, who had become acquainted with my mother, was I able to cut through the Japanese red tape and arbitrariness.

On the mountain top where we visited and where many memories from childhood flooded my thoughts, a large number of refugees had collected and were living in the spacious missionary Assembly Hall. A garrison of about sixty Japanese had fortified some missionary houses on the "north cape" of the summer resort. Daily I made trips to the Assembly Hall to mingle with the refugees and bring the Word of God to them.

A day before my departure I was waked up in the night with the whole mountain alive from the crackling of rifles. Men were running past my window and speaking in excited voices. Being unable to see, and not daring to light a lamp, I lay still until dawn.

All morning there was intermittent shooting. I learned that about four hundred guerrillas had come during the night and had bottled up the Japanese in their fortifications. However, the attack was not effectual. At noon, as we had just finished eating, I could see through a sheltered window straight to the Japanese fortifications, where I could make out a Japanese soldier with a machine gun creeping around the ridge to a vantage point, followed by others. It was a sign for the guerrillas to melt away as their old-fashioned rifles were no match for the superior weapons of the enemy.

Shortly after this, a delegation came with fear and trembling asking that I, as a neutral, hurry to the Assembly Hall to protect the refugees in case the Japanese soldiers should seek revenge on them because of the attack. I promised to go with them. Miss Lydia Hanson, who was working with my mother at the time, went with me.

At the Assembly Hall the atmosphere was tense, but we tried to quiet the people and used the time to bring them comfort from God's Word. Later I stepped outside and made my way along a path to consult with the Reverend Francis Joyce, a pioneer of the China Inland Mission, who had retired on the mountain and whose home was nearby. As I was approaching, some people in the back yard started shouting at me. Not hearing what they said, I began running toward them. Suddenly I came upon two women lying dead at my feet, one shot through the neck, the other through the chest. Then I realized I had been in the wrong place. Safe in the house I could see through a window that the Japanese had set up their machine gun on an abandoned Chinese fort and were shooting anybody who ran along that path. I realized that it could just as well have been I as those two women lying there on the way. Intermittent fog, however, had covered the fort and saved my life. God had given me a new lease on life and I prayed that I might use it more whole-heartedly for Him!

Back at the Assembly Hall after the battle was over, I waited for the Japanese soldiers who were sure to come and make a search. They respected a neutral and nothing out of the way happened as I made the rounds with them. The next day, all being peaceful, I was once more on my way, returning to Free China.

This experience at one small point behind the Japanese front revealed to me the ceaseless, nagging uncertainty which faced the Japanese along their overstretched lines of communications. In the aggregate there were hundreds of thousands of guerrillas scattered in small bands throughout occupied territory.

It was upon these small, patriotic bands, often poorly armed and ill-clothed, that the New Fourth Army, organized by Chou En-lai, was fattening itself. The Reds also had their agents spreading their propaganda throughout our district, as well as others, and making followers. They planted a cell in the mission school at the station where my sister Cora and I were working, giving us endless trouble. We uncovered a great deal of subversive literature in possession of certain students. In the fall of 1939 Miss Agnes Smedley came through fresh from her sojourn among the Communists and put up at our mission home. Her loud praise of the Communists did not make our situation any easier. Throughout the following year the New Fourth Army continued gaining strength until in December 1940 a clash with Government troops about thirty miles from us alerted the Kuomintang to the increasing danger of the Red threat.

We sensed that things were building up to some crisis. In a few weeks we were struck by electrifying news. It was in the beginning of 1941—that fateful year when the Japanese twice invaded our city, Junan, which had not been captured by bandit or warlord in three hundred years, and completely looted it, hundreds of army trucks jogging over the fields (as the highways had been dug up) with their prize take of goods, grain, silver and ancient furniture. It was also the year of Pearl Harbor.

In October the Government had ordered the New Fourth Army to proceed to the north bank of the Yellow River to engage the enemy. Surprisingly, they had moved southward instead, crossing the Yangtze River. While the Red headquarters staff and some thousand troops were still in Anhwei Province, the Government acted to disarm the rebels. In the ensuing clash on January 7, 1941, five thousand Communist troops were wiped out, Yeh T'ing the Commander was captured and Hsiang Ying, a former Vice-President of the Chinese Soviet Republic, was killed in battle. It was a setback for this Communist army, but only a temporary one.

True to form, the Communists were out first with their version of the incident, laying complete blame upon the Kuomintang and claiming that while they themselves were obeying orders to proceed southward over the Yangtze the Government troops waylaid them. By the time the propaganda dust had settled, most people took it for granted that the Communists had suffered deep injustice and the National Government was completely unreliable.

Meanwhile the Japanese were becoming aware of the growing power of the Communist armies. Hitherto they had paid little attention to them, considering them mere bandits who seldom troubled them. Now, as if overnight, the Reds had become a menace. The Japanese decided to take the offensive.

For three and a half months—from August 20 to December 5, 1940—there raged mortal combat between the Japanese and the Reds. The latter considered themselves strong enough to emerge from guerrilla tactics and engage in mobile warfare. To meet the Japanese onslaught the Reds had massed four hundred thousand troops in 103 regiments, for which reason the Communist historians love to call the encounter the "Battle of 100 Regiments." The ardor of the Reds for frontal attacks, however, was considerably cooled. According to their own *History of the Revolution* they lost one-fourth of their effectives and the population under their control was reduced from one hundred million to fifty million. For the next two years the Japanese, who also suffered considerable losses, continued with periodic anti-Communist campaigns, but their punch diminished when they had to transfer large portions of their armies to the war theater of Southeast Asia. The Communists after that were given a chance to more than recoup their losses.

During these years the Communists laid great stress on the training of young recruits for the Party. Because of their legal status in the United Front and the effectiveness of their propaganda they drew to Yenan, the romantic city of caves, the idealistic youth from all over China. Their slogans of "unity," "resistance" and "democracy" appealed to fervent patriots. Front line organizations such as "Young People's National Salvation Corps" or "Vanguards of Liberation" attracted the young as flowers attract the butterflies.

At Yenan, to take care of the influx of students, special institutions were established such as the "Anti-Japanese Military and Political Academy," the "North-Shensi Public School," the "Lushan Art Academy," the "Anwupao Youth Training Center" and others.

Following the Red Army expansion in the field and the sovietization of large sections of the country a still more welcome source of recruits opened up. As new districts were organized the leaders scoured the Youth Corps and Indoctrination Classes for those prospects which showed more ambition or a more ruthless nature than ordinary. After their preliminary indoctrination in their home village, these were sent to regional centers representing, perhaps, some dozens of villages. Here there were hundreds of students divided into manageable groups. From each section the most progressive and enthusiastic members were picked out for a few months of extra training after which they were dispatched to the county seat, where the school could accommodate a thousand or more students from four or five regional centers. The discipline and training became progressively stiffer and only some over a third of the students could pass their tests to be promoted to the Border Region headquarters. Again the most successful were sent on to Yenan where they joined students from all over China.

These so-called "war universities" of Yenan were greatly extolled in the foreign press; actually they were institutions for political indoctrination more than what we think of as universities. Candidates from the Border Region schools were already Party members by this time and were issued secret text books, including manuals by Mao Tse-tung, on each of which was printed the personal number of the student. At unexpected times census would be taken of the students and their books. If any book was missing, it meant severe punishment for the student.

Candidates were observed particularly for qualities of unquestioning obedience and leadership. Those who survived the harsh competition were selected for transfer to Chita, Siberia. Here the schools were under Russian con-

Special Indoctrination for Picked Students

trol and management and the students were kept in isolation from the population under rigid discipline. It was the last stage of preparation for going to Moscow, the Mecca of World Communism.

Thus we see how the most radical, the most fanatical, the most gifted and brilliant youth skimmed from the population of China, after passing through many stages of refinement, ended up in Moscow where they were given top training for Party activities. As stated earlier in this history, the Russians, for their long range program, had founded three universities in Moscow exclusively for Chinese. Before that the Chinese were admitted into other schools, as the Sun Yat-sen University was not set up until 1925. According to Nicholas Poppe, a former teacher of Oriental languages in Moscow, the Russians started with the training of one thousand Chinese students as early as 1921. The number increased progressively as the ball started rolling—as the Communist base in China spread and the universities were founded in Moscow. Had there been only one thousand a year graduated from 1921 to 1945—think of the impact that would have been made upon China by twenty-five thousand fanatical, Russian-trained Party workers highly skilled in sabotage and sub-version, flooding into all parts of China! Actually, the number was many times greater.

By the end of their training these students had lost their roots in China. They were no longer bound by the ties of blood to parents or relatives or native village. Their characters were steely, inflexible, fiercely anti-religious. They were now Internationalists, zealots for one Cause—the cause of World Revolution.

In the early part of the war when the National Government moved its capital to Chungking because of the Japanese advance, Chou En-lai moved there too, as the Deputy Director of the Political Department of the Government Military Council. From this vantage point he directed propaganda among Chinese and foreigners alike, planted Communist cells in the Kuomintang and military groups wherever possible in Free China, made valuable contacts with Russian and foreign diplomats and infiltrated the National headquarters with his agents. To underscore the illusion he was giving of humility and sincerity he chose to live in the poorest section of town in a simple house with peasant furniture.

Being an expert in the Communist trick of covering up atrocious acts with sweet reasonableness, he could tell a lie without blinking. He proclaimed the good intentions of the Communists with such apparent earnestness and honesty and patience that both correspondents and envoys fell under his charm. Perhaps no one has double-crossed or beguiled more people of importance than this handsome, suave, polite gentleman with the cultured Peking accent and a workable knowledge of French, Russian, German, and even English.

Before long American diplomats were reporting to Washington that the Chinese Communists were not real Communists at all. Later George Marshall was to speak of his "personal esteem" for this Chou En-lai—one among a group of "liberals" who would certainly "put the interests of the Chinese people above ruthless measures to establish a Communist ideology." Dag Hammarskjold on his mission to Peking in 1955 to negotiate the release of American prisoners was to become impressed with him as being the "most courteous" person he had ever met—this same Communist who in his Shanghai days commanded firing squads and liquidated his erstwhile comrades with such ruthlessness that he earned for himself the nickname of "Executioner"! The General Secretary's interpreter, a personal friend of mine, on the same mission was to be so convinced by Chou's attentions and gifts that he was to be blinded to Communism's oppression of the Church and become an unwitting mouthpiece for Communist propaganda. Chou En-lai's play-act of reasonableness and self-control put on at the 1955 Bandung Afro-Asian Conference was to be seen by us all.

After her honeymoon with the Kuomintang and the recuperation of her strength, the Communist Party realized that with the cross-purposes of the two sides coming to light continued smooth co-operation was an impossibility. In order to conquer China the Communists developed a two-pronged strategy: first, to undermine the reputation of the National Government both among the Chinese and abroad; and second, to increase their own power for the final assault, while hanging on to the United Front as long as they could.

One of the greatest gains which the Communists had made in the United Front was the permission to publish their own newspaper, the *Hsin Hua Daily News*. This organ and mouthpiece of the Communist Party became a whip to keep the Kuomintang in line. The official sanction for its publication in the war time capital gave the Party tremendous prestige and influence among the people. By means of it the Communists broadcast their own political views and flayed the Kuomintang, magnifying every little mistake. Corruption, bred by long years of hectic warfare and uncertainties, was indeed creeping into some quarters of Government and army, giving the Communists plenty to work on. They held themselves up as the champions of integrity and of national unity, progress, and resistance to Japan, while accusing anyone who dared to oppose them as being against the good of the country. The paper became a "hot potato" for the Government. If the latter suppressed the paper it would be given a black eye nationally and internationally; if not, it would soon be discredited with the public anyway. Yet, like an experienced dog hesitating to attack a polecat, the Government let the paper continue until the final break in 1947.

By cleverly aiming their propaganda, the Communists were able to sow discord in the Kuomintang ranks. Putting emphasis on the United Front, they catered to the leftist members while ridiculing and isolating the anti-Communist elements. A "Democratic League" was formed in opposition to the Kuomintang, but this eventually proved a "flop" when two member organizations were disillusioned and withdrew.

When on November 29, 1938, a telegram came from Wang Ching-wei, deputy leader of the Kuomintang, advocating surrender to the Japanese, the Communists seized on this not only to attack Wang but to ridicule the Kuomintang for its policy of trying to contain Communism, which policy, they said, was but one step from surrender itself. This line caused a good deal of disaffection toward the Government. Whenever the latter seemed on the point of adopting a stronger attitude against Communism, it was paralyzed by a barrage of still more severe criticism. The Reds believed firmly in the policy that the best "defense" was to be offensive!

In the Press Hostel and the Embassies of Chung-king Chou En-lai was busy persuading news reporters and envoys that the Chinese Communists were respectable and incorruptible people; that they were primarily "agrarian reformers" and "town-meeting democrats." The illusion was created that there was a "pro-Western" faction and that there might be a possibility of weaning the Chinese Communists away from Russia by the use of a correct policy. To back Chiang Kai-shek was betting on the wrong horse and throwing money down the drain. Why not give the Communists a try at running the country?

The theme was underscored at Yenan. Journalists and authors and important personalities from the West, as well as Chinese, were not only welcomed but invited to come to the Red capital. There they were treated royally, yet simply. Everyone was on best behavior. Copious transcripts were furnished the writers. Conducted tours were arranged into prepared areas. Guests were always impressed by the discipline of the army. The population was so docile, so regimented that they always moved together. This strange effect fooled transient observers into thinking that the actions and behavior were spontaneous and natural. If interviewed (generally through interpreters) no person would dare do otherwise than insist he was free and happy. Actually, it was not so much what these travelers saw that was wrong as what they didn't see. And the Reds had arranged beforehand what they intended their guests to observe.

An example of the extent of Red manipulation was once witnessed by a Catholic missionary, Father Raymond J. deJaegher. Early one morning he was amazed to find the screaming slogans against America and Great Britain erased from the walls of the city and complimentary posters in English put up in their stead all over town. On inquiry he learned that an American reporter had been invited by the Reds to inspect their anti-Japanese activities in that area. When he arrived a great show was put on for his benefit which undoubtedly left its mark. When he was gone the old signs came up again.

It is unnecessary to detail the names and circumstances of the dozens of authors and journalists (some of whom have since about-faced—but after the damage had been done) who visited Yenan, came under the spell and returned with glowing reports of the "real democrats" of China. Yenan's iron censorship (much worse than Chung-

king's), secret police and concentration camps were not
mentioned. Presently books rolled off the press and articles
filled the magazines and papers of the West, especially
America, extolling the Reds and fostering a smear campaign against Chiang Kai-shek and his government the
like of which has never been seen. Strangely enough, as
these books appeared one after another they were re-
viewed largely by the same set of people with their pro-
Communist viewpoints and given wide publicity.

The din of propoganda was strangely effective. Not
only in China, but throughout the world, Chiang Kai-shek
became the one who was blamed for the civil war and
all other evils! America was made to forget almost completely all that she owed to the man as an individual. Up
until a year before our getting into the war but after
Japan had begun her aggression against China, our country, in the face of frequent protest, had sent ten million
tons of scrap iron and steel to Japan unchecked by the
Administration. The weight of this scrap iron was ten
times the tonnage of the whole Japanese navy! We also
had shipped to Japan three million barrels of oil a month
for running her navy and for blasting the cities and armies
of China. Yet Chiang Kai-shek had not turned against us,
but had forgiven. He had the vision and faith to see that
the United States would ultimately be involved and come
to his country's rescue. During these critical years his
strong will had held things together and he had fought on
alone, spurning at least twelve attractive peace offers
from Japan. His deputy, Wang Ching-wei, had not been
able to resist the temptation. Had Chiang yielded to the
pressure, Japan could have organized China's resources
and welded the Far East into a mighty war machine
which would have required much greater effort to conquer. But he chose to stick with the democracies, not to

join with the dictators. We owe a great debt to this stubborn, tenacious character.

Simultaneously with this smear campaign against Chiang and the face-lifting for the Reds, the World Communist apparatus moved into action to support the great delusion. Stalin, the master, with his deceitful smile, joined the masquerade, confiding in Roosevelt his lack of interest in the "Marginal" Communists of China and his intention of dealing only with Chiang Kai-shek. Later he made the Sino-Soviet Treaty with the National Government, "ignoring" the Communists. The Red stooges like Alger Hiss, one of Roosevelt's right hand men, who had worked their way into our State Department, helped shape our foreign policy according to the great delusion. Fellow travelers in this country, and unsuspecting liberals, took up the chant which had now swelled into a mighty chorus. The voices of competent observers with insight and a true understanding of Communism, which were raised in warning, were drowned out in the general shouting. America, and not only China, was heading for disaster.

During the years of the United Front, the Communists were not only enlarging their own army and territories and trying to undermine the opposition, but also tightening up their party machine for the coming inevitable contest. In the highest ranks there had been going on for some years an unrelenting power struggle. As we have seen earlier, Mao Tse-tung reached the top over the dead bodies of his rivals. Since his accession to leadership in Kiangsi, there had been only one comrade with sufficient experience, prestige and audacity to oppose him in the open, and that was Chang Kuo-t'ao. The latter had been a charter member of the Chinese Communist Party. He had been President of the Honan-Hupeh-Anhwei Soviet

and one of the vice-presidents of the Chinese Soviet Republic. He had also been a leader of the Szechwan Soviet,
so he felt he was fully equal to Mao in wisdom and ability.
At the conference in Szechwan he had openly fallen out
with the latter and his clique, and the rivalry had continued in Yenan. By 1938 Mao Tse-tung had won complete mastery and Chang Kuo-t'ao was drummed out of
the Party, fleeing for his life to Hankow where he loudly
decried his recent comrades in subversion. (At present he
is residing in Hong Kong.) Following this purge Mao
Tse-tung's dictatorship was unchallenged.

With the influx of new blood at Yenan and the accession of thousands of new members to the Party, the danger
of quantity versus quality came to the fore. To cope with
this situation new schools of ideology were founded in
Yenan. "Forward Marx!" became the battle cry of the
Communist phalanx. The "Institute for the Study of
Marxism-Leninism" offered advanced instruction in Communist theories; the "Central Party Academy" gave specialized training for political workers. In these schools
Mao Tse-tung, Liu Shao-chi and other outstanding leaders
served as instructors. All Party workers and upper military
officers were required to refresh themselves with these indoctrination courses. One of the text books used was
titled *Party Reconstruction,* written by Liu Shao-chi and
based upon Stalin's *History of the Russian Communist
Party* (published in 1938) but incorporating the experiences of the Chinese movement.

The devious ways and zigzag policies of the Communist
Party were sometimes difficult for the lesser lights to follow. Many started to doubt and were confused as to
where the Revolution was leading. When Russia, which
had denounced the Axis Powers in no uncertain terms,
suddenly in August, 1939, made a non-aggression pact

with Germany, it left many of the Chinese Communists completely stunned. Once more they had to readjust their thinking when the German-Soviet war broke out. Another awkward development to face was Russia's recognition in in April, 1941, of Japan's puppet regime "Manchukuo" and Japan's recognition of Russia's "Republic of Outer Mongolia," both of which territories had been stolen from China. These kaleidoscopic developments required new and often embarrassing changes in propaganda. (What antics must not World Communists perform in the face of the current deflation of father Stalin! Even unbelievers have a hard time keeping up!)

When the switch from fighting the Kuomintang to uniting with the Kuomintang took place, there broke out an ideological storm. This was weathered in part by Mao Tse-tung's treatise in 1940 on *The New Democracy*, explaining the reason for co-operating with the opposition on the way to socialism. This important booklet became another textbook for the orientation of members in the correct line. An additional document which was used to set Party members straight on the reason for co-operating was titled *The Strategic Lines of the Party*. It bluntly stated that because of the weakness of the Party it was necessary to compromise temporarily in order to conserve their strength and increase their "power to strike." The United Front was merely an interim stage, a temporary makeshift on the way to absolute power—"a zigzag policy whose aim is to give the revolutionary forces time to recuperate" "so that the bourgeoisie may be overthrown."*

Mere indoctrination was not sufficient for maintaining one-hundred-per-cent purity in the Party. In the spring of 1942 Mao Tse-tung called for a general purge. On April

---

*Wan Yah-kang's *The Rise of Communism in China (1920-1950)*, pp. 48-49, courtesy of The Chung Shu Publishing Co., Hong Kong.

30 the order was issued by the Propaganda Department listing 17 (later 25) key works for use as standards by which to judge. Some of the main objectives were to eradicate "liberalism," to root out nationalism, which had been aggravated by the anti-Japanese war, and to plug for "internationalism"; and, finally, to confirm Mao Tsetung in his unquestioned supremacy while condemning all others who aspired to Party leadership.

Immediately, right down the line from Yenan to the farthest outposts of the Communists, committees were established in all the organizations under their proper heads. First of all, meetings were held for the thorough study of the documents designated, followed by the pathetic purge meetings where each person was compelled to expose his own errors in thought and life as revealed by his study of the documents. Then he was forced to accuse his fellow members. Tension ran high as nobody knew what lay in store for him. In abject fear and trembling he abused and reviled himself, painting his sins in the darkest color. After the heart-rending scenes everyone stood condemned by his own confession; as a result the leaders were justified in liquidating whomever they felt it was expedient to get rid of. This was done by having those present, following cues from their superiors, pass judgment upon their fellow comrades. By condemning others they themselves hoped to escape. Always there were those who were made to be an example. In the end the members who survived were put on their mettle to give more undeviating obedience to the Party line.

The following year there was put into effect the "self-exposure movement." Previously the weakest elements of the Party had been eliminated through the "struggle" meetings, characterized chiefly by having comrade pitted against comrade; this time the Party sought to keep the members in line by their own efforts through confession and self-condemnation.

Still the Party was not satisfied. A few months later, on August 15, 1943, the Central Committee ordered one more step to make absolutely sure that every member was loyal. The method of procedure was outlined in detail. Every group was organized beginning with a small nucleus at the top formed around the administrative head, branching into committees covering the entire staff. Doubtful cases of reliability were required to pass through mass interrogations, "struggle" meetings, self-condemnation, and tense, searching interviews with the committees. The nucleus of each group was required to check carefully over the thoughts and actions of every single constituent member. Those who varied stubbornly from the general pattern were branded as Trotskyites or spies and forthwith liquidated.

In this way undesirables were weeded out still further and the Party gained strictest control over the life and thought of individual members. It became a solid mass cleansed of all serious factionalism, moving forward in one column. The effectiveness of these "struggle" meetings, self-exposure meetings and checking procedures may be seen from the smooth operation of the Party in the coming conquest of China.

The great Dragon had been flexing its muscles as it was stalking its prey.

When unquestioned unity had been achieved, the Seventh Congress of the Chinese Communist Party was convened on April 23, 1945. Not since 1928 in Moscow had the Party held a national convention. Various reasons may be cited for this. First of all, the situation had been extremely dangerous for Communists. Furthermore, the difficulties of travel and communications had been a real obstacle. Chiefly, however, Mao Tse-tung, who had observed the strife and factionalism—leading to the unseating of previous leaders—at Party Congresses, must have been determined to take no chances until his grip on the Party had been completely assured.

For almost two months the Party met in grand deliberation. There were 544 voting, and 208 visiting, delegates coming from a membership of 1,210,000—a one-hundredfold increase of members since the adoption of the United Front. The Communist policy of "co-operation" had paid off handsomely! Mao Tse-tung could report nineteen "liberated areas" by this time and once more claim control over 100,000,000 people. The Red forces now included 920,000 regulars and 2,000,000 militiamen.

Besides the hearing of reports, the main business included the revision of the constitution and the "deification," so to speak, of Mao Tse-tung; his preeminence was written into the constitution, all dogmas opposed to Mao Tse-tungism were condemned. Henceforth the Chinese Communists were to call themselves the "Party of Mao Tse-tung."

GROWTH OF COMMUNIST PARTY

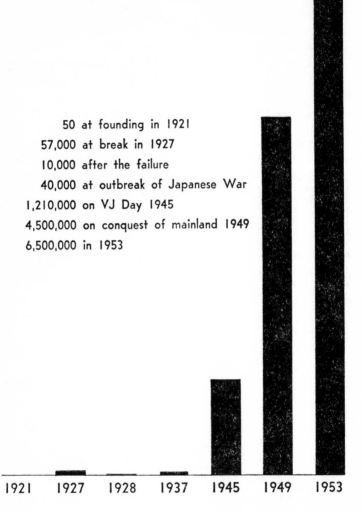

50 at founding in 1921
57,000 at break in 1927
10,000 after the failure
40,000 at outbreak of Japanese War
1,210,000 on VJ Day 1945
4,500,000 on conquest of mainland 1949
6,500,000 in 1953

| 1921 | 1927 | 1928 | 1937 | 1945 | 1949 | 1953 |

forlorn victim

ONE of the greatest tragedies ever to befall America is the loss of the friendship of that great country of China. For over a hundred years we have befriended China, been interested in her progress, and prevented her from being divided up as colonies among the great powers. We stood firmly for the Open Door Policy. Through the sacrifices of thousands of missionaries, through timely succor in years of famine and flood, a "reservoir of good will" had been built up. In spite of our periodic blunderings, the Chinese people as a whole looked upon America as their best friend among the nations.

All that has been changed. We have permitted Russia through her fifth column of Chinese Communists to take over the country. We have permitted over fifty million helpless civilians—including our staunchest friends and the brave souls who have valued liberty above life—to be slaughtered by a godless regime which demands absolute sway over body and spirit. As the old generation passes, we are seeing a new generation, which knows not freedom, being drilled in hatred of America and being subjected to such concentrated propaganda as the world has never seen before—except in Russia from whence it came. We see a whole nation of slaves being trained like robots and being forged into a machine to be used by Russia for the conquest of the Far East—and ultimately of the world.

While this dismal future was being hammered out before our eyes in the years following World War II, for the first time in our history our leaders were overcome with defeatism. From our State Department—in a "letter of transmittal" from Dean Acheson to President Truman prefacing the "White Paper" on China—came the amazing pronouncement: "The unfortunate but inescapable fact is that the ominous result of the civil war in China was beyond the control of the government of the United States. Nothing that this country did or could have done within the reasonable limits of its capabilities could have changed that result; nothing that was left undone by this country has contributed to it."

It was not only indefensible but ridiculous for the most powerful nation on earth to claim that we were helpless to do anything decisive for a friendly government which was engaged, not in a local war, but in a global struggle, and which was anxious for our help. We had not left Turkey to her fate, but had bolstered that plucky government in her resistance to Russia. We had not thrown up our hands in despair when the Communist penetration into Greece had appeared well-nigh hopeless. We had pitched right in and saved that country from imminent slavery. But when a huge and vastly more important country in the Far East was meeting the same onslaught of World Communism, our State Department formulated a "do nothing" policy and "waited for the dust to settle." While we waited, Communism marched forward and took the land.

For that policy we have had to pay—the first installment was Korea. There will be future installments—in Formosa, Japan, Southeast Asia, the world.

In Korea we expended 22 billion dollars and 33,600 young lives (not to mention the sufferings and destruction which came upon the Korean population). Had we possessed the foresight and the courage, we could have forestalled the frightful development with a fraction of such expenditure. We were quibbling about 2 billion dollars when 22 billion were about to be charged against us. Since World War II we have given outright gifts of 46 billion dollars to help other nations, but we could not afford a few billion to help save China.

It is useless to castigate the National Government of China for collapsing in the face of the Red onslaught when our own Far Eastern policy from the top down to the bottom collapsed largely through an undiscerning acceptance of Communist propaganda.

Before going to Yalta Roosevelt had remarked to a congressman, who was trying to raise the alarm against Communism, that he "saw a Red under his bed every night." At the conference where Alger Hiss occupied the seat of adviser, we urged upon Russia the unprincipled action of breaking her treaty with Japan and secretly sold China down the river, giving Russia special rights in Manchuria and subscribing to Russia's lopping off of Outer Mongolia.

On the field in China we employed men, many of whom had never made a thorough study of Communism or its workings. They followed the current statements and activities of the Communists but fell into the trap of taking these at their face value. Some of them were won over as strong supporters of the Reds and proved themselves totally inadequate for their positions in serious times like these.

There were, to be sure, men of insight and knowledge who raised their voices in protest, but our Government, which ought to have known its business, smothered their warnings.

In 1945 when General Patrick J. Hurley, our ambassador —who had started out with the idea that he could do business with the Communists but changed his mind—dismissed some of his pro-Communist subordinates, they went to Washington and were absorbed into the State Department where they could themselves issue directives to the ambassador. Whatever his other shortcomings, Hurley could not be accused of concealing his emotions. Later, after his resignation, with quivering mustache and pale face he testified before the Senate Foreign Relations Committee that these biased career diplomats had been sabotaging his work in China.

Mr. Walter Robertson, American chargé d'affaires, had unequivocally warned against the dangers of Chinese Communism, but his clear-cut, fact-supported pronouncements fell upon deaf ears.

One powerful voice raised at this time was that of Lieut. Gen. Albert C. Wedemeyer, a true expert on the China situation. If anyone was in a position to know what he was talking about, it was General Wedemeyer. Born a third-generation Army man, he was graduated from West Point at the end of World War I. He spent two years in Tientsin learning Chinese. During World War II he helped plan strategy in the Mediterranean, and in the Normandy invasion. In 1944 he replaced General Stilwell in China because of the latter's impossible personality clash with the Generalissimo. Stilwell—a man of power and character in his own way—who had no insight into the Communist problem, who was impatient over Chiang's delays and suspicions regarding the Reds, and who was only anxious to get along with the job of fighting Japan, had tried to impose his will on the equally unyielding personality of Chiang. The impact caused fireworks which sent sparks around the world. Naturally many American boys in China became prejudiced against Chiang, too. But Wedemeyer changed things. As Commander of the U.S. Army forces in China and Chiang Kaishek's chief of staff, he worked out a harmonious and skilful co-operation with the Chinese Government. When he was suggested for the U.S. ambassadorship to China the appointment was not put into effect because of Communist objections.

Wedemeyer was in the best possible position to know what was happening. He reported his reactions. He stated unhesitatingly that the Chinese Communists were not "agrarian reformers" but true Reds; that they could not possibly co-operate in a coalition; and that civil war would inevitably follow. He also maintained that the Government had been too weakened by the long war to gain control of China proper without American help. For Manchuria he proposed a three-power trusteeship.

The perfidy of Russia is easily seen from her actions in the Far East toward the close of the war and the period following. Japan had already sent out peace feelers and asked that Russia intervene as mediator. But Russia double-crossed both Japan and the Allies. Seeing the end in sight and anxious to grab the spoils, she mentioned nothing to her partners about peace proposals but broke her treaty with Japan and—six days before the war was over and two days after the first atomic bomb had been dropped—she marched into Manchuria against nothing more than token resistance. We had urged Russia to get into the Far Eastern war and now she was in it!

Immediately after Japan's surrender, Wedemeyer made a request for the stationing of seven divisions of American troops in North China to keep an eye on the Russians and to seal off Manchuria, "placing a barrier there so that I would know what was going on and could influence what was going on." Had this been done, the Chinese Communists could not have infiltrated Manchuria as they did later. All through the war the Japanese had successfully cordoned them off. But the request was denied.

So authentic a voice as Wedemeyer's ought to have been heeded or at least to have stirred up energetic investigations into underlying facts. An honest study of Communism's past would certainly have revealed the type of monstrosity with which we were dealing. But Wedemeyer's proposals were ignored and a few months later General of the Army George C. Marshall was sent to China to try to form a coalition government between the Nationalists and the Communists. Again Wedemeyer warned his chief and urged all-out support for Chiang; but the die had been cast.

As for the Communists, when Japan had surrendered, they had revealed their utter insubordination to their "Commander-in-Chief," Chiang Kai-shek, who had issued orders for them to stay where they were and await instructions. Instead, Chu Teh sent out from Yenan seven orders of the day for his troops to proceed to designated points to take over from the Japanese. Simultaneously he telegraphed the Japanese Commander-in-chief, General Okamura, to surrender to the Communists. These orders were immediately countermanded by Chiang Kai-shek. In Tokyo General MacArthur, realizing the possibilities, telegraphed to the Japanese to surrender only to the National forces.

Meanwhile our Government was working at cross-purposes to the advice of our military representatives on the spot. Pressure was being put upon Chiang Kai-shek to refrain from fighting the Communists and to form a coalition government. On August 28, 1945, Mao Tse-tung and Chou En-lai flew to Chungking in a U.S. Army transport with an American guarantee of safety. That night for dinner, with his characteristic lumbering gait, rigid arms, and clenched fists, Mao Tse-tung walked into the presence of his archenemy, Chiang Kai-shek, whom he had not seen for eighteen years. Six weeks of negotiations and "cordial" toasts followed. At length agreements were reached on a number of issues, including the convening of a People's Consultative Conference, and Chou En-lai signed the document for the Communists. At a farewell feast Mao solemnly promised that all outstanding problems would be solved *only* through discussions.

Two days before this, however, Red soldiers were already on the march. Orders had been issued to all Communist commanders in the field to tear up the railways and hinder the Government troops from reoccupying North China.

The forced march of the Government toward democracy involved not only the continued recognition of the Communist Party, but the acceptance of the freedom of the press and the immediate abolition of censorship. This was even more than the Communists could have hoped for. Almost over night a crop of sensational papers appeared, all against the Government. Communist propaganda ran wild. Much ado was made over the will of the people, free speech, free press, freedom for political prisoners, as though these were the monopoly of the Communist Party (whereas in fact the Communists had no interest in these things). The Kuomintang was constantly hit. Lest it be stigmatized as undemocratic in the eyes of the American people, the Government bore the malicious slander with dignity. The results, however, were disastrous. The gripes of the people after eight long years of war and privation were all directed at the Party in power. The belief was ingrained in the people that "the Communists can't be worse than the Kuomintang."

In the ensuing race between the Government and the Communist troops to occupy the chief cities of China proper, the former had the advantage, as four crack American-trained armies were air-lifted by Wedemeyer into Shanghai, Nanking, Peiping and Tientsin. But Communist troops were scattered in much of the countryside.

On the day of Japan's surrender, China, under American urging, had signed the Treaty of Friendship with Russia—actually, a bear hug of death. This "legalized" the secret agreements of Yalta, recognizing, in effect, Russia's grab of Outer Mongolia and giving her control over Port Arthur and, practically, over the Manchurian railways. The port of Dairen was to be internationalized. In return Russia gave categorical assurances regarding China's sovereignty in Manchuria and promised to support *exclusively* the National Government. Stalin had given our President his word that he was fully behind the principle of the Open Door in China! I shall never forget the bewilderment with which I received the news of these strange goings-on in the Far East!

Before the ink had a chance to dry, the Russians proceeded to break the treaty. Their armies which had plundered and murdered and shamelessly raped in public throughout Manchuria, continued their wholesale robbery. Rich stockpiles of food were removed to Russia, thousands of locomotives and railway cars. By September the Soviet Union began a systematic confiscation of industrial machinery, concentrating on certain types such as power plants, electric motors, transformers, newest machine tools. They would ruin whole plants and stop production by ripping out such key equipment as generators, often leaving the rest irreparably damaged. Like ravening wolves they looted and destroyed until the outside world began to hear strange rumors. Fed up with waiting for Russian permission to enter, foreign correspondents went in on their own. The tales they brought out were unbelievable. The following summer Truman sent the Pauley Commission to investigate; their "conservative estimate": *$2,000,000,000 worth of damage had been done.*

In other ways the Russians flouted the treaty. The U.S. Navy, in line with its post-victory obligations, transported two divisions of U.S. Marines to the Tsingtao and Peiping areas to help disarm the Japanese and maintain law and order. This raised a loud protest from Russia, who charged the U.S. with occupying sovereign Chinese territory! The Navy undertook to move several Chinese armies from the south coast to Manchuria to reoccupy their land. On arrival at the "international" port of Dairen the U.S. Navy was held at bay by the Russians who refused to let the Government troops land. To avoid a shooting war the U.S. Navy withdrew. Thereupon the Chinese intended to land at the smaller ports of Yingkow and Hulutao. When they got there they learned to their consternation that the Russians, contrary to their promise to keep Chiang Kai-shek informed, had already withdrawn and let the Chinese Communists take over.

Against the advice of Wedemeyer and others, Chiang Kai-shek persisted in his efforts to reoccupy Manchuria. He knew that whoever controlled Manchuria—a rich bread basket, a mine of mineral wealth and an industrial establishment for war or peace—would control China; he also sensed that politically his end would be near if he could not restore the territorial integrity of China.

Frustrated by sea Chiang Kai-shek pushed his armies over land. Some, bound for Mukden, two hundred and fifty miles away, started from where the Great Wall meets the ocean. Others, following the Pinghan railroad, were stalled about two hundred miles from Peiping because the Reds had destroyed the tracks and were blocking the way. After that Chiang Kai-shek decided to transport troops by air to the chief cities of Mukden and Changchun, but when he notified the Soviet ambassador the latter maintained that only a police force and not soldiers might be so transported. Only after much delay and trouble were National troops able to get to these places. In Russia's scheme of things, there was method in her madness; by these delays she was making indispensable provision for the Chinese Communist armies.

In the midst of these confusing developments General George C. Marshall arrived in China to make peace between the Chinese Government and the Communists.

In 1945, after furlough, I had returned to China. The following spring I flew to Chungking to arrange for the removal of our Lutheran Theological Seminary from the war-time capital back to its old home at Shekow, Hupeh, in Central China. In Chungking, where I stayed some months, I was put up at the same campus where General Marshall had his headquarters. Faithfully and patiently he was plugging away at the task assigned him—but it was foredoomed to failure.

News regarding the progress of the negotiations was not plentiful. Open warfare had broken out between the

Government and the Communists, and Chiang Kai-shek had a fighting chance of gaining the upper hand, but, under pressure, he reluctantly deferred to the wishes of General Marshall. For the Reds, the time gained was invaluable.

On January 10, 1946, a truce was signed. At headquarters in Peiping a Committee of Three was formed, Mr. Walter Robertson representing the mediators, General Cheng Kai-min the Government and General Yeh Chienying the Communists. All questions had to be settled by unanimous decision of these three. Truce teams under the direction of General Henry A. Byroade visited areas of conflict to prevent hostilities. On my routine travels I came across such a team in the Honan-Hupeh border region—an old stamping ground of the Communists. I tried to strike up a conversation with the Communist representative, a General Wang, but was met with deep suspicion and evasiveness. I wondered what could come out of such an attitude!

Almost every move we made regarding China during these years before and after Japan's surrender seemed to play into the hands of Russia. Marshall's chief Chinese secretary was the Communist Ching Nu-chi who did not show his colors until after the fall of Nanking when he went to Peiping with the valuable secrets he had learned. In Hong Kong he printed a book titled: *Secret Report on the U.S.–Chiang Conspiracy.*

Marshall had come to China with $500,000,000 to dispose of as he saw fit. This might have been used to bolster the National regime, but was not. Instead, pressure was applied to keep the Government from going after the Reds. Under Marshall's Military Reorganization Plan Chiang had suspended conscription and was working on the reduction of his armed forces. Later all military aid was cut off in order to impress the Communists with our fairness.

While we were putting pressure on Chiang's Government, Russia, on the other hand, had secretly invited the Chinese Communists to infiltrate into Manchuria. The negotiations and truce gave them the time and opportunity they needed. Russian delaying tactics had kept the National power out of the area. Observers were dumbfounded to see hundreds of thousands of unarmed Chinese streaming through the Great Wall into Manchuria. There the Russians armed them to their teeth. Before the war ended we had sent to Vladivostok hundreds of shiploads of American arms and equipment for the Russians to use against Japan. None of this was used against Japan; Russia turned it all over to the Chinese Communists. Besides that, the mountains of equipment and stockpiles of munitions accumulated by the Kwangtung Army, the cream of Japan's fighting forces, were turned over to the Chinese Communists, and tens of thousands of Japanese military technicians were forced to serve them. A stepped-up training program for the re-equipped troops was instituted by the Russians at Kiamusze near the Siberian border. The result was a spanking new crack Fourth Field Army of Lin Piao. This was the army that collided with the Nationalists in 1948 and initiated their total collapse. Moreover, it was these same men that drove the United Nations out of North Korea in 1950.

By January, 1947, General Marshall realized the futility of his efforts and gave up with a "plague-on-both-your-houses" report. On the day he left for the States he sought and received the advice of one of the most eminent authorities in the country, Dr. John Leighton Stuart—a man of over fifty years' experience in China. Stuart had been born in China of missionary parents. He was a noted educator who had been president of Yenching University since 1919 and whose weakness, if any, had been his liberalism, which had left him "open-minded" and friendly to the Reds until he had found out better—whom Marshall himself had suggested for the U.S. ambassadorship to China and who had been approved unanimously by the Senate on July 10 of the previous year. Dr. Stuart advised Marshall against a negative policy and urged that we support the National Government *actively* or pull out altogether. Stuart definitely believed that China could still be saved—and that with not too much assistance. But the venerable voice of experience was not enough to influence our Far Eastern policies.

The inevitable came to pass the following summer, 1947: the National Government outlawed the Communist Party and ordered its suppression. The civil war was on for a fight to the finish!

During these hot, steamy—and hectic—days, the Wedemeyer mission arrived from Washington on a fact-finding tour, spending four weeks in China and two in Korea. He and his staff of experts found nothing that contradicted the general outline of his earlier convictions; on the contrary, the current developments greatly substantiated his earlier views. From the mass of data collected the commission wrote out the Wedemeyer Report—recommending all-out aid for Chiang Kai-shek, with American supervision; urging a U.N. trusteeship for Manchuria; and warning that, unless a strong force of South Koreans officered by Americans was created, then, as soon as U.S. troops were withdrawn, the Russian-trained North Koreans would march on the South. In China the co-operation which Wedemeyer visualized with Chiang was not something new; it was merely an extension into the economic and political, as well as military, fields of what he had already carried out on a smaller scale militarily and found successful. Wedemeyer could testify that Chiang had never gone back on any promise he had given him. With Wedemeyer's type of friendly co-operation the Generalissimo was in hearty agreement, even offering to go along with a complete reorganization of his government with American supervision of economic and military aid. As Wedemeyer testified later: "We would have to get in as we did in Greece, get right into the area of combat, and help the Chinese tactically and explain to them the technique of the arms we were making available to them."

General Wedemeyer had performed his mission. He had gone to the Far East, *dug out the facts*, returned and submitted his report. Like the fabled ostrich that hides its head in the sand, the U.S. Administration suppressed the report.

Other high U.S. officials—top Navy officers; MacArthur in Tokyo; Congressman Walter Judd, a former medical missionary to China; and subsequently Consul General Angus Ward (who was confined under "atrocious conditions" by the Communists for over a year after the fall of Mukden, and publicly humiliated)—proclaimed the facts, but nothing could change the "do nothing" policy. U.S. troops rushed home to be demobilized before their task had been completed. The Marines were withdrawn from North China. Major General William Arthur Worton, Chief of Staff of the Third Amphibious Corps, with over twelve years' experience in China, called the withdrawal of his forces from the Peiping-Tientsin-Chingwangtao triangle the greatest mistake we had made. Continued occupation, he said, could have kept the Reds from moving south of the Great Wall.

The "do nothing" policy was later extended to the

publishing of the White Paper (which shocked and amazed Ambassador Stuart), attacking a friendly government and all but inviting the Reds to help themselves to whatever they wished; it was extended to the secret circularizing of our diplomatic corps to write off Formosa. Then the policy was projected into the Korean situation where it became the "limited war" and the dismissal of General MacArthur who understood the global Communist situation as few others and looked into the future with eagle eye. Divided Koreas and Germanies and Indo-Chinas will not bring peace to a distraught world, no matter what European allies ar any others may seem to think.

CHAPTER ELEVEN

devouring the land

HAVING been betrayed by allies and double-crossed by Russia; with no *positive* backing from the U.S., and hence no guarantee of victory; beset with inflation, where people carried money in bushel baskets and used hundred-dollar bills for lighting fires; with completely inadequate revenues (the National Government had not learned from its enemies the technique of killing rich farmers to get their wealth or of terrorizing and enslaving the people to get their obedience); undermined by Communist subversion and infiltration; with troops underpaid and underfed, and utterly weary of continued strife; fighting a wily, vigorous, fanatical and unbelievably persistent foe which had the full support of Russia; with decay and corruption, accelerated by the hopeless situation, eating into the vitals of the Kuomintang; with Government malpractices greatly magnified by Communist propaganda (deep freeze and pastel mink remind us that corruption is the monopoly of no special government—and who could be more corrupt than the Communists themselves who murder millions of innocent victims and en-

slave the rest to further their own pet schemes?), resulting
in loss of confidence by the unknowing common people
and by the foreign powers, whereas peace and a Paradise
were promised by the enemy; with the masses ignorant regarding slave labor camps and liquidation programs connected with Communism's march through other countries;
and with a stupid lack of proper counter-propaganda, the
National Government collapsed quickly before the blazing
civil war which galloped over the country like a forest
fire. And outsiders wondered at how the Government
could be defeated so rapidly!

As the Communists plunged into their show-down
struggle, they simultaneously instituted their second large-
scale purge which occupied the latter part of 1947 and
some of 1948. This ideological purge was called the
"Three-fold Let-Us-See Movement." In the same inquisi-
torial manner previously described the comrades were put
through the mill, being tested on three searching points:
"Let us see your social status," "Let us see your background," and "Let us see your stand." As before, large
numbers failed to qualify and were mercilessly liquidated.
Membership was growing so rapidly—in one year's time it
almost doubled—that standards of discipline had to be
strictly maintained.

In the renewed civil war the Government seemed to be
getting the upper hand to begin with by forcing the Reds
out of Yenan in Shensi, Kalgan and Chahar, and several
cities in Kiangsu and Shantung—even before the official
break-up of the United Front. But in September of 1947
the tide turned with the Red storming of the highly important communications center of Shihchiachwang on the
Pinghan railway. Other Red troops freshly trained and
armed by the Russians in Manchuria used junks to cross
the gulf secretly from Dairen to the Communist-held port

of Cheefoo in Shantung, turning back the Government campaign which had been successfully launched in that Province.

It may be enlightening to consider the specific case of the attack on Shihchiachwang in order to understand the general strategy of the Communists in capturing Nationalist cities. At this time the Government held most of the cities and the Communists held much of the countryside.

The city of Shihchiachwang on the Peiping-Hankow railway was an important communications center which the Japanese had built into a strategic fortress. At the time of the Japanese surrender it contained factories, arsenals, stockpiles of materials, and half a million inhabitants. When the Nationalists had taken it over they had occupied the surrounding country within the radius of a hundred miles. From the time of its transfer—for two years—the Communists worked on its downfall. They worked on the inside and they worked on the outside.

First of all the Communists planted their fifth column inside the city, secret agents unobtrusively worming their way into the administration, the police force, the various strata of society. Many were conscripted into the National Army or volunteered for service, always behaving well until their position was assured.

On the outside the Communists applied their guerrilla tactics which they had learned so expertly. They kept up an incessant attack on the lines of communication—digging up and hiding rails, burning ties, dynamiting bridges, destroying engines, cutting off the hands of loyal engineers, blocking roads and waylaying buses. Government repair gangs ran out of materials and many of them were killed. Eventually the city was isolated from other large cities.

Then the Communists put on the squeeze, tightening the

net around the city. They used lightning attacks to over-whelm one outpost after another. If they found a strong-point garrisoned by a thousand soldiers, they would col-lect from all directions and hurl against it five thousand, ten thousand. In a huge, amorphous, undeveloped country like China, such strategy becomes outstandingly success-ful. With poor communications and an insufficient number of troops to station everywhere, the Government was not able to rush reinforcements to the outpost before it was too late. The Government tactics of defending cities proved to be its downfall.

When the Communists captured Government troops, some of the latter, those that were strong and young, they incorporated into their own units, dispersing them widely so that they could be watched. Others they treated well and set free to become unwitting bearers of Red propa-ganda. The severely wounded were cared for, then sent back to their own lines with a small allowance in order that they might become a burden on the Nationalists. Sometimes the captives were used as expendable spear-heads in human sea tactics.

Having taken the outposts and occupied the villages in between, the Communists not only increased their own supplies and manpower, but applied a strict blockade against the city. No food of any kind was permitted to slip through. As the Reds closed in, one hundred thousand refugees swelled the tide of starving people inside the city, increasing the problems of the Nationalists. Soon food and supplies for the troops had to be air-lifted in, but the Government did not have enough planes or re-sources to take care of all, and the refugees were left to starve. There was no one to tell the people that this was the way the Communists wanted it.

Among the refugees were many Communist agents

smuggled in. These fanned up the unrest and resentment in the city. They complained bitterly, blaming Chiang and the Government for not taking care of their people. They slyly insinuated to the soldiers that Chinese ought not to fight Chinese. As opportunities presented themselves the agents glorified the life under the Communists, saying the food supplies were with them and further resistance was useless. Stacking up lies and promises, the agents tried subtly to break down morale and work despair among the troops. What they said was taken up and repeated by others. The result was sharp internal contention between the anti-Communists, many of whom had learned from experience, and the pro-Communist victims of propaganda who also thought they knew.

When the time was ripe, the Communists struck with a series of sporadic attacks, ever growing in intensity. When they found the opposition surprisingly strong, with a feigned attack on Paoting to the north they drew off many of the defending troops, and, about halfway between, annihilated them with overwhelming force. Surging back to the storming of Shihchiachwang, they released the riots and insurrections arranged inside the city. These might have looked spontaneous, but they had been prepared long in advance for the hour and the day that the signal should be given. Rumors were started among the militia that the soldiers had defected and among the troops that the militia had surrendered. In the confusion the commanding general did not know whom he could trust. When the enemy broke into the city, their fifth column joined their ranks by the thousands. Shihchiachwang had been captured.

The loss of this strategic center in the heart of China was a serious blow to the authority and prestige of the

Central Government. It was a turning point in the war. A few months later, in 1948, Tsinan, the key city and communications center of Shantung Province, fell to the Red General, Chen Yi, through the same tactics. Then in quick succession followed the loss of the beleaguered and starving cities in Manchuria. The National soldiers, holed up in their fortresses, with steadily dwindling supplies and with the inhabitants in misery and starvation, lost all hope for their cause. At Changchun the fabulously expensive airdrop of supplies was so inaccurate that much of it landed behind the enemy lines. At length the city with all its American-trained soldiers and equipment surrendered to the Communists. Shortly thereafter Mukden fell. It was too late to escape; the National soldiers, ordered to break out and fight their way south, were annihilated on the road. The "liberation" of Manchuria released Lin Piao's three hundred thousand or more troops for use elsewhere.

After the capture of Tsinan, Chen Yi had moved his men southward for an attack on the vital junction city of Hsüchow with its tremendous stores of munitions. Chiang Kai-shek ordered its evacuation and the destruction of the supplies which could not be removed. But with the help of the "One-eyed Dragon," Chen Yi cut off the retreat and a titanic struggle ensued involving over half a million troops. Casualties on both sides were frightening. The news of Hsüchow's fall struck us like a thunder clap.

The battles and developments of 1949 came in too rapid succession to be recorded. With the Communist armies bearing down on the Yangtze River barrier in three columns, the Government moved its capital from Nanking to Canton and for its own prestige asked that the foreign embassies move also. Seeing that the National Government was doomed to collapse, not one of the North

Atlantic Group embassies moved to the new site. But keeping up its masquerade, the *only country* which ordered its ambassador to move was Russia!

In January 1949, Tientsin and Peiping surrendered. On April 20 the Communists pushed across the Yangtze with little opposition—as they had previously bribed the commander of the Kiangyin Forts—and on April 24 occupied Nanking. Thereafter Taiyuan with all its arsenals succumbed—Taiyuan, where the bankrupt Government had spent $300,000 a day on the airlift and where thousands of civilians had starved to death from the Communist encirclement! In quick succession followed Hangchow, Wuhan, Sian, Nanchang, Changsha, Shanghai, Tsingtao, Lanchow, Canton, and places between.

And so the shadow of the Red Dragon raced over the surface of the land, as when the sun is being swallowed in an eclipse. But it was not a shadow; it was the real thing. China itself was being devoured by the Great Red Dragon.

With the fall of Chungking—whither the Government had moved from Canton and whence it moved to Formosa —and Chengtu, toward the end of the year, the chapter of conquest was virtually closed. But just before it ended, the new Communist regime—now boasting a Party membership of 4,500,000 (which has since increased to about 6,500,000)—declared with great fanfare on October 1, 1949, the establishment in Peking of the "People's Republic of China." *The very same day,* the hitherto "disinterested" Russia—followed by her satellites—recognized the so-called New Democracy!

the aftermath

FOR the Chinese people, what has been the aftermath of this catastrophe?

First of all, it has meant the tying of China's fate to that of Russia.

The month following the establishment of the Red Government, Mao Tse-tung made his long trek to Moscow to make obeisance to his master, Stalin, and to work out the next step in the Communist World Conquest. He stayed there a long time—almost three months—until rumors started flying that he had been imprisoned. That was not the case. Stalin had much use for him yet.

Many people speculate over the possibility of Mao's becoming a Tito; they have no idea what they are talking about. *There is no possibility* of China's breaking away from Russia's iron grip in the foreseeable future. There are many reasons one could list offhand why Titoism can't apply to China:

1. Russia has had one experience of Titoism and will be doubly on guard against a repetition of the occurrence. China is too great a prize to lose through carelessness.

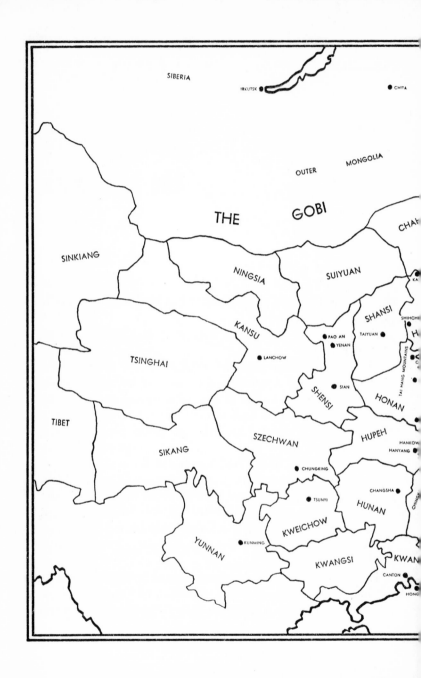

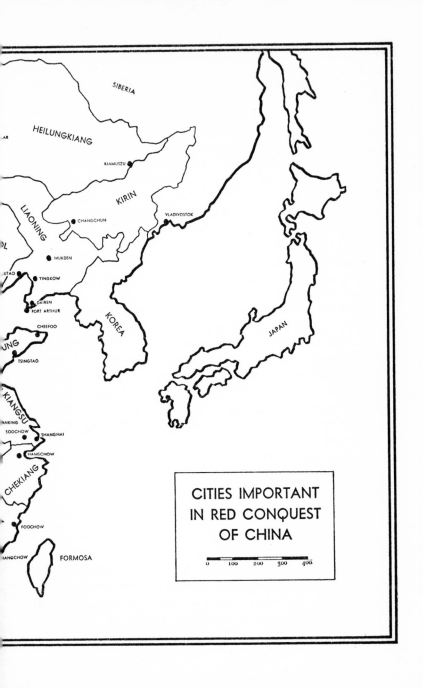

CITIES IMPORTANT
IN RED CONQUEST
OF CHINA

0   100   200   300   400

2. China and Russia have thousands of miles of common boundary, making a break away well-nigh impossible.

3. The whole history of the Chinese Communist Party from the beginning has been tied up with the Kremlin.

4. The Chinese Communists have a common faith with the Russians in the basic Hegelian-Marxist view of the redemptive process of history—the inevitability of *World Revolution*—and in holding that the Communist Party is the sole agent for achieving the goal. Mao Tse-tung merely introduced a new dimension to the process by emphasizing peasants.

5. All the methods of organization and terrorism have been learned from the Russians. China's propaganda is timed with Russia's and echoes Russia's.

6. Tens of thousands of the leaders have been trained and indoctrinated by Russians.

7. China Reds have always *considered themselves* to be orthodox Marxist-Leninists and true followers of Stalin; those liquidated were time and again accused of Trotskyism and "deviation." When the split between Tito and Russia came into the open, Mao Tse-tung wrote an acid article for the "Cominform Journal" condemning Tito for his stand

8. From the beginning Mao and other leaders have proclaimed their loyalty to Moscow. They continue to do so today.

In January, 1940, Mao Tse-tung wrote in his *The New Democracy:*

"The world now lives in an era of revolution and war, a new era, where capitalism is definitely dying and socialism is beginning to flourish. In the international environment of the middle of the Twentieth Century, there are only two ways open to all decent people in the colonies and semi-colonies. They must either go over to the side of the imperialist front or take part in the World Revolution. They must choose between these two. There is no other way."

On March 11, 1949, Commander-in-Chief Chu Teh said in a speech at the graduation exercises of the North China People's Revolutionary University:

"In our revolutionary work, we are not alone. We have many friends, particularly our elder brother, the Soviet Union, who has been furnishing to us direct military aid as well as indirect economic and political assistance. In the military field, I know far more than you do. Practically 80 per cent of our 'Liberation Army' were trained and equipped by the Russians. Our arms and ammunition were not necessarily Russian made, but they were handed to us in Manchuria by the Soviet Union.

"Frankly speaking, as we Communists always do to fellow Communists, there are Soviet advisers in every department of our government; and we have patriots from other countries, such as India, Indo-China, Burma, Malaya, Siam, taking an active part in our work.

"In Manchuria, we have an aviation school in Kiamusze, in which over 2,000 cadets from South East Asia are receiving the best training in aviation from Soviet Russia. Similarly, Chinese comrades have been sent to these countries to work and learn; this is necessary for the purpose of exchanging intelligence.

"In conclusion, I must tell you that without the assistance of the Soviet Union, the proletarian revolution of other countries would not have been possible."

In his opening speech before the Chinese People's Political Consultative Conference in Peking on September 21, 1949, Mao Tse-tung said:

"Internationally, we must unite with all countries and

peoples loving peace and freedom, first of all the Soviet Union and the New Democracies, so that we will not stand alone in our struggle to safeguard the fruits of the victory of the People's Revolution and to oppose the plot of domestic and foreign enemies in staging a come-back. So long as we uphold the People's Democratic Dictatorship and unite with our international friends, we shall ever be victorious. . . .

"Let the reactionaries at home and abroad tremble before us!"

The same year on July 1 Mao Tse-tung proclaimed to the world:

"We belong to the anti-imperialist front headed by the U.S.S.R., and we can only look for genuine friendly aid from that front and not from the imperialist front. The victory of the Red Revolution in China would have been impossible without the aid of the U.S.S.R. We also oppose the illusion of a third road. Not only in China, but also in the world without exception, one either leans to the side of imperialism or the side of socialism. Neutrality is a camouflage."

From Moscow a few months later he declared:

"For many years the Soviet people and the Soviet government have repeatedly given aid to the cause of the liberation of the Chinese people. These acts of friendship on the part of the Soviet people and the Soviet government, which the Chinese people received during the days of their severe trials, will never be forgotten."

At the inaugural meeting of the Sino-Soviet Friendship Association in Peking Chu Teh said again:

"The Soviet Union is China's most intimate and most dependable friend. The victory of the Chinese people's democratic revolution cannot be separated from the friendship of the Soviet Union."

Pronouncements to the same effect by Chou En-lai and others have been voluminous and need not be quoted.

9. Russia's cultural aggression in China has been most pronounced. Posters of Russian leaders are displayed everywhere. Russians are eulogized and called "elder brothers" instead of the former "big noses." In all the important cities Sino-Soviet Friendship Societies are functioning. Russian portraits appear on Chinese stamps —an unheard-of thing in the past! The Russian language has displaced English and is being taught by compulsion in all the schools throughout the country, including Middle Schools (high schools). The writings of Marx, Lenin and others have been substituted for the old Chinese classics which have been banned. Stalin's *Dialectical and Historical Materialism* has been one of the basic text books used. By the middle of 1953 more than ten million copies of Stalin's works had been published (but not a single edition of the writings of Buddha!) and over three hundred Soviet technical books had been translated. In an ever-growing stream Soviet Russian books and periodicals are issuing from the presses of China.

10. In China proper today there are some one hundred thousand Russian military and technical advisers distributed throughout the country, pulling the strings behind the scenes. In Peking the Russians have a shadowy figure, the "political representatative," who outranks the Russian ambassador and is present at all the meetings of the Chinese Politburo itself.

11. Russia's grip on Manchuria, the Ruhr of China, is unbreakable. Since the Communist conquest, Russia has been pouring in settlers by the thousands. She has already established several farm settlements, the one at Hailar consisting of five thousand Russians. It is estimated that about five hundred thousand Soviet citizens have spread

themselves over the Northeastern Provinces from Manchuli to Port Arthur, including advisers, farmers, railway workers and regular troops. Though nominally a part of the People's Republic of China, Manchuria has its own regional government with treaty-making powers and issues its own currency. Advanced sovietization along Moscow lines is proceeding apace.

12. The Soviet Union has strong naval and submarine bases, not only in Dairen and Port Arthur, but also ringing the China coast at Tsingtao, Shanghai, and Hainan Island, as well as lesser points between. She also has many troops and anti-aircraft crews on Chinese soil. China would be at the mercy of Russia in any struggle.

13. China's whole military-economic system has been integrated with Russia's. Chinese slave laborers have appeared as far afield as in Eastern European countries. China is completely dependent upon Russia's heavy industry. Not only has she received her tanks, planes, submarines, engines and heavy artillery and other equipment (not to mention industrial machinery) from Russia, but she in entirely dependent upon her for replacements and parts.

14. Finally, Russia possesses the atomic and hydrogen bombs, whereas China has not even begun to enter the arena of nuclear accomplishments.

The Moscow-Peking Axis seems to be well greased for many, many years of smooth running with the Kremlin in the driver's seat!

After Mao Tse-tung's conquest of China he set in motion wave upon wave of terrorism such as the world has never seen before—not even Russia's can come up to it in scale and furor. Not in the heat of battle when passions reign and discipline may lapse or run low, not in the sudden rising of the long oppressed to throw off their shackles and wreak vengeance on their tormentors—but in the calm of peace after victory, with power already in their hands, in cold-blooded, calculating, diabolical planning, the Communists unleashed their reign of Red torture, anguish and death.

A glimpse at what is meant may be helpful. After the Communists had taken over Shanghai and the people were beginning to breathe a little easier, the authorities required that everybody write out his biography from the time he was seven years old up to the present. Everything must be written in detail telling what he did each year, and what he thought. Nothing must be skipped over. Reams and reams of paper were used. Sometimes the biography had to be rewritten seven or eight times before the authorities would accept it. Each person was required to confess his sins to the Government. If he had ever cheated anyone, committed adultery, been in a fight, done anything evil—he must confess it to the Government.

"Do not be afraid," said the authorities, "only be frank. If you are honest, you have nothing to fear from us. We are only out to get the crooks. If you are not frank we will know that you are trying to hide things and that you must be a spy; but if you frankly confess your sins, then you have nothing to fear. If you have served the former government, if you have been mayor of a town or a clerk in a bank or an officer in the army, just report it honestly and you will be all right."

Most people dared not do otherwise than write out a frank biography and confession. These were collected in the various Communist-organized associations and digested.

Then the Communists posted throughout the city small containers like mail boxes into which people were asked to insert accusation slips, condemning others for crimes or sins which they had committed. These slips need not be signed. Whoever had a gripe or desired vengeance on others had a wide-open opportunity to accuse, whether for real or made-up offenses.

When these things had been attended to, martial law was proclaimed and from this time on police vans went from house to house, mostly at night, picking up tens of thousands of victims who had written out their confessions and jamming them into prisons. These were often so overcrowded that the people arrested had no place to lie down but had to stand up day and night. Thereafter daily the police vans drove through the streets with sirens screaming bringing their victims "trussed up like pigs" to the execution grounds where they were publicly killed.

Thousands of people were forced to come out and witness the executions. Representatives had to be sent from every family. School children, kindergarten youngsters were required to come in a body, led by their hysterical teachers, waving Communist flags, shouting Communist slogans and singing Communist songs. To begin with children would vomit from being emotionally upset; after a few times they learned to enjoy the excitement. The Communists aim to put iron into the blood of their youth so that they will be steeled to the rigors of the World Revolution. They want them to get used to blood and thunder. Through these public executions the authorities instill fear into the hearts of the populace so they become more pliable.

When the reign of terror was at its height in that large, formerly cosmopolitan city of Shanghai, the inhabitants were so filled with dread and forebodings, fearing that the knock on the door at night might come to their home next, that from two to three hundred people were committing suicide every day. So many people were jumping down from the skyscrapers that pedestrians not yet ready to die didn't dare to walk on the sidewalks but used the middle of the street lest these unfortunates fall on them from above.

A Chinese truck driver who fled from Shanghai and came to Hong Kong reported:

"I was conscripted by the Communists to drive one of their death trucks. I did not drive in the daytime, but at night. By far the greater number of the executions were done secretly and after dark. The victims were tied up hands and feet and loaded on to our trucks like logs—120 of them to a truck. All night long I drove back and forth from the prisons to the river bank. The authorities didn't even bother with wasting shot on the victims. These were simply dumped into the river and drowned. I could not stand this nefarious traffic nor bear to hear the screams and moans of the helpless prisoners; one day I jumped from the truck and fled. I was lucky indeed to make my escape."

Another truck driver, known personally to friends in Hong Kong, came out from the opposite direction, from Canton, with essentially the same story. Meeting him unexpectedly one day my friend and former colleague asked:

"Where have you come from?"

"Oh," replied the man, "I am just out from Canton. Couldn't stand it there any longer. The Communists are killing people like flies—many more than you see published in the Communist press. You have no idea what they are doing."

"How do you know they kill more than the numbers they publish?"

"Know! I have seen with my own eyes the thousands they butchered whose fate was never disclosed to the people."

"What were you doing?" queried my friend.

"I drove a truck at Canton for the Government; they gave me good pay."

"Why, then, did you leave your job?"

"Leave my job!" replied the former chauffeur, "How could I take it any longer? How could I bear to see those dead people piling up and to hear the cries and moans of the dying? Every night after dark the Reds made me drive truck loads of suspects, tied up like pigs and gagged —dozens loaded on one truck. There were six trucks and every night we worked, driving these people out of town where they were machine-gunned. We kept going till dawn. The Red newspapers then reported 60 or 80 re-actionaries had been killed during the week! You could add zeros to that figure and still be inside the truth. I realized they would finally kill me, too, so I fled; I knew too much."

During the first years of their rule the Communists kept the people constantly in hot water with one purge after another, and drive upon drive, not even giving them a breathing space. Though the Communists had massacred large numbers of people in various places where they had held sway for some time, the wholesale killings did not take place until after their conquest of the country.

The general program was the liquidation of the land-lords and rich farmers first, after having wrung from them their money through studied tortures. With China's par-ticipating in the aggression against Korea, the anti-mis-sionary campaign came to full bloom and has continued to the present. Some scores of missionaries have been tor-tured to death but most of them have been expelled after enduring various degrees of suffering.

Throughout the Korean war the farmers were impover-ished through unheard of taxes and money was squeezed

out of the people rich and poor by means of the forced
sale of "voluntary" Victory Bonds, the Resist-America-Aid-
Korea movement, and the movement for "voluntary" subscriptions to buy planes, tanks and guns for the war. Sometimes homes had to be sold in order to provide funds for
payment. The aim of the Government was to convert
every individual into a pauper so that he would be totally
dependent upon the Government for his job and livelihood. Money is power, and the people must not have
power—that is, of their own.

In 1951 the land reform purges continued full pace. On
February 15 the "Bamboo Curtain" was lowered *to hide
from the outside world what was happening within, to
shield the slaves of Communism from outside influences
and to block the way of escape for the hapless victims of
the State.* During the year six movements were launched
one after the other, the bloodiest of which, perhaps, was
inaugurated on February 21 when Mao Tse-tung proclaimed the "Regulations of the People's Republic for the
Punishment of Counter-revolutionaries." Millions were
felled under this show of mock justice. Then the "New
Marriage Law" was put into force, breaking many homes
and liquidating undesirables. During this year the Communists started their campaign of blackmail, sending
countless ransom notes to the Chinese overseas. In December the "Anti-three Campaign" (against bribery, corruption and bureaucracy) was launched, which amounted
to a small-scale Party purge.

Early in 1952 the "Anti-three" evolved into the "Anti-
five Movement," a hair-raising nightmare in which the
middle classes of the nation—the merchants, traders, shop
keepers, white-collar workers—were more or less thoroughly raked over. Other millions perished and the survivors
were made docile and obedient. In October Mao Tse-tung

launched the "brain-washing" movement for professors and intelligentsia. In Peking and Tientsin over three thousand professors from twenty institutions were put through the mill. Those that did not wash clean in the third or fourth attempt had their heads washed off the following time. Proceeding from Mao's throne the "thought reform" movement spread throughout the nation. The same year a "reinvestigation" of "land reform" was instituted—but this was merely a device for catching the fish that might have slipped through the net when the "land reform" liquidations had been carried out.

By 1954 executions had tapered off. In 1955 another Party purge in the top ranks was instituted, Peking radio announcing on April 5 the startling liquidation of two top leaders. First was Jao Shu-shih, a stalwart from Shanghai, who was a member of the highest politico-military council of the country, Political Commissar for one of China's four Field Armies, and ruler of six big eastern provinces comprising one of China's seven major military districts. The second victim was Kao Kang, 53 years old, who cheated the executioner's ax by committing suicide. It will be recalled that he had given refuge in his area to Mao Tse-tung and the bedraggled remnants of the Long March. Kao Kang was the "Manchurian Stalin" who during the Korean War ruled over thirty-six million people. He was one of the six vice-chairmen of the Peking government, a Communist whom Mao Tse-tung had once characterized as being "consistently correct." He was boss of China's faltering five-year plan. After announcing the liquidations, the Peking radio proclaimed the creation of "Party control committees" at all levels to carry out a careful purge of undisciplined members.

In some six years of rule the Communists have executed or killed over fifty million victims. We all realize the horrors of World War II with the death and sufferings showered upon the nations; yet the Chinese Communists have tortured and killed more than three times as many civilians as all the soldiers that perished on all the battle-fields of World War II. The total of military and civilian casualties combined cannot compare with the destruction of life with excruciating painfulness wrought by the Communists.*

We hear a good deal from certain quarters about the immorality of relying upon the atom and hydrogen bombs for staving off the enemy, implying that it would be better to surrender to the Communists than to defend our country by such means. But let us consider that if the enemy laid down atom bombs on every square mile of our country from the Mississippi River to the Pacific coast, annihilating every man, woman, and child in that vast area—yet the number of slain would not equal the number of people butchered by the Chinese Communists during the "peace" they established in China after the civil war was over.

The number of executions, of course, is merely an estimate—but an estimate that can be arrived at from different directions.

First of all, compiling independent first-hand reports from all over China, not counting suicides or starvations, one comes to the conclusion that an average of twenty-five thousand people killed per county is a conservative estimate. In some populous counties there have been twenty thousand or forty thousand people killed in just *one* or

---

A Survey of European Civilization (Houghton Mifflin Co., 1952) by Ferguson (New York University) and Bruun (Cornell University) on p. 978 places the total number of forces engaged at 70,000,000 with the cost in lives at 10,000,000 soldiers and 12,000,000 civilians. Other sources set the figures higher.

two waves of liquidation. According to the 1952-3 *China Handbook* there are 2,031 counties in China besides 51 municipalities like Shanghai and Peking. The resultant figure of over fifty million victims is thereby arrived at.

By another method a like figure may be computed. Throughout China the Communists published partial lists of people whom they executed in order to put fear into the hearts of the survivors. However, from overwhelming testimony, twice as many people were killed secretly as openly. These Communist reports have been compiled and the numbers added up. Though partial and incomplete, the figures by August, 1951, had reached over fifteen million. With liquidations taking place since that time and with the double number of secret killings added plus the missing reports not taken into account, one arrives at an estimate far exceeding fifty million.

In 1954 Bishop Quentin K. Y. Huang, who himself escaped after arrest and imprisonment, published a book titled *Now I Can Tell*. In this book he gave the figure (which could take one through 1953 only) of 43,400,000 massacred by the Communists, including almost two hundred thousand Christians. How he obtained his estimate, I do not know.

According to experts on the Soviet Union, Russia slaughtered fifteen million people in her purges. It is not surprising, therefore, that China (where life is cheap), having almost three times as large a population and using the perfected techniques of Russia, should exterminate a somewhat proportionate number of people.*

In this connection one meets an interesting sidelight from a document released by the American China Policy Association on July 16, 1950. The text contains the Mao-

_____
*The Statesmen's Yearbook for 1955 gives Russia's population in 1931 (when liquidations were still unfinished) as 160,430,300.

Stalin Secret Pact attached to the treaty made between Mao and Stalin. The Association announced that the document was smuggled out of China but there was no way of checking its authenticity. However, other points set forth in the document outlining China's coming participation in the Korean War and her mixing into the Indo-China situation, were amply demonstrated before the year was up. Article 7 states:

"The population of the Chinese People's Republic must, owing to the existing lack of resources, be diminished by one hundred million, since otherwise they cannot be sustained. Its detailed procedures are to be determined by the Chinese People's Government itself." In Hong Kong we heard rumors of this agreement but had no proof on which to base its reliability.

Not long after this time the Communist Government broadcast to the world in order to cover up her own black crimes that the population of China had risen to six hundred million. She might have announced seven hundred million and a gullible public would not know the difference! Who will be able to check the facts before Communism has conquered the whole world?

In the general terrorism the Christian Church has not escaped, but many warriors of the Faith have fallen in the battle. In many places true Christians have had to go underground—but the promise of Christ remains that the Gates of Hell shall not prevail against His Church. The Communists have set up a puppet Church of compromised Christians who have often helped in the liquidation of their brethren. These "reformed" Christians will say what the Government wants them to say and act the way the Government wants them to act. They have the form of godliness but have denied the power thereof. True Evangelicals suffer untold persecution in China today.

Communism's reign of terror is necessary from their point of view to achieve three primary objectives:

1. To gain the wealth of the people for the State. Individuals have never been so poor or lived on such a low standard as they do today. Conversely, never in four thousand years of history has the Government of China been as powerful as it is today. The individual counts for nothing; the State is everything.

2. To liquidate the opposition. There is nothing so effective as killing off the opposition. In the process a suspect is the same as a criminal. The Communists believe in the principle: "It is better to have ten thousand innocent imprisoned or killed than to let one guilty go free."

3. To gain absolute obedience. After having been through the machine and the wringer, there is not much starch left in the people. They are cowed and docile and mellow. They will praise the Government and do its bidding. An occasional execution will keep them in line.

Then the Government can start on its construction programs of large dams and trunk railways, of skyscraper Government buildings and public parks. Having lost their soul, the people are expected to build their Utopia.

The Great Red Dragon is a gory creature.

PART TWO

they saw it

*The fool says in his heart,
"There is no God."
They are corrupt, they do
abominable deeds.*

PSALM 14:1

creeping paralysis

I TOLD it to members of the Rotary Club and to other groups in Shanghai—the things I had seen and heard —but they said, 'It may happen in the interior; it will never happen here.' Yet today it has happened in Shanghai—the terrors of Communist barbarity—and it will happen elsewhere if we are not alert."

So spoke one of our Lutheran missionaries who had come from the plains of Honan where he had observed the very beginnings of Communist infiltration and where he had been able to carry on for some time after the Reds had taken over. Those had been the early days when the Communists, not yet sure of themselves, had not dared to drive the foreigners out.

And here is the story my friend told:

"When the Communists first came to an area they kept absolute order. They required much less grain and taxes than the old regime. Their soldiers were polite. The old militia, receiving little wages, had been reduced largely to the practice of stealing and squeezing for a living. Now the people were not pestered with these abuses. The new soldiers did not bother the populace. When the Reds occupied a place for a day or a week, they generously figured up what they owed and wrote out receipts to be applied against future taxes. If anyone offered the soldiers part of his house they would say, 'Oh, no, that will make it too crowded for you!' If he offered them a quilt or other article, they would reply, 'Oh, no, you keep that. That is yours!' In this way the good behavior of the Red troops won the hearts of both rich and poor and disarmed their hostility. Even the wealthy began to say, 'Well, if this is Communism, then we want it, too!'

"As the fighting seasawed back and forth, government troops would take over briefly, looting and raping as they came. When the Reds got back they would say, by way of contrast, 'See what Communism can do for you?'

"By the end of 1946 when their power had increased, the Red soldiers would come to a village, spread out in every direction, and ask the rich, 'May we be quartered in your home? We are so tired tonight.' From their previous contacts they knew just where the better class people lived. They would not molest them but would find out all about them, how many acres of land they owned, how many houses, how many animals. They would take detailed inventory of every piece of furniture and other possessions. They even would try to find money cached away in walls or other secret places, but whenever they found it they left it alone, merely took note of how much was there.

"When the Reds felt that their power was sufficiently consolidated in a community, they would begin their program of creating class hatred. Every home with two *mu* (a third of an acre) or less was considered poor and would be required to send representatives to an indoctrination course. All the riffraff and 'good-for-nothings' would be required to attend, too. Most of the members would be from the poorer classes, but sometimes the well-to-do would be roped in for the purpose of flushing them out into the open and making life intolerable for them. At the first meeting the authorities would hand out a bushel of wheat to each representative. They would tell the people how wonderful Communism was. They would make use of slogans such as 'Help the poor,' 'Equalize wealth.' They would preach against America and the Nationalists.

"After a series of meetings, when the people had been warmed up, the leaders would come to the climax of their efforts to stir up class hatred. They would point out some rich man in the community and say, 'Have you noticed so and so, how much he has—and you have so little? He wears silk—and what do you wear? Is that right? See what he eats—meat every day! And you?—only coarse bread! Is that fair? He lives in a good house. How much land does he own? Who does all the work on it? He sleeps late, but you get up before light and work. Yet you get nowhere. He travels to Peiping and Shanghai any time he wishes, but you have to stay with your work. Is that fair? You see, you do the work and he reaps the benefits. What he has really belongs to you. Now today we are going over there and you are going to get what belongs to you.'

"Thereupon the whole class, about two hundred strong, would troop over to the rich man's courtyard. Communist guards would be standing at the gates. Everyone would be ordered to help himself to some article or piece of furniture and to take it home for himself. The guards would see to it that no one left empty-handed. When some peasants, who were related to the rich man or had received kindnesses at his hands and loved him, would try to leave with only a stick of wood, the guards would grab the sticks and beat up the bearers.

" 'Get something worth while!' they would bawl. 'What does a stick amount to?'

"When nothing was left to take, the Reds would tell the people, 'Help yourselves to the rafters of his house. Take the tiles for your own use.'

"Through this procedure the poorer people would get a lot of loot. However, if some obtained too much, the Reds would get those who were still poorer to work them over.

"When the landlord had been stripped of all except what he wore, that was not the end of it. The Communists knew that he had money hidden away. His tenants would be forced to accuse him, and large fines—always larger than he could pay—would be imposed upon him. Through tortures he would be forced to disgorge his last penny and then he would have to borrow from others to make up the difference. When the landlord had been brought to utter destitution, the Communists knew that they had in this man an enemy for life, one who could never be converted to Communism. Therefore the best policy was to do away with him. Trumped up charges would be brought against him and a large public trial organized.

"After a harangue by the Reds the leader would shout to the mob, 'What shall we do to this rascal?'

"Red agents scattered through the crowd would bellow out, 'Kill him, kill him!'

"Soon everybody would be hollering for his blood. Not to do so would be highly dangerous, stigmatizing one as a sympathizer and fellow-reactionary. After condemning the victim, the Reds would make a public spectacle of the execution. Often many victims would be handled at one time.

"On one such occasion one of the victims was a 72-year-

Trial by Mob

old man who lived four miles from our place and whose
family we knew. After condemning him the authorities
rigged up a frame or gallows about thirty feet high
equipped with rope and pulleys. They made the man's
own children and grandchildren hoist him up by his wrists
which were tied behind his back, thus wrenching his arm
sockets and causing excruciating pains. They even forced
the children to laugh while doing this.

" 'Do you see Chiang Kai-shek?' the Reds asked, as he
was hanging there.

" 'No!' he replied.

" 'Then hang there awhile,' they continued. 'Perhaps you
will see him presently.'

"Racked with pain the poor man hung there for several
hours.

" 'Now do you see Chiang Kai-shek?' they taunted.

"When he replied 'Yes' this time, they said, 'Oh, fear and tremble!'

"They thereupon forced his own sons to stick a pitchfork directly beneath him and to let go of the ropes so that he dropped on the pitchfork. The process was repeated until he was dead.

"This method of punishment was used over and over again throughout the countryside when we were there in 1947. The wholesale killings hadn't started yet, but still the Reds killed a *lot* of people. Even at that time the masses were deeply struck by fear and they realized that the promises of the Communists were worthless.

"At one of our outstations lived a Christian who owned two and two-thirds acres of land, thus being classified as a rich farmer. He was zealous in witnessing for Christ. He had donated to the church some of his land on which a house was built and used as a preaching place. The congregation, one of our most aggressive ones, was collecting funds in preparation for building a church. Donations were put into buying cotton [as a precaution against inflation] and lumber, which were stored at this place. Once when the authorities tried to get this Christian leader involved with the other peasants in looting a landlord's quarters, he feigned severe illness and so got out of it. He didn't want to go and take what belonged to others. It was not long before the Reds came and completely looted his home and all the savings for the church. However, this Christian could not be downed. With everything gone, he was still happy in the Lord and kept right on preaching the Gospel. One day a Communist confronted him with a revolver as he was witnessing.

" 'Haven't we forbidden you to preach?' he bellowed. 'From this day you stop preaching or you will find out who is the boss—you or this thing in my hand!'

"Five of our outstations were closed and the people forbidden to preach. However, during those early stages
of Red occupation most of our outstations were able to
carry on in some way.

"In 1947 our city changed hands thirteen times. There
was terrific fighting. We had hundreds of Red soldiers
coming through our place and visiting our house, to whom
I had a chance to talk. Some were ugly, others friendly.
One soldier said to me, 'You are all right now, but it won't
be long before you'll have to get out of here.'

"On one occasion an officer was going to drag away my
brand new bicycle from an inner room in our house. I
stood in the doorway and said, 'You're not taking that bicycle out of here.'

" 'Of course not,' he replied. 'We don't take anything
that belongs to you.'

"In a short while he was back again with others. I said,
'Why do you insist on taking it, when you have promised
not to take what belongs to us?"

"One of the soldiers thrust the butt of his rifle into
my chest, but I held my ground at the door to block
their way. The other members of my family, alarmed at
developments, pleaded with me to let the Reds take my
bicycle, so finally I yielded and let them have it.

"At that time the Reds started with their program of
dividing the land. Each peasant was allotted about half
an acre. Many got land but were not used to farming.
Some in possession of manure were not able to sell it, as
the rich had fled or had been done away with. By the
spring of 1948 the people as a whole were so fed up with
the new regime that even the poor cursed the Reds to their
faces. But it was too late.

"The people were enslaved."

murder in manchuria

DURING 1949 a number of missionary friends from various parts of Manchuria passed through Hong Kong on their way home. Several spoke at our Seminary there. Since they had stuck it out under the Reds as long as they could, they had been eyewitnesses to the Communist methods and persecutions. A few had themselves suffered disgrace and privation in prison. Now when they were forced to leave, they were able to give us a clear picture of what had been happening in the far north.

The testimonies of the missionaries were remarkably similar. It was a conservative estimate to say that from half a million to seven hundred thousand civilians had been murdered by the Reds in the three northeastern provinces, most of them for no other reason than that they owned property and were well-to-do. Ninety per cent of the people hated Communism and were hoping for a world war to break out so that they could be set free.

Said one of our friends, "In one of the villages up our way the Communists, though atheists themselves, forced everybody to paste up paper gods. This measure **was** aimed against the Christians. One of the Christians who yielded was later struck with remorse. Thinking all hope was lost, that God had rejected him, he wanted to commit suicide. His family was perturbed.

"'Why don't you first go to the missionary,' they said, 'and see if he can help you? He will pray for you.'

"Finally the man was convinced that this was the right thing to do. Over the dusty roads and the long miles he hurried, following the gleam of hope. With open arms I received him as with tears of repentance he confessed his sin. I told him of Peter's denials and of the Lord's loving concern and of Peter's subsequent restoration. Through the Word of God he was led to the assurance of forgiveness and to full freedom again in Christ.

"After the Communist occupation the people, and especially the Christians, endured unspeakable sufferings. In one of our counties forty thousand people had been killed. Property was confiscated wholesale. One of our Christians whom I had baptized twelve years previously could not bear to see all the injustices of the new regime. Being very outspoken, he felt he had to make his voice heard. He rebuked the Reds, telling them that what they were doing was unrighteous.

"'To take away people's property—no one can stop you from that,' he said. 'But to kill people right and left—that is intolerable!'"

"So zealous was he to have the outrages corrected, he even wrote to the authorities about the matter. Of course he could never get by with such frank and outspoken criticism of the sins of the Communists! He was hauled before a 'People's Court' where the Reds accused him of many crimes against 'the people.' They ordered the crowd to march by their victim, each one giving him a blow with a club or stick until he should be beaten to death.

But this time their tactics misfired. The people refused to obey, saying, 'He is a good man.'

"Frustrated in their designs, the Reds had to condemn him to death themselves, without a show of right.

" 'If you renounce Christ,' they challenged, 'you will be set at liberty—what do you choose, Christ or Communism?'

"With a loud voice the Christian cried, 'Jesus, Jesus, Jesus!'

"Thereupon they led him out to the river bank for execution. The crowds were forced to follow along and watch. On the way the man sang with a clear, ringing voice, 'Jesus loves me this I know' and the twenty-third Psalm set to Chinese music. Before his death he was granted his request to make a prayer. After kneeling in prayer he turned to his persecutors and said, 'I have done according to my desire. Now you do according to yours.'

"The Communists make a practice of shooting their victims in the back. These then usually fall on their face and grovel in the dust. However, as this Christian was executed, he fell backward as into the arms of Jesus, with his face looking up into the skies.

"The whole community was rocked by this Christian witness."

CHAPTER FIFTEEN

marked for destruction

THE day was hot and sultry; our apartment seemed unusually stuffy. I offered a fan to my friend, and over cups of tea we relaxed and visited. My friend was one of the thousands who have become Christians since arriving at Hong Kong. He was baptized in our little church across the valley. When our conversation drifted to the topic of his past and of how he had become a Christian, his muscles tensed. There was a strange glow in his eyes as he told the following story:

"After my graduation from college in Shanghai I went into government service and worked at Hangchow, Nanking, Changsha, and, last of all, at Canton. With the collapse of the National government, I returned to my home in Kwangtung. As my wife did not wish to leave the folks and flee with me to Formosa, we stayed put during the Red occupation.

"For three months I experienced the uncertainties of life under the Communists. To begin with, all seemed to go well. During the first few weeks the authorities did not indulge in wholesale killings. Though I was a landlord and had been in government service, I was not afraid, for I believed the Communist promises. From the beginning they had broadcast their assurances: 'People, be perfectly at ease. Whatever your past has been, it makes no difference, just so you don't resist the new regime. Landlords and Kuomintang officials have nothing to fear from us as long as they are law-abiding and obedient.'

"After the Communists had consolidated their hold on our area, they began inviting me out to meals. They had learned that I was formerly a man of position. My wife became alarmed and said it was a bad sign, but I felt the procedure was quite in keeping with old-time custom. One day the county magistrate would invite me, the next the mayor, and so on. With much flattery they said they needed my help to rule the country. I had determined to accept no position, but only to retire and spend my time in studying.

" 'Don't you think for a minute that it will be as easy as all that!' insisted my wife. She had been a lawyer and her judgment and intuition were sharp. As a Christian she early and late urged me to become one too, and even tried to teach me to pray. I smiled and asked her what all the fussing was about.

" 'The Communists are simply trying to get me to accept a public office,' I said. 'All I have to do is to refuse. Who can harm me for that?'

"Earnestly my wife pleaded with me: 'Unless you pray to God and He delivers you, you will never get out of here alive. If you accept a job with the Communists, they will kill you, and if you don't accept a job, they will kill you.'

"This idea seemed fantastic to me!

"Then, during the second month of their occupation the

Communists began extorting money, torturing, and killing. They came to us and levied one thousand piculs of rice [about one thousand sacks containing 133 lbs. each]. Not only was everybody forced to pay levies, but the people were compelled to bring their contributions to the state granaries with dragon parades and drum-beating as a demonstration of the great joy and spontaneity of their actions. The papers were then filled with accounts of the wonderful zeal of the people and their large voluntary contributions. We paid the one thousand piculs without questioning, as we had that much on hand and were able to scrape it together.

"A friend of ours, Mr. Liu, was assessed sixty piculs, but he hesitated to pay it. When it did no good to plead with the petty officer, he went to a higher official, the county magistrate.

"'Surely we will cut down your allotment,' said the latter. 'Tell the officer in charge of your village that I said you need only pay forty piculs.'

"Mr. Liu returned, joyful. Upon being told what the county magistrate had said, the petty officer flew into a rage.

"'What business have you to go over my head? What does the county magistrate know about local conditions? Now you pay one hundred and twenty piculs, and not one catty less!'

"The man paid the forty but no more. He was thrown into prison where he was tortured until he gladly produced the whole amount, borrowing from friends to make up the total. Later he was assessed more, and being unable to pay, was finally tortured and killed.

"But to return to our own case. Some weeks later the authorities demanded another one thousand five hundred piculs of grain, which we furnished them with great diffi-

"The petty officer flew into a rage"

culty. The policy of the Communists when they get into power is to put levies on everyone, the rich and the poor, until the rich become poor and the poor come to starvation. As a result everybody willingly works for the government in any job he is assigned. Having no resources he becomes a slave and a tool of the government. Laborers are paid on the basis of work done, so that those who are not able to do much get insufficient to eat and those who put forth superhuman effort are awarded a trifle more. Thus the highest producer sets the norm. In this way the Communists get public works a-going and completed in no time compared to formerly.

"During the second month while I was still home the Reds in their first wave of executions killed on an average two thousand people per county. With wave after wave of executions since that time I would estimate that, besides women and children, they have killed four or five out of every ten males above twenty years of age.

"At the time the Communists came, I had discarded my Western clothes and had made a rustic peasant outfit which I always wore, and in which I later escaped. One day I went to attend the wedding of a relative. Not five minutes after I had gone the local official, toting a revolver and accompanied by four armed guards, entered our home.

" 'Where is your husband?' he growled.

" 'He's not at home,' replied my wife.

" 'When will he be back?'

" 'I don't know.'

"Refusing to believe my wife, the Communists made a thorough search of our compound.

"When the official left he was all politeness and said, 'You have nothing to fear. I only brought a private letter from the magistrate which I was supposed to hand to your husband personally.'

"When my wife took them to the gate, she noted that a cordon of soldiers had been thrown around our sprawling quarters.

"Immediately after this experience my wife sent my younger sister by round-about ways to inform me that the authorities were after me and I must by no means come home. Then, for the first time, I was almost felled by the *realization* of what the situation was. Before the wedding ceremonies were finished I slipped out the back way. As I left, I saw the Red soldiers surrounding the quarters of the bridal pair in order to trap me.

"I knew what it meant to be hunted. For over a month I was fleeing, hiding, trying to get away. Every stage of my journey was fraught with dangers and suspense, but the lowly, friendly farmers helped me in my escape. Without their kind help I could never have reached safety. At every stage a farmer would escort me to the next stopping place where I was left with trusted friends. We dared to travel only at night and over unfrequented pathways. By day they hid me in their homes.

"I arrived at the railway, but bypassed the large city of our district. The next two stations southward I also bypassed. I figured that the secret police might pick me up so close to home. I thought surely, though, the danger would be over when I reached the fourth station. There I rested in the home of a friend, hoping to catch the train the next day. That evening a farmer came to warn me.

" 'Don't you dare catch the train in this city,' said he. 'I know the secret police here and they are lying in wait for you.'

"This was startling news. I realized that God had saved my life once more.

"The following nights I continued my southward trek through the country on foot. After passing three more stations I finally took the train without further difficulty. In those days travel had not yet been severely restricted. People who could speak Cantonese could travel back and forth. Only Northerners were detained. Thus I arrived safely at Canton where I stayed about a month. I owned a store in the city but did not go near it, for I knew the secret police would be looking for me there. They were also repeatedly taking census, in order to keep tab of the people and to trap fugitives. Not daring even to live with my friends, I moved about from one place to another among my friends' friends in the country. When the Reds instituted a universal census, there was no question about it—I had to get out at once. Fortunately, travel restrictions were not yet under full control and I slipped into Hong Kong on a beautiful day in December, 1949. My joy of freedom, however, was clouded with anxiety for my dear ones.

"After I had left home, my wife did not dare to stay around but lived in hiding in the country. About a week after my arrival in Hong Kong, she together with our son appeared on the scene, to my great joy. But a deep grief remained. My old mother, my sister, and my two daughters in their teens had been trapped.

"After my escape the Communists tightened the screws on those left at home. It was the last straw when they demanded that our savings in gold bars be turned over to them. When some of the gold was given up, they insisted on getting more. They strung up my sixty-eight year-old mother by her thumbs and beat her till she had forked out everything. Upon that, the authorities demanded still more and tortured further. Whether my mother is living or dead today I have no way of finding out. My younger sister, weeping for her mother and seeing how hopeless everything was, jumped into the river. When the farmers rescued her and tried to restore her, the Communists forbade them and buried her alive.

"From my experiences I know that it is God who has delivered me. The untiring prayers of my wife saved me. Had I left home five minutes later I would have been finished. Had I left the wedding ten minutes later I would have been caught. Had the farmer not warned me against the secret police on the railway, I would have been taken. Now I have truly learned to pray. Here in Hong Kong I have studied the Gospel and become a Christian.

"Before I left home, the Communists had destroyed all the country churches in my district, about ten of them. Some they tore down, some they burned, explaining to the people that these were symbols of Imperialism's cultural invasion of China. I have vowed to the Lord that if China becomes free and I can return, I will go back and work for the Lord till these churches are rebuilt!"

the intrepid wayfarer

OUR bicycle tires were pumped up, our packages containing Gospel portions, wadded garment and other supplies had been securely fastened to the carriers behind the seats, and we were off bright and early for the market town. We started out single-file—two Christian laymen, an evangelist and I.

There was something unforgettable about the simplicity of our fellowship. Though from widely different circumstances, yet we were one in purpose, one in love. As we bumped along the rutted, dust-laden ox-cart roads, we shouted to each other in conversation. For odd stretches one could pull up alongside another. Then it was easier to talk and to hear. God had been good to us. He was giving us another opportunity of bringing His Word of Life to the multitudes.

That was in those days, during the war, when the Japanese made foraging raids into our territory from their outposts farther to the south. Never shall I forget a hair-raising incident which occurred one night when the Japanese were ravaging our city. One of the two above-mentioned laymen, who was "refugeeing" in our Mission compound together with hundreds of other Chinese, asked me to go along to inspect his home to make sure it had not been destroyed by fire. Armed with hoe and pitchfork for digging in the rubble we slinked through the alleyways, avoiding the Japanese guards, and arrived at his courtyard. All was quiet, except for noises in the distance. As we were checking on damage done and whispering in the darkness, suddenly from the shadows there flashed a bright light and two Japanese soldiers with fixed bayonets jumped out at us.

"Who are you?" they cried in their fright, mistaking us for guerrillas.

Just as frightened I replied, "I am a missionary taking my friend to inspect his house."

"Don't you know it is dangerous to be out like this? You could just as well have been dead men by now!"

We had a hard time explaining ourselves. My friend was dragged to headquarters for questioning.

"You may return," said the officer to me.

"No," I said, fearing the worst. "He is my sheep and I am pastor of the flock. I will wait until you are through questioning him and then we will go home together."

They permitted me to stay and my friend was questioned civilly.

All this had happened before Pearl Harbor, when we Americans were still considered neutrals. Just one month before Pearl Harbor the Japanese had left our city and we were in free China again. The following year furlough time had come and I had returned home via China's back door, flying from Chungking to India, then taking a transport around South Africa through submarine-infested waters to the shores of America. After the war I had not had the chance to revisit this district. Now the

Communists had taken over and the institution with which I was connected was operating in Hong Kong. Hope had died that I would ever get to see these friends again.

"Do you know that Mr. Liu has come from the interior on a business trip?" asked one of our students. "He is fearless and has traveled far. He wants to see you."

"Of all things!" I replied. "Are you telling the truth? Please invite him to come to our home for dinner—and you come along."

And so came the unexpected moment when my friend and I were brought together once more. He was introduced to my family whom he had not met before as they had been in America during my second term on the field.

"And how is everything on the other side?" I asked. The question triggered a one-sided conversation:

"Do you remember our encounters with the Japanese?" he said. "My nerves still tingle when I think of them. But the Communists are ten times worse. You knew where you were at under the Japanese—but not so under the Communists. Everybody lives in uncertainty and fear. Most of the landlords in my county have been imprisoned or killed. People shudder to think of the Communist prisons. They are refined torture chambers. When you get inside, every move is regulated. You can't cough without getting permission from the guard. If you do, you are severely punished. Prisoners are packed into a room and lie on the brick or mud floor at night. They have to get permission to turn around. They have to get permission to go to the toilet. Some with dysentery pollute the room, but nothing is ever cleaned out, so all the prisoners are made to suffer for it. Some victims with their hands tied behind their backs are suspended by their thumbs just high enough so that they can barely stand on tiptoe. Others are handcuffed with paper links. If they break them they are half killed. The fear and tension of trying to keep the links intact almost drive the victims crazy. Yes, the Communist prison is a living Hell; people will do anything to escape it. In all matters they have learned to obey the authorities.

"Remarkably, I have managed to do a good deal of traveling. I made the rounds of our outstations and found that the Communists had occupied practically all of the churches. I tried to locate the Christians, but was afraid to make too many inquiries lest I and they come under suspicion. In my contacts I have found the great majority of the people against the new regime. Even the laborers and ricksha coolies hate it. They have to work terribly hard and barely get enough to keep themselves alive, not to mention their families. And they don't have nearly as good food as formerly.

"I tried to keep the fire of faith burning in my home. One day two of my relatives came from the country. I reported their arrival to headquarters, as one has to do this to avoid grave trouble, and I got permission for them to stay at my home overnight. That evening while having devotions I talked about obeying the regulations of the government. I also said, 'We belong to the Kingdom of Heaven and must obey Christ.' I do not remember having said anything out of the way. During devotions, without my knowledge, two spies had come from headquarters, carrying a little lantern. Upon entering the courtyard they demanded that my door-watchers remain silent. They put out their light, went to the rear where our meeting was being held and stood outside the door listening. Without their presence being known, they heard everything. Nothing happened that night, but the next morning when I went to headquarters to get permission for my guests to return home, a young boy about sixteen curtly told me, 'They can't leave today—and don't you dare come again to this place to inquire. Wait until we inform you.'

"Day after day passed without any word from head-quarters. Both my guests and I became very anxious. It was an economic problem for me to keep guests for such a long time—my friends also had things to tend to. Besides, their families would become greatly concerned about them. When there seemed to be no solution to this problem, I took things into my own hands. I wrote out a notice purporting to come from the home town of these guests asking for their return. This note I smuggled out to their home where the people got the local official to sign it. This was sent to the headquarters in the city where the authorities were finally forced to act and let my guests go home. In numberless ways like this the Reds deliberately make life miserable and full of fear for the people.

"Making it a point to study the new situation, I traveled extensively through Honan, Shansi, and other provinces. I found that many evangelists and preachers had been martyred for their faith. I stayed in the home of a widow who told me about the courage of her husband who had been the leader of their congregation. The Reds imprisoned and tortured him.

" 'Now you may go,' they said, when releasing him, 'but don't you dare to preach any more.'

"He answered firmly, 'You can force me to do this and that, but when you command me not to preach, I cannot obey you.'

"The head official became furious and snarled, 'Then you must die, you poor, miserable lout!'

"Calmly the Christian replied, 'I am not the one to be pitied. You are poor and miserable,' and he started to preach to him. As in the case of Stephen, the Communists could not withstand his words. Grinding their teeth in rage they seized and shot him without further ado. This man would not compromise his faith.

"On the train coming south I noticed a fellow passenger who had his mouth full of gold fillings, though he was dressed in the poorest of clothing. I took the opportunity of getting acquainted with him and inquiring about his circumstances.

" 'How is it,' I asked, after getting his confidence, 'that you have gold teeth and yet are dressed in rags?'

"When nobody was looking, the man unbuttoned his clothes and showed me his body. He was covered with terrifying scars.

" 'I used to be well-to-do,' he said, 'but the Communists not only confiscated my wealth, they also put me through their torture chamber. They smeared my body with patches of kerosene and set fire to it, burning me horribly. However, I did not die but at length escaped.'

The time had come for our party to break up. It was not easy for my friend to return to the dragon's lair, but his family was there and guarantors would be involved if he did not show up.

"We may never be able to see each other again," he said. "God be with you!"

I escorted him down the road. A last wave of goodbye —and he disappeared over the hill into the night shadows of a Communist-dominated land.

Four weeks later rigid clamps on travel were applied and the Bamboo Curtain enclosed the borders of old Cathay.

student with a limp

HE WALKED with a characteristic limp. I had known him in my classes but our acquaintance had been casual as we had never met before he came to school. One day while we were conversing he said, "Do you know how I got my limp?"

"No," I replied. "I am interested in hearing."

"Well," he went on, "that was quite an experience! It happened in the interior shortly after the turn-over. I was traveling peacefully when secret police came along and for no reason whatever arrested me. I was not particularly disturbed, for I was not doing anything wrong. But I misjudged the temper of the new regime.

" 'You are a spy,' said the police. 'You are a Nationalist agent.'

" 'No,' I answered, 'I am a Christian.'

" 'Nonsense!' insisted the chief as he began searching me. He pulled from my pocket a letter which I had received from the American pastor of my home congregation to deliver to a friend at my destination.

" 'What did I say?' he continued, after examining the

letter written in English. 'Look here, you are a running dog of American imperialism!'

"I realized it was getting serious. I was without defense. Nothing I said counted. They were taking me to Peking for questioning.

"At the capital I was thrown into prison and put through a course of torture. For one thing they placed a board along the front of my leg, tying it down tight at the ends. Then they inserted a brick between my knee and the middle of the board, bending my leg the wrong way like a bow.

" 'Now will you confess?' they nagged.

"I maintained my innocence. What else could I do?

"They inserted a second brick, then a third. I cried out in pain. My leg was breaking. The terrific pressure was driving me mad.

"At this point a Red official chanced by, a boyhood friend of mine. He recognized me and said a few words to the torturers. I was released—but not before my bones had been warped and my ligaments stretched and permanently damaged. That is why I limp today."

When Mr. Chen's scholarship ran out, he left our institution and tried to make a living as a small trader between Red China and Hong Kong. He often called at our home, showing us the knickknacks and embroideries he was peddling.

On one such occasion he showed up in great agitation. It was January 27, 1951, and he talked steadily from 3:30 in the afternoon till 8:00 in the evening. He had just arrived from Hankow and brought us a gift of beautiful slippers embroidered by a former helper of ours.

As the words cascaded from his lips, we recognized a picture of human suffering and slavery that, in spite of its horror and tragedy, was becoming commonplace in Hong

Kong where hundreds of thousands of refugees were piling up, each with his tale of woe.

We shall listen to Mr. Chen as he tells his own story:

"I was in Changsha purchasing articles for my business when the police took a census. After endless questioning they learned that my home town was in Honan.

" 'What are you doing here so far from home? You are a landlord, a corrupt oppressor, a Nationalist spy!' they charged.

"It was the same thing over again. I tried to prove my innocence, but it was useless, hopeless. They shipped me to Honan to face a People's Court in my own home town.

"What was my surprise when I saw a former bandit, a scoundrel, occupying the seat of head official! That's the way the Communists do it. They make use of the most wicked and ruthless fellows to carry out their purposes. These devils get drunk with power and don't realize that they are mere puppets who come in handy for the purging out of the old ruling and influential classes of society, but who will be kicked aside when the Communists are through using them.

"Cruel death stared me in the face. In the cold of winter, as I knelt before the crowd, sweat started out on my forehead. Trying his best to instill fear in me, the swaggering official kept cocking and brandishing his gun until I was anxious that I might be shot by accident. The situation looked ugly, dangerous, terrifying. There was no law, no justice, no self-defense. I was completely at the mercy of the mob. The meeting was being whipped into a crisis—a crisis which was about to decide my fate—when, unexpectedly, an old woman, one who had formerly helped in our home, jumped to her feet and called all the women to arise.

" 'I have known this young man,' she cried, 'for many years, and I know that there is nothing seriously wrong with him. What do you say? All of you who agree, raise your hands, and you who disagree, keep them down.'

"All the women raised their hands and the assembly followed suit. I got a new lease on life. A letter was written for me to take back in which they said that they had proved that I was not an oppressor, nor a landlord—but whether or not I were a spy the authorities would have to investigate for themselves in Changsha. Thereupon I was released.

"Having been cleared, I took the opportunity to look around. Orders had been handed down for all Christian services to be discontinued. Since the authorities had already occupied the large church in town, the Christians had been meeting in homes. In the country the congregations were much worse off because of the ignorance and unreasonableness of the petty officials. Casually I wandered over to our old church.

"I was accosted.

" 'What are you doing here? Are you a Christian?'

"A convulsing fear clawed at my heart and I said, 'No, I am not a Christian, I am just passing by this way.'

"Yes, I know I sinned. I denied Christ. I was also forced to shout with the people, 'Down with imperialist America!' Everybody shouted, as I did, but I have learned that countless of them mean just the opposite. The newspapers blared forth 'Victory, victory,' while the people asked, 'Why hasn't America thrown her atom bombs on China yet?' They still look to America and have faith that their deliverance will come from her.

"In my home county seven thousand victims had recently been executed and four thousand were in prison in danger of liquidation, among whom was my cousin. I tried to look him up, but the authorities would not permit me to see him.

"The Russians have a stranglehold on China. I saw many of them in Peking, I saw them in Hankow and in Changsha. Stalin's picture was everywhere, given more prominence than Mao Tse-tung's. The government is pressing the study of the Russian language in the schools. Yet the great majority of Chinese hate the Russians and 88 per cent of them detest the new regime. The only ones in favor are the Reds themselves and the former riffraff and scoundrels and the most poverty-stricken individuals who are now on top and have obtained something out of it. Though little, it is more than they had before. The ordinary poor, however, are fed up with the Communists who have worsened their lot instead of bettered it.

"Everywhere I saw huge storehouses and granaries built by the government for storing its grain taken from the farmers. All wealth and power are now concentrated in its hands. Through taxation, confiscation and other methods the whole country has been pauperized and the State has become all-powerful. The ordinary people, forced to subsist on two meals of poor food a day, are undernourished and have difficulty earning a living.

"Young people in China are helpless victims of the Communist State. Methods of coercion are most subtle and diabolical. Unless the young folks join in the work of the State, there are no jobs for them, no future, no hope.

" 'If you join the Movement,' they are told, 'you will have plenty to eat and to wear, and you will have a wonderful time.'

"Just before an enlistment drive the Reds will put on a great show; the young folks working in government jobs will parade in their warm clothing, let the public see the wonderful food, with meat dishes, which they eat. In one place they invited the public to watch them dance far into the night, men with women, to show the voluptuous time they could have in government service. After that young folks are urged to join them. When they are practically starving at home, how can they withstand the temptation?

"The Communists are past masters at applying what is perhaps the greatest pressure there is in the world—social pressure. Whenever a group of youth join up, they are praised to the skies and a public meeting is called where others are urged to give gifts. Those who respond are in turn held up for great honor while those who resist are ridiculed and told that their thinking is not straight, that they are in need of more indoctrination. Then others are asked to volunteer and when they do they are held up as examples of patriotism and progressiveness. The die-hards are despised, cursed and buffeted. The crowds, led by Communist agitators, have learned what way is profitable for them to act.

"In the interior, as people are not allowed to listen to short-wave radio, no one knows much about the outside world except what the authorities want them to know. You who live here in Hong Kong get a much clearer picture not only of the world situation, but of the situation throughout China. The people who are bottled up in the inland only see what is around them, but to you who are living here news trickles out from every quarter."

When he left our home, the former student with the characteristic limp promised, on his next trip, to return and visit us. His ties with the interior were more than he could lightly sever. He turned, in his fatalistic way, to face an uncertain future. The bamboo curtain then screened the land, and our friend was never again seen or heard from.

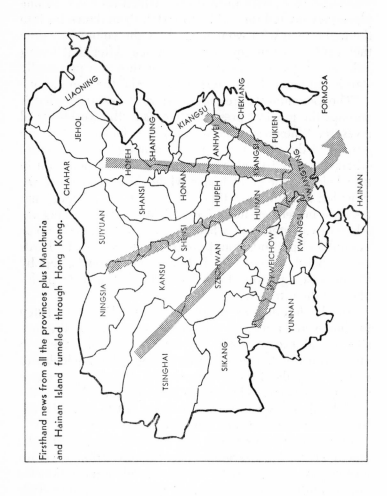

Firsthand news from all the provinces plus Manchuria and Hainan Island funneled through Hong Kong.

the confucian scholar

ONE hot summer morning with the Bible in one hand and a folding fan in the other—in Chinese fashion—I stood before an attentive audience in the small stifling quarters which had been rented for a preaching place in Shatin village, Hong Kong. My text was the words of Jesus: "Every one who drinks of this water will thirst again, but whoever drinks of the water that I shall give him will never thirst; the water that I shall give him will become in him a spring of water welling up to eternal life" (John 4:13-14).

"We may take the water in the physical well," I said, "to symbolize all the temporal things of this life—the things that men desire supremely. But are they satisfying? What do you long most to have in life? . . . money? . . . education? . . . power? . . . fame? . . . pleasure? All these things are of passing value and, like the water in the well, cannot quench the thirst of the undying soul. Man was made for eternity, for God—and until he rests in Him he can find no rest. Jesus said, 'But whoever drinks of the water that I shall give him will never thirst.' Jesus died

for us and through His atonement offers us living water—
His salvation, the forgiveness of sins, a new life, the in-
dwelling of His Spirit. For the believer this becomes a
spring of water within him welling up to eternal life."

Three days later I received a letter from a stranger
asking for an interview. That was easily arranged. When
the time came, I met at the door a polished, kindly gentleman of middle age dressed in simple, coarse garments.
He hesitated a moment, wondering if he dared intrude
upon my time.

"I am happy to meet you!" I greeted, sensing his uncertainty. "Come into our inner room." Those whom the
Chinese honor most and welcome dearly, they invite into
their innermost chamber.

Tea was poured and for the first hour I let Mr. Chin
do the talking.

"I was in a Gospel Hall the other day," he began, "for
the first time in my life, and what you talked about fitted
my needs exactly. I am in a desperate situation. Everything in this world has proved to be undependable and
empty, and my soul is bitter. I have been seriously thinking about ending it all, but now the Word of God holds
out new hope. I want the Living Water!"

Having a makeshift hut for home, Mr. Chin had been
called upon one day by a graduate of our Seminary who
was serving as evangelist, and at his invitation had come
to church to hear the Word of God that Sunday morning.

"I can see you have been through some bitter experiences," I said. "Tell me about them. I am anxious to
hear."

"I am living in tragedy," he went on. "My home has
been ruined, my family broken up. I cannot sleep at
nights wondering about my dear ones. Sometimes I think

I will go insane. But perhaps your God can save me out of all these distresses?"

My heart wept with my friend as he relived his experiences. Yet the heartaches and agonies of this one man were but a tiny mirror of the ocean of sorrows and misery brought upon the human race by Communism.

"My home was in Hunan," continued Mr. Chin, "where I had a happy family circle with both my parents living. I was prominent in the community, a member of the Nationalist Party, and a teacher by profession. When the Reds took over the city I was the principal of a thriving school. Figuring that the Communists would not trouble me in this position, I continued my work. Then things began tightening up and I realized that difficulties lay ahead. I had accumulated a wonderful private library of ten thousand volumes of which I was really proud. To my dismay the secret police called one day and sealed up the whole establishment. Fear gripped my heart—and forebodings for the future. Then to my consternation the authorities came and destroyed my entire library of precious books! The labors of a life-time went up in smoke. There could be no remonstrance, no way of resisting.

"'Come,' I said to my father in the secret of night, as I realized the net was closing in on us, 'come, let us escape as a family or we will be liquidated.'

"My aged father replied, 'I'm too old to float around the country. What means of livelihood would we have away from home? No, I shall remain here. Who will harm a 70-year-old man? I stayed through the Japanese occupation—nothing could be worse than that—and no harm came to me. You may leave, if you must, but I'm too old to flee now.'

"We had a family consultation and decided that we

could not leave the old folks alone. There was no question about me—I must leave or the ax would fall. But my immediate family would stay on, as my wife was needed at home to take care of my father and mother. I fled alone to Canton, that large city where I would be lost in the crowd.

"As Chinese New Year's approached I turned with longing thoughts to my family circle. You know, that is the one time of the year that we Chinese really celebrate in our homes. I became restless, could find no peace until I decided to risk everything in order to join my family circle once more!

"I studied carefully the train schedule which my friend brought me from the depot. As it was the south-bound trains which were being checked for escapees, I should have no special difficulty getting on the train and traveling northward. I decided on the schedule that suited my needs, one that would bring me home after dark.

"Since I did not wish to hang around the depot, I bought my ticket shortly before the train was to leave. My heart pounded, but I tried to look casual. There was no questioning by the police and I boarded the train with the rest of the passengers and sat inconspicuously in my seat. Endless hours rolled by and I pretended to be sleeping most of the time. However, my restlessness increased the closer I got to home. Now it was getting dark. What if some policeman should recognize me? What if I were held for questioning? Hopes and doubts pursued each other in my mind. The train stopped, and there was no more time for reflection. Though my knees shook, I walked bravely off the train and, seeing the police busy elsewhere, I glided through the depot and out into the streets. The dim, eerie lights were my allies. Stealthily I found my way through the alleys, out into the country, then by familiar bypaths to our village.

"I had made it!—and not a soul outside of my family was aware of my presence. Never before had I experienced such a welcome home as I received that night and for seven days we enjoyed a glorious reunion, the only discordant note being the atmosphere of uncertainty and fear hanging over us. During those days I renewed my pleas with my father, but he remained adamant.

" 'No crack of doom has descended on us yet,' he argued. 'If I must die I will die at home, not as a wanderer in a far country.'

"I realized that it was impossible for me to remain longer. Sooner or later my presence would be discovered, and then vengeance would be merciless. Taking my older son along I departed, leaving my parents, my wife, our seventeen-year-old daughter and our six-year-old son. Finding the atmosphere in Canton charged with suspicion and tenseness, we pushed on and arrived in Hong Kong before the border was closed. I was still able to correspond with my family, and my daughter wrote faithfully, saying that all was well at home and I must not worry.

"Then the ax fell. I no longer got letters from my daughter, but, instead, horrible stories through the grapevine concerning Communist atrocities and purges. The landlords were being exterminated through mob trials and mass executions. Like those of a huge octopus the Red tentacles were reaching down into every village, every hamlet. No one could escape. The will of the Communists was being imposed upon the masses and it always turned out to be the 'will of the people.'

"The Communists manipulate the crowds like a master magician. However the people may feel, the authorities twist their wishes to serve their own ends. At one village trial the leader shouted to the peasants, 'Is this man a landlord?' Petrified with fear they all raised their hands. Then he announced: 'By the judgment of the people this man is a criminal. The people have sentenced him to death!' Forthwith he was murdered on the spot. At the next trial, since the crowds realized that a good man had been killed because they had raised their hands, they stood glumly silent in response to the leader's challenge. Then he shouted exultantly: 'By your silence you have shown your acquiescence in the death of this criminal. He has been judged by the people to pay for his crime with his life!' Through the consistent use of fear and intimidation the Communists train the multitudes to respond correctly to their suggestions. After a time the people mechanically raise their hands or shout, 'Kill him, kill him!' when challenged by the leader.

"Before long I heard rumors in Hong Kong that my beloved father had been purged. An old man, kindly and much loved, a philanthropist of his day who had inherited a certain amount of wealth, he had been seized by the government and dragged off for public trial. Under the perfect Red manipulation this old gentleman together with many others had been sentenced to death by the mob and executed. My anxiety increased as I received no definite word—only still more rumors, that my mother, seventy-one years of age, was begging on the streets, that my wife in fright and despair had committed suicide. The uncertainty of it all was devastating.

"Then a letter came through. It was from my seventeen-year-old daughter. My hands trembled as I opened the letter. I dared not read it—I dared not leave it unread. The news fell on my soul with searing effect as I read about the holocaust which had enveloped our home.

Communist Leader Calling for Accusers

Murder, suicide, living death—all was confirmed. My daughter's six-year-old brother had been completely lost track of; she herself had been roaming the countryside like a hunted deer. Thrice she had fled to Canton, trying to get out to Hong Kong, but each time she had failed. Her money had run out. She borrowed enough to get to Hankow where she had an aunt and there she got a permit to stay for three months. Now the three months were over and she must move on. Though the authorities had not yet caught up with her, there would be no more foolproof method of falling into their clutches than to overstay her time limit. Then she would come in for suspicions and endless questionings until her fate would be sealed. Where should she turn to next?

"My eyes blurred and my heart was torn to shreds as I finished the letter. Where should I turn to next?"

I remained speechless for a while. Who is sufficient for these things? In deep sympathy I handed my friend a Chinese Bible and looked up passages for him to read, after which I enlarged on their meaning.

"I do not understand these passages," he remarked, "until you explain them. It is just like with Mencius and Confucius. You cannot understand their sayings until the teacher explains them."

The Word of God was something entirely strange to this man, but already the Spirit of God was speaking to his heart through that Word.

"Have you ever prayed?" I asked.

"No," he replied.

"Would you like to pray?"

"Yes—but I don't know how."

"That's all right," I said. "I'll say a sentence and you pray it after me."

In simple words I prayed: "Dear Jesus, I accept you as my Savior. Send your Holy Spirit to enlighten my heart and to strengthen my faith in you. Through your grace and mercy forgive me my sins and cleanse me in your blood shed for me on the cross. Grant me your full and free salvation—the Living Water which you have promised. O God, you are my Father! Comfort me in my distress. Look to my dear ones who may still be alive in the interior and save them! . . . Hear me for Christ's sake. Amen."

Sentence by sentence he repeated the prayer after me like a child—this scholar trained in the ancient wisdom and culture of China.

the strapping guerrilla

H E WAS the picture of health with the strapping physique of a northerner, close-cropped hair, bronzed face, sparkling black eyes, a straightforward look. Intelligence was written over his features just as strength had been built into his frame.

Here was a sturdy specimen of the hard-working peasant of the northern plains—a model of strength and self-possession.

"I grew up on the farm," related my friend, as I inquired about his past. We had just been introduced and I had been told that he had recently escaped from the interior. To impress on me his acquaintance with toil he showed me his calloused hands and he took off his shirt to let me see the horny skin on his shoulders, which had come from bearing heavy burdens with a pole. "I loved hard work," he continued, "and our clan, being industrious and frugal, achieved substantial prosperity.

"After the outbreak of the Japanese war I joined the army. There I was promoted to *Yin Chang* with seven hundred soldiers under my command. No sooner was one enemy, the Japanese, defeated than another monster reared its ugly head—the Chinese Communists. When the government troops were defeated in West China, I and my men joined the guerrillas in the mountains. After operating for some time we ran out of supplies and conditions became so unbearable that we decided to disband. I gradually made my way homeward and arrived at Tanghsien, Honan, in October, 1950.

"Since the land reforms—during which thousands of people had been killed in our county—had already taken place, I was too late to get any land to cultivate. My wife and I obtained a little donkey and we set up business grinding wheat. Everybody has to be engaged in some productive occupation.

"My, what a relief it is to be breathing the free atmosphere of Hong Kong! Life under the oppression of the Communists is unbearable. Even the formerly poor have become disillusioned. During the first year after the redistribution of land the Reds were not too bad to the farmers and the poor. They required little taxes and tried to win the confidence of the masses. Gradually, however, the strings were tightened and, especially after the outbreak of the Korean war, the taxes became more exorbitant than they had ever been. Because up our way the country was thickly populated, each farmer had received only one sixth of an acre of land. Now the authorities were collecting from 70 to 80 per cent of the grain raised. When the farmers complained that there was not enough left for them to live on, the authorities politely told them: 'Let your children join the government. There they will have plenty to eat—rice, flour, meat and vegetables to their heart's content.'

"Whether they liked it or not, the young folks were being forced along to follow the new regime. When I came away there were hardly any young men left to be seen in the country. It was mostly old men and women and children who were cultivating fields. Many young and middle-aged men had been killed during the liquidation and others had joined the guerrillas or fled to Taiwan, while the remaining young people had, as a rule, entered government service or been sent to Korea as 'volunteers.'

"How wonderful it is to breathe freely again! Why, the reports the papers here in Hong Kong print about conditions in the inland aren't anywise as bad as the actual situation! You can't imagine what things are like unless you have been through them yourself!

"After the widespread killings connected with the land reforms, things calmed down until the first part of this year (1951) when orders came from Peking for a further purge of reactionaries. Suddenly, throughout the county, arrests were made. About six thousand victims were brought into our city all at once, filling five improvised prisons to overflowing. There was one large Temple system which could hold about three thousand people when packed in Communist style. With this extraordinary influx of humanity into town, the authorities provided for them by making special allotments of wheat to the millers who then brought the flour to the prisons. As I brought my portion each day, I could see for myself what the situation was like. As arrests continued, the prisons needed emptying. This was done by sending groups of prisoners into the different country districts for execution. Terror was distributed by this means throughout the countryside. Farmers and traders coming into town brought the reports, but we had to be very careful that no stranger was around when we talked. Plain-clothes spies were everywhere.

"The arrests and executions continued unabated for

several months. Anyone whom the authorities wanted
to kill, they "put a hat on his head"—called him a spy, a
reactionary, or a Kuomintang special agent. That finished
him. There was absolutely no chance for self-defence.
That there was not an iota of truth to the accusation made
no difference. Even old-time Communists were suddenly
transferred and liquidated, so they came to fear nothing
more than an unexpected transference. It might mean
a new place of work or a promotion, or it might end in
liquidation. There was security for no one.

"So many of my relatives and friends were killed in the
liquidations that there is no way of calculating their number. The forms of torture used are so many that they
cannot be enumerated. I shall tell you about my maternal
grandfather who was tortured and killed. He had four
sons. Two were put to death and two disappeared without
leaving any trace. Two grandsons were killed. My grandfather had been a landlord highly respected by the people,
one who believed in 'doing good.' But the Communists
have coined a new term—*shan pa* (benevolent despot) in
distinction from the common term *o pa* (wicked despot).
Both of these classes must be exterminated.

"At the public trial the leader called for accusations but
the people would not denounce my grandfather. Then
came pressure.

" 'So you are in cahoots with these landlords, are you!
If you do not accuse them, it is proof that you are their
dog-legs.'

"The people had to produce some charge, however trif-
ling. Yet the least accusation becomes devastating. For instance, if one from the crowd, hoping not to harm the
accused, gets up and says, 'Twenty years ago this man's
donkey passing by my field ate a bean off of one of my
plants,' such a small accusation is no obstacle for the Reds!

The debt of this landlord is figured out. Had the bean been planted, it would have borne so and so much. The next year all the seeds would again have been planted and the yield harvested. Every following year the previous harvest would have been planted until by geometric progression the amount of the debt would become so staggering that no one could ever pay it back. As a result this debt must now be paid in torture and blood.

"For his retribution my grandfather was given the 'cold and hot treatment.' It was in the dead of winter. The Communists soaked a wadded cotton quilt in water, wrapped him up in it, laid him outside on a slab of stone, then turned the threshing fans on him until his teeth chattered.

" 'Are you cold?' they asked with feigned concern.

" 'Yes, very cold,' was his natural reply.

" 'So you are cold, are you?" they taunted. 'We will have to warm you up.'

"Thereupon they built a bonfire around him until the blanket steamed and sizzled, but they were careful not to apply the torture to the point of death. My grandfather's body was one mass of blisters. In their frenzy these torturers sometimes use broken pieces of tile and scrape off the half-boiled flesh of the victim until the ribs are bared. In this condition my sixty-nine-year-old grandfather finally had his ebbing life beaten out of him.

"You ask if these tortures and methods are not just local and exceptional. They are not! The Communists follow the same pattern *everywhere*.

"Up our way in Tanghsien, a county with some over four hundred thousand people, by the time I left, there had been about twenty thousand victims killed and there had been countless suicides. Conditions were still worse at Wuyang, a much smaller county where the same number of people were killed. All the counties around there suffered a similar fate. Many Christians fell in the general slaughter and the churches were closed.

"In the midst of these mounting arrests and executions my wife with tears urged me to flee.

" 'You know,' she said, 'that one of these days your turn will come and you will be dragged off. It is better to die on the road than to die hopelessly in their hands.'

"My father and mother also urged me to leave: 'Regardless of what happens to us when the authorities find out that you have left, you must get out!'

"I could not resist their tears or their logic. The die was cast; I would leave! An air of suspense and excitement pervaded our home as we held consultations and laid plans for my flight. My only chance was to escape to Hong Kong, yet how preposterous the idea seemed—what with all the secret police lurking around the corners, the travel passes that always had to be shown, the unpredictable and endless questionings, and I with my northern dialect traveling through strange regions where circumstances could so easily trap me! But there could be no turning back—only one mad plunge into the unknown.

"The first difficulty to hurdle was the matter of getting a travel pass. It was absolutely essential that this step— the most important—be carefully and successfully negotiated. One miscalculation, and life would be worthless!

"Exhausting thought and painstaking efforts were put into this project. From a public proclamation posted in the city I tore off the corner containing the official seal of the authorities. I bought a cake of soap and carved its face so that the official seal stood out in reverse. I secured some paper and wrote out a permit saying that the bearer was of the medical profession, that he had a brother who was a doctor in Hong Kong and that he was traveling to that place to buy medical supplies. All this, of course, was pure fiction. Using the cake of soap and printers' red ink I stamped on the corner of the permit the official seal. This exacting work, done in my spare time, took me about two weeks to accomplish.

"When all was ready, armed with my forged pass and with money for the long journey, I took leave of my parents, my wife and my six-year-old son. I walked over a hundred miles to the railway and boarded a train for Hankow. Fortunately, no inquiries were made until I got to Wuchang, across the river from Hankow, where one has to change trains for Canton. There I was challenged to produce my pass. When I had started out on my journey I had made up my mind that under whatever circumstance, even torture or death, I would firmly maintain my innocence. If I didn't I would be finished anyway, of course. Trying to look innocent and natural, I handed my forgery to the guards. Happily for me, so many of the officials and agents used by the Communists are so grossly ignorant and stupid that they cannot possibly tell the difference between a genuine pass and a counterfeit. Many of them cannot even read or write. The inspectors took my pass and looked at it this way and that. When they saw the red seal in the corner, they asked no more questions. I boarded the train and was on my way to Canton.

"On the train I kept strictly by myself. Except when I bought food from peddlers, I talked as little as possible, lest my northern dialect get me into trouble. Time and again the security police boarded the train, walking up and down the aisle questioning people hit and miss, especially those who looked suspicious or scared. They pounced upon an unlearned farmer in front of me. My heart leaped to my throat, but I pretended to pay no attention. The poor man was so shocked at the brusque treatment and sharp cross-examination, that he couldn't answer straight.

"'Get off here,' they shouted at him, 'and give an account of yourself! Your travel pass is o.k., but your statements contradict it.'

"The police looked my way but passed on. Not once at

"The police looked my way but passed on"

the various stops did they come to me, whereas several other passengers were pulled from the coach and bundled off for questioning. Of course they lost the train—and it is anybody's guess as to what might have become of them.

"I thought we would never get to Canton, but even that trip came to an end. Once more I had to go through the dreaded process of changing trains, this time for the last leg of my journey. The guards looked at my pass but did not seem to understand it. They let me through. However, when I arrived at Shumchun, across the border from Hong Kong, the officials seemed to know their business.

" 'Now,' I thought to myself, 'I am surely caught.'

"They examined the pass over and over again, conferred among themselves and examined me.

" 'This pass is no good,' they said. 'Where did you get it?'

"I thought my heart would stop. Yet I must have looked calm and self-possessed, because I held them at bay. Acting the personification of innocence, I stared them straight in the eyes and said, 'This is what the authorities at Tanghsien gave me, and I don't see why it shouldn't be all right!'

"After sparring around for some time I was still unable to dissolve their doubts and they clapped me into prison. Now I feared the end had come. Under repeated questionings I firmly maintained my position. As I did not give way I rocked their confidence, and they finally called me out.

" 'This pass,' they explained, 'is out of date. They are issuing printed passes of a different kind now. You must go to Canton and get it changed for the new kind.'

"Personally, I knew that if I did that it would mean my life. Here I was—so close to Hong Kong that I could see the hills across the border—and yet so far away!

" 'I have used up my money,' I pleaded, 'and don't have enough to go to Canton and come back again. Being so close to Hong Kong, can't I go across to my brother who has the funds I need?' All my pleading was in vain.

" 'You go back to Canton, and you go at once!' was their strict rejoinder.

" 'That is all right,' I added submissively, 'but may I at least stay here a few days until I can get funds sent to me from my brother?'

"With this astonishing concession they let me go.

"I betook myself to an inn where I stayed for eleven days. During the daytime one could move about quite freely, but in the evenings there was grave danger. The secret police would come around unexpectedly and take census. For this reason I spent much of my time in the out-house. I noticed that I was not the only one with this bright idea. Other fugitives seemed to be making it their habitat, too.

"The innkeeper was a sympathetic man and gave me invaluable help and advice, warning me of dangers and outlining for me a plan of escape. He drew a map of the area and told me what barriers to avoid and in what direction to go.

"Some days I would take a short stroll outside and casually survey the countryside, getting my bearings. From a distance I would view the border over which I was to flee, but the task seemed hopeless. Aside from the river and the barbed wire entanglements that had to be negotiated, there were the guards, posted everywhere, rifles and machine guns in hand.

"As day after day dragged on, I was at times overcome with pessimism. To get across the border was next to impossible. To return inland was sure death. To remain—I was penniless and would sooner or later be discovered. Anything would be better than to fall into the hands of the secret police. More than once I viewed the rafters of the roof. I contemplated suicide as the only solution available to me, but a voice kept saying: 'If you kill yourself, all is lost. If you make one dash for liberty you *may* succeed—and you cannot do more than die!' The one glimmer of hope won the day. I would gamble all on the possibility of making an escape.

Taking Census in Hotels

"On August first the great opportunity came. The inn-keeper himself had disappeared a few days before. Perhaps he had made his own escape, I do not know. Three of us refugees, one from Nanking, one from Shanghai and I, planned our get-away together. A howling typhoon was lashing the countryside and rain came down in torrents. We set out in the dark. Every few steps, as we approached the border, searchlights poked out into the darkness and flashlights of the patrols flickered off and on. My two companions were more cautious than I and at such times would drop to the ground, but I pressed on. I do not think the patrols could see anything in that blinding rain, anyway. I lost track of my companions. Coming to the river, I plunged in and swam across. I crawled over the barbed wire entanglements on the other side, tearing my clothes and my hands. But I was over! I had made it! A burden rolled off my back. I had regained freedom—freedom, which one misses only when it is lost! I have endured much hardship since I came to Hong Kong, penniless and destitute, but I am *free*, and that makes up for everything!

"Once beyond the barrier, I set off alone across the mountains of the New Territories. I finally came to a railway and I followed that into Hong Kong. Now I thought that I was in a free country, that all my worries were past.

"I blithely came up to a policeman [employed by the British] and asked, 'Where is the Nationalist Bureau where I can register?'

"He looked at me in amazement and said, 'There is no such thing here. Where are you from? Don't you know that if you have come across illegally you will be deported back again?'

"Cold chills went up and down my spine, but the man continued, 'I am from Shantung and I can understand your situation. Had you accosted a Kwangtung policeman, your goose would have been cooked. Now hurry on your way.'

"I was given directions as to how to get to the camp where tens of thousands of refugees are staying. There I am eking out a bare existence by making paper flowers early and late until my eyes smart and my head aches. Yet I must say once more, what a relief it is to be breathing freely again! Under the Communists there are so many plain-clothes spies and informers that no one dares to talk. You have to be absolutely sure of the one to whom you are speaking. Death is preferable to that kind of life. The people had a saying that to live under the Communists was like sitting in prison under an indeterminate sentence. Ordinarily you have hopes of getting out of prison when your time is served—say after two years or ten years—but today the people have no hope. Besides, there is less security in China today than in prison formerly. You never know when your turn will come and you will be dragged away for questioning and perhaps for torture and death."

When his tale was ended I asked my friend, "Have you ever been in contact with Christianity?"

"As a child," he replied, "I attended the Mission Primary School, but I had little contact after that."

"Do you know that God has graciously spared your life and given you a chance to believe on Jesus Christ as your Savior?"

"Yes," he replied. "Every day I am attending the Lutheran Mission at the refugee camp."

After prayer, as he was about to leave, he said wistfully, "I have arrived safely at Hong Kong, but my family will not know about it. If they are still living, I dare not endanger their lives by writing to them."

model communist prison

T HE following report is of special interest because this lady, a Free Methodist missionary for over thirty years, had been well-disposed toward the Reds, considering them agrarian reformers with whom one could do business. She bought a good deal of medicine in Shanghai to take inland, figuring that as a medical worker her chances of co-operation with the authorities would be assured. For a while the Communists played along, and glowing reports of their good conduct and their excellent treatment of her were published in the *New York Times*. Some months later a letter was smuggled out in the hub of a cart wheel and we learned that things were not going so well. When she was finally able to evacuate from China during the latter half of 1951 she gave us her version of the situation substantially as follows:

"I had left the provincial capital where I lived and taken the train to a nearby city, when I was unexpectedly arrested. I explained to the police that I had obtained permission for the trip, but they refused to honor my pass and only repeated, 'You have broken the regulations and must be punished.' When I 'talked good words' to them, as the Chinese say, one of them barked gruffly, 'Nothing doing—she's the ringleader!'

"A number of mission boards in the homeland had been sending funds to me for distribution among their respective groups on the field. As a result workers from many places had been coming to my office to obtain their money. I imagine that is why the Communist official called me a ringleader.

"I was taken to police headquarters where I waited in silence to see what they would do with me but, though hours passed and daylight was now fading, nobody showed up to look into my case. Nor would they permit me to inform my friends as to where I was. I was given two black buns to eat and was confined to the room for the night.

"Another day—and nothing happened! It was not until the third day that I was summoned to the chief's office and told that I must return home at once. I was effectively intimidated and after that didn't dare to set my foot outside of our city.

"Some time later I had three missionary guests calling for funds. According to regulations I reported their presence to the police. When we had finished evening prayers and were getting ready to retire, loud voices were shouting downstairs. It was the secret police. After examining our registration certificates, they dragged the four of us off to headquarters.

"When I asked what it was all about, they shook their heads and said, 'A little questioning won't hurt you any.' I had meticulously followed their regulations—yet they were taking us to police headquarters! The Communists are liars all the way through. You can't believe a word they say!

"At headquarters we were approached by a youth in his twenties. To begin with he was so polite that an uninitiated person could easily be fooled into thinking the politeness was genuine. It was not. Very soon his real nature broke out.

" 'Be frank,' he charged us sharply. 'What were you people scheming?' Without waiting for an answer he added, 'You folks!—not satisfied with living well, you have to plot against the People!'

"After explaining I said, 'I've told you everything; don't you believe me?'

" 'Believe you!' he snorted, 'Huh! you deceitful Americans!'

"When they had finished questioning us separately they shut us into a dark room, the four of us, two men and two women. It was in the cold of winter; the wind howled and the snow flurries blew through the window and stung us in the face. In the darkness we could feel no bed nor any quilts for covering. Fearing I might not survive the bitter cold of the night, I pounded on the door and called for attention.

"Immediately a guard directly outside our window cursed and said, 'Are you looking for death?'

" 'We are cold,' I pleaded, 'and there's not so much as a piece of straw on the ground to lie on.'

" 'Go to America,' he retorted, 'and live in luxury!'

"That night we did not sleep a wink but prayed for inward peace and waited for the dawn.

"When daylight arrived we heard doors squeaking on their hinges. Presently our door was pushed open and we were told to go outside. We saw that our cell was connected with a large courtyard which had about thirty small rooms opening to it. There must have been no less than one thousand six hundred prisoners. We had to line up for roll call and other duties and, being newcomers, we were among the last. This prison was connected with the security headquarters. There were several other prisons in the city connected with various departments of the government and we learned that ours was the smallest of the lot.

"The second day we were allowed to keep some quilts and cots brought to us by church members. There was only enough space in our tiny room to put up two cots. One of the men slept on the ground at night. We were not permitted to leave the room except once in the morning and once in the late evening. We had two meals a day of black buns frozen hard from the cold, but hunger drove us to eat them. Later, on our release, we were required to pay for our 'board' during the imprisonment. Since the weather was bitterly cold, we never took off our clothes. There was so little water available that we could wash our face only once in four days.

"The first three days we were questioned separately more than ten times, with each session consuming over three hours. They expected to get a quick confession of plotting, but we could only say my friends had come for funds. After our release I learned that the authorities had repeatedly prodded our Christians to make up accusations against me, but they had refused. Our last inquisitor at the prison was that same cocky youth. Staring at us with wicked eyes he said, 'All right, you crooks, sit here then the rest of your lives!' After this we were questioned no more.

"I was not too anxious about our own situation because, being foreigners, we were treated infinitely better than the Chinese. Besides, our prison was not as important as the others, since it contained only second-rate victims, and treatment was not as severe. There was, however, a large turnover as people were constantly being transferred to the other places. At the Military Affairs prison or at the prison of the Justice Department people were condemned to death on the spot.

"Even so, it took only a few days for a strong man to be worn down. The fear, the hunger, the cold, the cruelty, the being questioned under torture—all these things left a person half dead. The prison's qualifications for being a torture chamber were more than sufficient.

"On the thirteenth day, not knowing why we had been imprisoned, I could take it no longer. I asked a guard standing near the door: 'Well, how about it for us?'

"Pretending to be cautious he replied, 'So you want to get out of here, do you?'

" 'Certainly,' I answered. 'They ought to be done with their investigations by this time and found out that we have committed no crime.'

"With a sneer he retorted, 'Whether you're here or at home, what's the difference? It won't be too late to wait till imperialist America has surrendered.' Then he strode off.

"I marveled that every agent trained by the Communists should show such identical hostility toward us and toward all the prisoners. There was not a speck of sympathy in their make-up. Some of the things we witnessed showed their complete lack of any feeling of humanity.

"In our cell there was a small window through which we were not permitted to look. Stealthily we peeked out at times to see what was happening. A few feet away was the entrance to a prison room crammed with prisoners, who were not even allowed to talk to each other. In this respect we were far more fortunate than they as we had not been forbidden to do that. We even sang under our breath, and quoted Scripture to each other from memory since our repeated requests for a Bible had been denied.

"For over an hour one morning we heard the weak but agonizing groans of a woman from a room to our left. The questioning by the police during the night must have been severe. When the prisoners were lined up in the yard for roll call and morning indoctrination, she was rudely dragged out, as no one, whatever his condition, must skip these classes. But in her pain she had fainted away.

"As she lay there I recognized her—a Christian teacher in our primary school, the model mother of four little children. Her face was deathly white, her eyes sunken and dark, and on her forehead was a large clot of blood. Her disheveled hair covered the one side of her face while her dirty, torn clothes revealed bloody wounds. She lay like one dead.

" 'So you pretend to be dead!' growled a guard as he spat a mouthful of sputum into her white face.

"Roughly he grabbed her by the shoulders, shook her up and down and threw her back on the ground with a heavy thud. The woman came to for a moment, opened her eyes, then faded away. The fellow prisoners looked the other direction, but the curses of the soldier pursued them and they heard the dull sound of kicks as he shouted, 'You rat, you ought to die!'

"People under questioning or those who had made infractions of the rules were tortured in various ways. From our cell we could hear their groans and sometimes see their sufferings. A favorite method of torture was to tie a person's hands behind his back, then fasten a rope to his wrists, loop it around the neck, bring it down again to the wrists where it was tied securely. When the rope was made taut the victim nearly strangled. If he tried to relieve his wrenched and aching arms and sockets by pulling down on the rope, he would choke himself. Thus he was forced

to struggle to exhaustion. If he wasn't struggling sufficiently, the guards would tighten the rope. My three companions were Quakers and Pacifists, but when they heard
and saw the tortures, one of them remarked: 'I am a Paci-
fist, but when I see all this and hear the groaning, then I
wonder. If they laid hold on my wife like that, I am afraid
I would start fighting!'

"During the night of our thirty-eighth day of imprisonment one of my fellow missionaries became violently ill.
To be sure, we were all sick people, but this man came
down with high fever and was in a critical condition. I
had had nurses' training, but I could not determine what
his illness was.

"Next day I appealed to the guard: 'Will you please
find a doctor for us at once?'

" 'Not without permission from the top,' he snapped.
When I saw he remained motionless I said—with a tinge
of authority in my voice—'If you do not report it to the
higher officials, it will be your responsibility. After all, a
man's life is in the balance.'

"This must have impressed him because half an hour
later three uniformed men appeared. One of them examined the patient, shook his head and turned to me:
'What sickness does he have?'

"I replied, 'Please get a doctor to examine him.'

" 'I am the military doctor,' he huffed. Then turning to
his comrades he remarked, 'Huh, this is a strange imperialist sickness!'

"Addressing me once more, he said, 'We'll do it this
way. Whatever kind of medicine you say he should have
we'll give to him.'

"He made as though he were leaving.

"I took this opportunity to plead that we carry the man
home and nurse him.

" 'So you want to open another meeting, do you?' wheezed one of the officers standing by.

"I was about to make a short explanation when he broke me off. For some reason or other he evidently did not wish to have the foreigner die in prison, so he said, 'All right, you may all leave—but be mighty careful how you act!'

"We immediately rolled up our bedding and sent word to our Christians who came and helped carry our friend to the mission compound. We had escaped from the devil's lair! The next day our patient recovered from the illness. It was the marvelous doing of the Lord.

"After our release we witnessed the Red terror grow worse and worse. In our city one hundred people were being executed each day. In the county thousands were being liquidated. Often the police didn't bother with shooting the victims, but forced them to dig a long trench, pushed them in and buried them alive. This I know from eye-witness accounts. Besides those that were being executed openly, the Communists carted truck-loads of victims away at night and did away with them secretly.

"Of the several prisons in the city the largest held five thousand inmates. Prisoners were crowded together so tightly that they could not lie down, but only sit, nor could anyone get up without permission. When the prisons were filled to overflowing room was made for fresh victims by executing the old ones or transporting them away for slave labor. One day all traffic was forbidden on the streets and the people were strictly ordered to remain at home. All that day thousands of prisoners were brought in from the surrounding countryside and shipped off on freight trains to the North for slave labor.

"The Communists don't do a thing of what they promise. They have deceived the farmers who now must pay so much of their crops to the authorities that many would gladly give up their land if they could. Though the Communists promised religious freedom, there is nothing of the sort. They are determined to destroy Christianity. Of this there is no doubt whatsoever. One third of the churches in our area have been closed. In many places the Christians have had their Bibles taken from them and have been forbidden to hold meetings in their homes. A large percentage of the Christians have fallen away from the faith. In the former missionary middle school no two students were allowed to pray together.

"The Communists are destroying the morals of China. Standards of conduct are purposely being degraded. In the government institutions and in the schools of our city the boys and girls were not segregated in separate dormitories, but lived together. They slept in the same rooms and shared the same beds or mats placed on the floors. To give birth to illegitimate children was not a shame but a glory. The government established public nurseries where the babies could be brought up.

"In our city six Protestant pastors and three Catholic Fathers were imprisoned. They were the leaders of the churches. Three of the pastors had been taken because they had received funds from the mother church to last for three years and they were accused of misusing the funds and not registering them properly with the authorities. An accusation meeting was arranged for these pastors. At this meeting representatives had to come from the churches of the various denominations. At the first meeting they opened the proceedings at eight in the morning and continued till three in the afternoon, and the following day they continued from eight to six o'clock. No one entering the hall was permitted to leave until the meeting was over, and no one was given anything to eat. The three faithful pastors had to kneel on the hard platform during the whole time. One of them who had suffered from tuberculosis and had once had three ribs removed fainted from weakness. He was revived with cold water and ordered to continue kneeling. When he collapsed again, they allowed him to sit during the proceedings. Accuser after accuser—members of the churches, intimidated and taught by the Communists and trying to curry their favor or save themselves—rose to give their speeches. As they came forward to the platform they slapped, kicked and spat on the victims. Sometimes they handled them so roughly that the guards had to step in to hinder them. So terrible was the meeting that our own pastor and principal of our school (who was forced to attend and who afterwards reported everything to me) said that he became so nauseated that he vomited during the meeting. At the end of the second day, as the victims were brought out, streams of tears gushed down their faces.

"Following these meetings the government made up mimeographed lesson sheets covering the accusations and the proceedings. These had to be studied at numerous indoctrination courses. A whole month after the accusation meetings they were still keeping on with these lesson sheets. After Sunday services the church-goers had to continue with an indoctrination class which they were not allowed to open with prayer. After the long course examinations were given. My pastor shook his head when telling me about some of the questions. 'Either you have to expose yourself,' he said, 'or else you have to ruin your conscience.' The questions he referred to were of the following type: 'Do you approve of this accusation meeting which has taken place?' 'Would you welcome holding such an accusation meeting in your own church?'

"You have read about the spy system in Russia—but such a thing is unbelievable until you have seen it! Under the Communist system everyone is made to spy on everyone else. The people become so frightened that they do not dare to talk to each other. The average Chinese says that the Japanese occupation was heaven compared to the Red regime. The Communists have such a stranglehold upon the people that there is absolutely no chance for any organized insurrection. Salvation must come from the outside.

"And behind the scenes the Russians are in power. There were scores of them in our city; I saw them on the streets, even their womenfolk. No one can tell me that everything is not made up in Russia! The Russians have control in China, with their officers and advisers in charge. I am glad that I stayed in as long as I did, for now I have seen for myself and I know the truth."

western panorama

NORTH, Central and South China have spoken. No matter from which area the testimonies come, we notice the same general pattern of wickedness. We now hear West China speak from one of its largest cities through a missionary of the China Inland Mission:

"The Communists took over our city the latter part of 1949, so we have been living under the Reds for almost two years. For the first year we were free to carry on our work with little hindrance, except that we were not permitted to go more than a mile and a half outside the city. The Communists had their hands too full carrying out their program in the country to pay much attention to us.

"Gradually things began to tighten. Since spies sat in on all meetings, one had to be very careful about what he said. People never know who may be a spy or an informer; everybody lives in fear. Even church members are forced or enticed into acting as spies. One such member was an itinerant barber, who, because of the nature of his job, could collect a great deal of information about people. The authorities offered him one hundred catties [approximately 133 lbs.] of rice a month—a considerable amount of remuneration in these times! For every conviction he brought about they offered an extra two hundred-fifty catties of rice. The man thought he was 'in clover.' But, after he had secured much information for the authorities and they had no more use for him, they got someone else to accuse him so he in turn met his downfall. Through fines the authorities got back much of what they had paid out and they then condemned him to a slave labor camp.

"In our city lived a prominent police officer who had filled his office in an exemplary way under the Nationalists and was well spoken of by all. As he had been an upright man he thought he had nothing to fear from the Reds, so stayed on when they took over. He and his wife lived in an attractive, semi-foreign style house which they owned. Both he and his wife became interested in the Gospel.

"Unexpectedly this man was thrown into prison where he languished for months. The authorities had secured a woman to testify that the officer had killed her husband. This may have been a false charge or it may have been true—an incident occurring in the officer's line of duty—but the Communists are not interested in that angle of the problem. They expelled the man's wife from the home, sealed up the property and, eventually, gave the house as a reward to the woman who had accused the officer.

"While her husband was in prison, the wife was baptized and became an ardent Christian. She prayed continuously for her husband. A few days before his execution she fasted and prayed and came to a definite assurance of his soul's salvation. She was not permitted to see him in prison, but the day before he was killed she was able to send him some food with a bowl containing meat. This

man and another Christian were executed together and
were the first two from our group to lose their lives.

"One cannot deny that the Reds have brought about
certain improvements. Houses which they have confiscated from their victims are whitewashed so they look outwardly clean and attractive. The streets are kept more
sanitary. There is much less trouble with the coolies than
before, as they charge a set price and do not dare to
haggle. The government is making and improving roads
in every direction. But no one can tell me that there is
no more graft! There is still plenty of it—only it shows itself differently from formerly. Communists caught in
graft are being executed right along.

"The Communists are all out for capturing the youth.
They do not 'give a rip' about the older people—whether
they suffer or starve or die. They terrorize them and indoctrinate them in order to keep them submissive, but it
is the youth to whom they give their full attention and
care in order that they may create tough Communists for
the future. For the young people there is actually no livelihood unless they join the government.

"The Communists have a fiendish skill for organizing.
Sooner or later everybody becomes involved in indoctrination. There is no escape. Even I had to attend an indoctrination course together with the Catholic Fathers
and other leaders in the community. During the discussion each of us had to get up and say something. We were
required to take some point from our lesson sheet and
enlarge upon it. It was difficult to find a point on which
to talk without damaging one's conscience or getting one-
self into hot water.

"One day at indoctrination when the Communists were
attacking the belief in God, in order to give a good im-

pression one of the Catholic Fathers, who later went insane from the pressure, chimed in saying: 'Yes, I agree with this point. Some people say God is in everything, but I wouldn't say that He was in that electric light bulb.'

" 'No,' I said, taking issue with him, 'you're wrong. God *is* in that electric light bulb.'

" 'Nonsense!' joined in the Communist leader of the meeting. 'How can God be in the light bulb? We Chinese made that bulb.'

" 'Who made the electricity,' I asked, 'that burns in the bulb?'

" 'We Chinese,' he answered, 'dug the coal that powered the plant that created the electricity.'

"I persisted: 'And who put the sunshine into the coal which produced the electricity?'

"The Communist leader was nonplused and said, 'You are not permitted to bring religion into these discussions!"

" 'You are the ones,' I replied, 'who brought it up first and not we!'

"The Communists did not like such frankness during the discussions and later they threw us foreigners out of the meetings entirely.

"Whenever one got stuck, it was good strategy to have stock questions which would puzzle the leader. One time I asked, 'We learn about Marx and Lenin and Stalin, but what about Engels and Hegel? Can you please tell us something about them?' The ignorant leader turned to some of his colleagues for enlightenment. At length one of them got up and mumbled a lot of stuff in a strange tongue and then sat down. It did no good when I objected that nobody could understand what he said. They changed the subject and went on to something else!

"Another time I remarked that there was much we could learn from the Communists, especially regarding their spirit of sacrifice. 'But,' I said, 'you sacrifice too much.'

" 'How so?' asked the Communists.

"I grabbed the opportunity to say a few words for my Lord and continued, 'You have left out the most important thing of all. You have sacrificed Christ, and without Him everything else is worthless.'

"On one occasion the indoctrinator was grilling me on the introduction of opium into China. I told him, 'I don't know too much about the introduction of opium into China, but I do know who has been trying most to get rid of it. The *Church* has always been in the forefront of the battle against opium and against all other social vices.'

"From my experiences I learned always to give first place to spiritual conversation and fellowship. Whenever anyone called on me, I started to preach to him about Christ right away. In this way our conversation was edifying and also enabled me to find out to what type of person I was talking. If he were safe, we could later talk about other things, such as the prevailing conditions.

The last six weeks we were inland the people had to meet six hours a day, every day, holding accusation meetings against us foreigners. I suppose they are still continuing with them! At these meetings every family must be represented and the *chia chang* [boss of ten families] and *pao chang* [street boss] are responsible for attendance. If any family is not represented the informers report to the authorities and the bosses are punished. The same holds true for attendance at public executions. The authorities designate how many people must be present from each street—and they have got to be there, even little children.

"The Communists secure complete obedience by relying on a system of imprisonment and intimidation. Besides using the old prison buildings, they were filling all kinds of houses with their victims. On all sides of us huge, new prisons were being constructed.

"The Communists are ruthless in their handling of the people. In the country they kill off the rich and influential and put coolies and illiterate riffraff into power. Such people are easier to command and control. They are more apt to believe what the Reds tell them, and since they cannot read or write they will not dispute the information which they receive. Using them as tools the Communists torture and kill mercilessly. Even girls in their teens are killed—thirteen-year-olds, eighteen-year-olds. Not only outsiders, but even Communists themselves and their collaborators are being shot.

"I would judge that one fifth of the population up our way had been killed by the time we came out. The executions were still continuing, but they seemed to be diminishing in number. I base my estimate on reports I received from Christians and farmers coming in to town from all sections of the county. Old trusted friends, if they saw nobody around, would come into our compound and call on us. During the time we were there we were never restricted to our compound but could go about the city freely. The last months, however, most of the people were afraid to recognize us on the streets, but we were still able to get together secretly.

"The forms of torture used are innumerable. One favorite method is to tie a man's hands behind his back and to suspend him by his wrists from a beam. He is then swung back and forth and the people are forced to beat him as he swings close to them. One man was suspended in this way all night and a millstone was placed on his arms back of his head. By morning he was deformed and his arms were completely out of their sockets. For some reason this man was not killed but set free. Fortunately, he had a relative in the medical profession who helped get his arms back into their sockets and otherwise treated him. In the winter the Communists often give their victims the cold and hot treatment—first strip them and make them freeze, then, if they complain or show signs of suffering, build a fire under them.

"Many of the political prisoners whom the Communists do not execute they send to slave labor camps. There was such a camp only two and a half miles outside our city. There the government housed about twenty thousand prisoners. Every day under armed guard these prisoners went about their work. Many of them who had never carried burdens before were forced to carry coal into the city from a mine thirty-five miles away.

"During the last five months we cooked our own food and did our own shopping at the market. Our cook had to go into the country to get his share of the land distribution. Thirty-some miles from town there was a cluster of homes inhabited by a clan of thirty-two souls. Every single one of this group—men, women, gray-haired grandmothers and tiny babies—was annihilated. It was on their land and in their houses that our cook was placed. Being unable to return to us himself, he showed his concern by sending his wife to see what she could do to help us. This woman told us much about the conditions in the country and about what she had seen with her own eyes. She told how she had seen the authorities force the peasants to stick pieces of broken glass into the ground and then roll their victims back and forth until they were gory with blood and grimy with dirt. All the villagers had to witness these proceedings and even take part in them so that their hearts would be filled with terror and no one would dare to oppose the government.

"Just outside our city lived a thirteen-year-old girl who became a convert. Every Sunday she walked to church to hear the Word of God and to fellowship with God's people. Informers among the neighbors told the police that this girl was going out every Sunday. They investigated and learned that she went to church. This they forbade her to do, even taking her Bible from her. As she continued attending services, they imprisoned her for several days. After that they would not permit her to go outside without a pass—and yet they would not issue any pass to her. In this way her connections with the Church were broken.

"Some of our Christians were tortured by having their wrists tied so tightly that their fingers swelled up, after which they walked around with hands that looked like footballs. They were tortured in order that they might confess things of which they were innocent. I knew these people personally—and the things the police tried to make them confess were preposterous!

"Under the terrific pressure some Christian groups in our city had succumbed, but our congregation and the Lutheran Church were still holding firm. So far they had refused to sponsor accusation meetings. Our pastor was adamant in his refusal to permit Stalin's picture to displace the poster of the Cross on the altar piece. 'The moment Stalin's picture goes up,' he said, 'that moment I resign from being pastor.' With such leadership the congregation held with him. I am convinced that the only way for the Church to meet the crisis is to refuse to co-operate with the government and to be prepared for martyrdom.

"Because of his non-co-operation, on one occasion the Lutheran pastor was arrested and tortured by being strung up by his thumbs. His thumbs were tied with hemp and the dry hemp was soaked with water until it contracted and bit through his flesh to the bone. As he was thus suspended, the police tried to make him confess the crimes of having mishandled funds and of having poisoned others. They got youngsters to come and accuse him to his face, saying he had used them to put poison in people's food. I do not know what the ultimate fate of these faithful pastors will be, but, by God's grace, after much suffering, this pastor was finally released. When his wounds were healed, deep, white scars marked his thumbs. Undaunted he said: 'I thank God that I had this experience, for now I bear branded on my body the marks of Jesus.'"

CHAPTER TWENTY-TWO

the red passport

DEPORTED missionaries—or plain evacuees—punched holes in the bamboo curtain, so it was always an event when such friends called at Gospel Breeze Mountain. On such occasions our small community would often gather to visit over a cup of coffee or to partake of a fellowship meal. Having dedicated our lives to bringing the Gospel to the Chinese people, our deep concern continued for their unfortunate land which had fallen victim to the all-devouring Red Dragon. We were always interested in learning about developments in the interior—and always saddened as we heard the facts.

At a Christmas dinner, 1951, I had the opportunity of sitting next to a University professor, a Norwegian citizen, just released from China. Since he had been well-disposed toward the new regime before the Communist take-over, it was quite a jolt for him to meet the reality of their rule.

"For the last ten months," he related, "my wife and I have been trying to obtain permission to leave China. There wasn't a thing we could do for the Chinese. In fact our presence there was a detriment to the Christians, for which reason I resigned from teaching at the University last February. We haven't been to church since last March.

"Conditions in the interior are hopeless. There are supposedly no beggars in China, but we saw plenty of them—as many as ever. Though we were not in direct touch with the farmers, we heard that they were worse off than formerly. There is still much corruption, as the government is making an issue out of purging and executing corrupt officials. Those in power are taking for themselves the best of everything. They drive around in the best cars, live in the best houses, wear the best clothes.

"I was able to smuggle out a number of important Communist documents and papers by having them bound into the covers of books by a Western friend who knew how to do this type of work. These were mailed to Hong Kong and arrived here safely. I would not have dared to take them along with me when evacuating.

"The morals among the Communists are very loose. In order to destroy the ancient family institution of China, the authorities scatter the members, sending the husband to work in one place and the wife in another. One high Communist official said in a speech: 'Don't be worried if we send you to work far away from your wife. We will furnish you with another one.'

"The number of executions in our region was tremendous and the suicides countless. In some places, if a person commits suicide, his relatives are punished for it. The sadistic behavior of the Communists is revolting. I know of one case in which they shot their victim in the back of his head, blowing out his brains with a dumdum bullet, then forced the other victims to eat the brains.

"The country is filled with propaganda against the United States. For example, they print such statements: 'The United States soldiers in Korea are so barbaric and misbehaved, that we are forced to restrain them. We give them towels with which to wash, but they are so filthy and uncleanly that they don't even know what the towels are for and go for weeks without using them.'

"We foreigners were met with *exquisite impoliteness* on the part of the authorities, as we experienced all the way while traveling out. When we came to the border, we had to wait four hours before we were permitted to cross. Since the police insisted that every single Chinese must go first, we were the very last.

"For the first stage of our journey we flew. We were surprised to see so many airplanes on the fields. The airports were full of them, American and Russian makes. Travel facilities have been greatly improved, but many of the Communist officials are stupid—plain stupid. One young, impudent officer at Canton made quite a display of searching people, making them take off their shoes and examining their persons. When he came to me, he asked what nationality I was. I replied, 'Norwegian.' When he saw my passport with red covers—with a show of authority he waved me by, saying, 'Oh, you will have no trouble.' Evidently he thought I must be from some Red Satellite country because of my red-covered passport! As soon as he came to my wife and saw her red passport, with the same air of importance he waved her on.

"As for Christianity in China, I see no hope for the *organized* Church. Only about one-tenth of the former Church activity and attendance in our area was continuing. Many of the Protestant leaders seem to have bowed to the Communist force. One prominent pastor in the Protestant church, in accusing someone, told a bunch of lies. I met him later and chided him for so doing.

" 'Why,' I asked, 'did you say those things when you knew they were false?'

"He did not like that I approached him on this question. 'You foreigners,' he said, 'are mistaken on this. You don't understand Chinese psychology. We give in on the non-essentials. But if the authorities should touch on our religion, then we would stand firm to death.'

"With this attitude, the leaders are defeated from the beginning. How can you separate Religion from Ethics! Because of this compromising attitude on the part of the leaders, many Christians will not go to church, lest they become involved in the new policies. They are the future hope of Christianity in China!

"In spite of the dark picture, we had some encouraging experiences before we left. Up until our departure my Chinese co-worker, a pastor, refused to accuse me. Twice he was forced to write out an accusation sheet and submit it to the police, but both times the sheet was rejected because it was too mild and not to the point. Another co-worker, a bishop, who had resigned two years ago, said as his parting words: 'If you hear that I have been executed, sing "Hallelujah!" That is what I am looking forward to. It will be wonderful for me to get away from this life of torment.' On the day we left, no one dared to see us off officially, but the night before, many Christians came to us secretly to say good-by. Some faithful women assured us, 'Do not be worried—we will not give up Christianity!'"

communist justice

IN THEIR anti-Western hatred the Communists not only baited Americans but attacked other nationalities as well, even those who had recognized their regime. The following experiences related by a Norwegian missionary lady who was deported as a criminal in December, 1951, reveal the keen sense of justice and propriety possessed by the Red atheists of China:

"Our city was 'liberated' in August, 1949. When the Communist army arrived, the soldiers were orderly and well disciplined. They slept on the streets and refused to disturb the people in their homes—a marked contrast to the National troops who had been looting and oppressing the people. As a result, it was almost with a feeling of relief that the people adjusted themselves to the idea of the turnover. The Red soldiers were well-behaved and polite. If they borrowed something and broke it, they would pay for it. Later we found out that the army had been given strict orders to behave in this manner. A Red soldier told me one day, 'Yes, the army is good, but you beware when the political workers come around!' And so it was. Though things looked quite hopeful in the beginning, it wasn't long before the situation took on another color.

"Once, when a group of armed agents came to usurp one of our mission buildings, I hurried to the stairs to try to head them off. Immediately the agents poked two revolvers into me, one into my chest and one into my ribs.

"On seeing their attitude I said, 'So this is the meaning of your posters, points six and eight!'

"During the 'liberation' posters had been set up throughout the city and the above-mentioned points guaranteed the freedom of religion and the protection of foreigners and their property. All these promises of the Reds are only theory, not practice. Such virtues as honor or truthfulness are entirely foreign to the Communists. There was no stopping them in their evil designs. Time and again we had guns and bayonets pointed at us.

"The Communists said much about loving the people and about being concerned for their welfare—but they themselves always ate the best, lived in the best houses, wore the best clothes, whereas they taxed the poor people to desperation. Whether excessively polite or brawling mad, the officials were always *devilish*. That is the one word that describes them best.

"By killing so many of the populace the Reds instill fear into the people until they will do anything they are told to do. Through intensive training and pressure they bring out the deepest evil of the human heart and make it so that wives can no longer trust their husbands nor husbands their wives. Parents are even afraid of their own children.

"After the occupation, in spite of difficulties, we were able to keep on with our work until Easter, 1950. Then things broke. Simultaneously the leaders of the Church, of the mission schools and of the mission hospital were arrested. It was a terrible Easter! Instead of anthems of joy ringing forth praises to God, the Communists forced the congregation to hold accusation meetings in the church all day.

"A faithful friend of mine, who was forced to attend all these meetings, reported everything to me secretly. For six hours the principal of our school had to kneel before the audience while Communist-inspired accusers reviled and abused him. Almost beside himself with pain, he tore off his jacket to kneel on, but the authorities snatched it from him. Agitators cried out for his execution. Worked up by the Communists the students seized the wooden cross on the altar, smashed it before the principal and trampled upon it like madmen. At the end of the day the government leader of the meeting announced that the Christians were still backward and needed to learn more. Hence the following morning there would be services in the church followed by Communion and in the afternoon there would be continued studies in mental orientation. The Christians must have felt that the setting was not fitting, for the Communion services the next day did not materialize!

"Before their arrival we had been under the delusion that the Chinese Communists would be different. But now it became clear to us what we could expect for the future. From this time on there was no peace to be had. I was accused by the secret police of using a radio transmitter which I did not have—and for half a year they kept pestering me regarding this radio. There was only one period of two weeks in which they did not come to our house to search. Otherwise, they were around two and three times a week, questioning me for hours and searching everywhere, even digging gaping holes into the walls and tearing up parts of the floors. They specialized in night visits and even insisted that I keep the doors open so that they could come in conveniently without having to wait for me to open the doors! This I refused to do. When I delayed a couple minutes while dressing at night, they kicked up a big fuss, pounding on the door and cursing violently. Then when I opened the door, they burst in like barbarians with obscene and vile language on their lips. Most of the time it was youngsters, nineteen, twenty years of age, who came swaggering around on these searches.

"Finally, in December of that year I was called to the police headquarters for questioning. At such times they always ask what a person *thinks* about the land reform, or what he *thinks* about the executions, or what he *thinks* about the accusation meetings, and so forth. For days in succession they made me return to the police station for grilling. They asked me when I had come to China, with whom I had associated on the boat, what we had talked about. I told them I could certainly not remember all that! Had I remembered, I would not have told them anyway.

"The police wanted me to report what I had been thinking since I was seven years old. They insisted that I write out in Chinese my life story and a confession. I replied that I could not write Chinese. They said I had to write it! At length they suggested a Chinese lady whom I should get to help me. Afterwards they made it exceedingly difficult for that lady whom they themselves had suggested, because she had helped me with the writing!

"When Christmas arrived I saw clearly the Communist manipulation of mob psychology. My fellow missionary lady and I prepared large batches of cookies, as we expected crowds of people, including the school children, to come and call as formerly, bringing the best wishes of the day. Aside from one old woman, nobody called on Christmas Day!

"On the following day what was our surprise when three hundred primary school children invaded our house, tearing down our Christmas tree, stamping and spitting on it, breaking what they could lay hands on or stealing fountain pens and other valuables! Little children, six and seven years of age, who had been in our Sunday School, with tears streaming down their faces, pleaded with us: 'Don't believe in Jesus any more! We didn't know any better before, but now we have learned how terrible it is!'

"Once more the police came to question us. Just as they were searching the house, a group of Middle School students came and accused me before the police of having poured boiling water on them from the second story as they had been entering the building, also of having chopped them with a knife, which instrument was now at the police station. The police took notes of the accusations and told the students to leave and they would take care of the matter. The whole put-up job was timed to the minute. We explained to the authorities that the knife was no butcher knife but only a bread knife and that it belonged to my fellow missionary and wasn't even in my part of the house for me to get hold of. But the police were not interested in getting at the truth, of course.

"That same Christmas all our Christian workers who had been assigned to the various outstations to help celebrate the festival were arrested. Now we missionaries realized that our presence among the Chinese was worse than useless and we applied to the authorities for permission to leave China.

"Because of the indoctrination and political involvement, it became a detriment for true Christians to belong to church. Humble believers began to stay away, dropping out of church and relying upon devotions held in their homes to keep their spiritual life going. While we were there, the attendance in our large church, which formerly was crowded with eight hundred worshipers, had dropped to six or seven or eight. There was no spiritual meat for Christians to get, so why should they attend?

"My heart was sick. It seemed that so many of the leaders of the Church had yielded to the enemy. One Sunday morning through the open windows (my house being next to the church), I heard the evangelist preaching on a text from the Sermon on the Mount.

"'*Love your enemies*,' he said, 'this statement is bad, indeed, and must be rejected. Who could pray for one like this Norwegian missionary? Christ was an imperialist, just like the Americans.'

"One thing surprised us. The people we didn't expect much of were the ones who were standing firm, whereas those we expected most of went astray. After the accusation meetings the bishop of our synod wrote and published in the papers such vile and hideous and ridiculous charges against our pioneer missionaries as well as against the rest of us, that they sound like the words of one possessed. Later, when I left China I felt that I must take a copy of this article with me, so I folded it up and hid it in my stocking by the toes. When, at a checking point, I was searched by a Communist girl, she asked me to take off my shoes and started to pass her hands over my feet. I jerked back as though afraid of being tickled. She smiled understandingly and said, 'All right, that will be all,' and let me put on my shoes again. Thus I still have that article in my possession.

"In July of 1951 I was dragged before my first accusation meeting where I was accused vehemently by church members. The Communists always get people on the inside to carry out their plans and to do their dirty work. They then pretend that they themselves have nothing to do with the nature of the proceedings. Everything is 'the will of the people.'

"I shall never forget the shock which came to me as I stepped inside the church where the accusation meeting was to be held. From the altar up in front the Reds and their stooges had removed the cross—a smaller one which had been taken from the chapel and which had been used to replace the one previously smashed—and had set up in its stead two huge crossed flags, the Russian and the Chinese Communist, with the portraits of Stalin and Mao Tse-tung beneath!

"The weather was stifling. I was led to the front where a platform had been erected on top of two church benches. On this I was placed and was forced to keep silent while all kinds of wild statements were hurled at me by one person after another. For one, the milkman—from whom I had not bought any milk and who had not even been in my house—accused me of having a picture of Truman in my room, of displaying imperialist flags, and of living an immoral life.

"When I saw another of my accusers—one of the leading 'Christians'—gesticulating and acting in a frenzied manner, frothing at his mouth, with spittle dribbling to the ground as the words flowed from him, I could not help but laugh at the fantastic scene. Had I not been able to see the funny side of things in spite of the heartbreaking sadness, I believe I would have lost my mind.

"As I stood there with my hands tied behind my back, youngsters obtained cigarette stubs from the people who were smoking and repeatedly pressed the burning ends against my skin—all this while the Communist leaders were sitting by meekly watching. When the youngsters lifted up my skirt to burn me, I lost my temper and sailed into the leaders of the meeting.

" 'Have you no sense of shame or of decency,' I fired my words at them, 'to permit the children to carry on like this! You know the responsibility is yours!'

"Evidently they had not expected this, and they told the children to cease their operations.

"As I refused to admit the ridiculous crimes of which I was accused and to bow in submission, the Reds gave me a blow on the back of my head which sent my head forward. They then tried to force me to kneel as a sign of my guilt. When I refused, they took hold of my wrists which had been tied behind me and wrenched them upward so that I lurched forward and fell off the platform. I was in grave danger of smashing my face on the cement floor—and, as I fell, I thought of this, threw my head back and landed on my chest.

"Trembling from the experience, winded and bruised, I was returned to my perch on the platform. From there I could see the police waiting at the door, and without depending upon the outcome of our meeting I knew what my fate would be.

"From the church I was taken to police headquarters where I was confined in a small room. Due to the exertions I had gone through I was completely soaked with sweat and covered with grime, but there was no water with which to wash. I was thrown into the room—and forgotten. Yet my Savior stood by me and comforted me. There was a hard, uneven, wooden bed, like corrugated iron, but no bedding or mattress. There was no sleep for me that night. Mosquitoes were eating me up on top and bed bugs below.

"The following day I was left without food; yet in the

afternoon I was hauled off again to a continuation of the accusation meeting. Later, however, they permitted me to buy some food and my faithful servant brought me some clothes and bedding as I was returned to my cell.

"When night came I was exhausted—but this time, I thought, I would get some proper sleep. I was able to obtain a small amount of water for washing, took off my dirty clothes, cleaned up in a fashion and went to bed. No sooner was I soundly asleep than there was loud pounding at the door. As soon as I opened up, the guard came barging in.

" 'You're wanted immediately at the chief's office,' he said.

"As he did not budge I replied, 'If you want me to go, then you have to step out of the room so that I can get dressed.'

"This he did, and soon I was ushered upstairs to the chief's office. It was about one in the morning. I was met by the officer with profuse politeness. I had come to dread this politeness even more than brutality. He offered me cigarettes which I refused. I had to explain to him fully why I did not smoke! He lectured to me about the wonders of Communism. He also said that if I confessed my crimes, it would go easy with me, but if not, it would go hard. I still maintained my innocence.

"Straightening up seriously the chief looked at me and said, 'You behaved very bad at the accusation meeting.'

" 'How did I behave bad?' I asked.

" 'You laughed,' he replied.

"I told him that my conscience was clear so consequently I could laugh at the ridiculous charges. Nevertheless, he took a serious view regarding my reactionary attitude. After a couple of hours of questioning and lecturing I was sent back to my cell.

"On the fifth day of imprisonment I was summoned to appear before a Red 'court.' Six of my accusers were there too and their accusations were recorded in detail. At the accusation meetings I had not been permitted to say a word, but now I was called on to answer the charges. Again I refused to admit my guilt.

" 'These people,' I said, 'that know very little about me accuse me. Ask the people with whom I have been living, then you will find out that the charges are false.'

" 'Do you know,' asked the judge, 'that America is just a "paper tiger"?'

"I pretended to be dumb and he lectured to me lengthily about the impotence and stupidity of America.

"Presently he returned to the subject in hand. 'Don't be afraid,' he said gravely, in keeping with the dignity of his high office, 'just be honest and confess your crimes.'

" 'I am not afraid,' I assured him, reiterating my position. 'You can investigate the charges and see that they are false.'

"Becoming impatient, he commanded me, 'Write out a confession and make it in Chinese!'

" 'I can't write Chinese, may I write it in English?' I asked, determined, after my previous experience, not to involve a Chinese friend by getting one to help me.

"After much ado about nothing, he finally gave me permission to write in English. 'Tell everything,' he confided, 'and in ten days you may leave the country.'

"I was not impressed. I had learned that no Communist was to be trusted. Seeing my lack of enthusiasm, in Chinese fashion he pointed to his nose and said, 'I guarantee that you will be out of China in ten days.'

"After writing out a statement according to my ideas I was released in the evening to return to my mission quarters.

"Days and months passed by—but I was not given permission to leave China. My colleagues had long ago received their permits and had gone. I alone was left behind.

"One day my servant informed me that he had overheard the authorities remark that my exit permit had been granted for some time. Yet they had never told me. Every few weeks I had been called to headquarters to fill out new blanks with endless details and each time they had told me that the previous request had not been granted.

"Soon I was summoned to the police station again.

" 'Are you anxious to get out?' they asked.

"I had learned that it was best to act indifferent and not to let on that one was anxious. Otherwise, they would purposely make it more difficult.

" 'Oh,' I replied, 'that would be all right, but if you wish to have me stay, I can stay. That is all up to you.'

" 'Fill out a blank,' one of them ordered.

" 'You want me to leave, then, is that it?' I asked. 'There is no need,' I added, 'to fill out another blank as you already have my exit permit.'

"The man reddened in his face. 'How do you know that?' he stormed. Taken by surprise he had given himself away and did not pursue the matter further. The session over, I returned to my home.

"Shortly after this episode my servant came to me trembling and white. 'The authorities are threatening to kill me,' he said. They had told him: 'If you don't accuse this woman we will kill you.' He had replied: 'I don't have anything to accuse her for,' to which they had answered, 'If you can't find anything against her, we can supply you with what you need.'

" 'How can I accuse you?' mourned my faithful cook.

'I shall jump into the river and end it all! I can't live under
these circumstances!'

"He was dreadfully in earnest and I had all I could do
to dissuade him from suicide.

" 'Think of your family,' I urged. 'If the Communists
force you to read something, it won't hurt me. You know
it is not true, and so do I.' At last he consented.

"The secret police gave my servant two long sheets of
tightly written accusations to memorize. Day after day
they pegged away at the task, trying to coach him in
memorizing especially the important passages. Though
he had been to school in his youth and knew how to read,
he pretended to be very stupid and always managed to
memorize only the unimportant statements.

"One evening in November he came to me completely
shaken up. 'They are arranging another accusation meeting for you,' he informed me, 'but don't let on that you
know. Don't tell anyone that I have been here to see you.
Be sure to dress warmly as they are likely to take you
away.'

"The day arrived. I was escorted this time, not to the
church where I was accused the first time, but to a large
hall where three thousand people were gathered to try
me. Every school and institution in the city had been
ordered to send delegations. I was brought to the platform where dozens of government representatives were
present, sitting behind me and to the sides. Five or six
of them sat nonchalantly below the platform, pretending
that they were only taking notes and that they had nothing to do with the proceedings as such. The latter were
entirely the 'doings of the people.' Yet these same Reds
are the ones who determine everything behind the scenes.

"As the meeting got under way, the Red leaders tried

to whip up the audience into a frenzy. Chief among the accusations brought against me were these: that I had murdered twelve people—with the years and dates supplied—that I had been an interpreter for the American army, that I had a radio transmitter and that I had lived an immoral life. As I had a clear conscience, I laughed at these absurd charges, especially the one of having killed three Chinese several years before I had even come to China! My lack of fear angered the adversaries. 'Aren't you afraid,' they roared, 'after committing such outrageous crimes?'

"As the meeting warmed up, two men on the platform wrenched my hands behind my back and held them there. When they got tired of that, they took the belt from off my dress and tied my wrists. The government representatives pretended to be present merely to keep order while it was 'the people' who were rising up against imperialism. Their put-on indifference encouraged acts of cruelty. That is the way they wanted it.

"Presently the two men beside me forced me to kneel and then stood on the calves of my legs to be sure that I stayed down. This was a most painful experience. When the men tired of standing on my legs, they sat on my shoulders. Thus I was kept kneeling for close to two hours.

"When the trial was over, I was marched through the streets. They had intended to take me from the one end of town to the other, but I pretended to be stupid and not to mind or understand the disgrace. When we came to headquarters, about half ways, they took me in and the parade was ended. As the people shouted to have me taken the rest of the way, I heard an officer say to them: 'She's too stupid to care, why bother any further?'

"I was next transported to the capital of our province. There the authorities brought me to our mission compound. An insolent young church member, an evangelist whom I knew well, met me at the gate and refused me permission to enter. The compound now belonged to the Chinese and I had been excommunicated from the church so they would have nothing to do with me. I had to leave but finally found refuge in a doctor's home.

"In this city I experienced my third accusation meeting or trial. But this time, since I was not the only missionary present, I was spared the brunt of the attack. The same impudent worker who had said that I had been excommunicated was now 'yell leader' for the mob. When former Christians fall in with the Communists, they become like demon-possessed, their faces turning dark and wicked. This man's face looked exactly like a devil's face as he called out the slogans which the mob was to cry out after him.

"Having suffered indignities at this meeting, we were paraded through the streets. As we walked along stones and dirt were showered upon us. The mobs which the Communists had worked up were now out of control. Covered with dirt outside my clothes and inside, with blood running down my face, I was taken to the depot and expelled from China.

"I was given an exit pass with the reasons for my expulsion written on the inside. I pasted these pages together so the inspectors on the way noticed only the front and the back of my pass and did not know that I was being deported. In this way I was twice accorded better treatment than I would otherwise have gotten.

"Only a short railway bridge between Red China and Hong Kong—but when I had trudged over it I had stepped from slavery into freedom, from a mockery of justice into a due respect for basic human rights!"

"marxianity" in action

*I know your tribulation . . . and the slander
of those who say that they are Jews and are
not, but are a synagogue of Satan.*

REV. 2:9

A COMPROMISE of Christianity with Marxism pro-
duces a monstrosity—a hybrid that has been called
"Marxianity," whose head is Marxism and whose tail is
Christianity.

The amazing transformation which takes place, relig-
iously, when the Church becomes wed to Communism
may be seen from a translation of parts of two articles occupying over 35 percent of the contents of a "Christian"
magazine connected with the New Church Movement. Of
the eight other articles in the issue all are political with
such titles as "To Reform the Church We Must Incite the
Mass of Believers," "The Problem of Reforming the Thinking of Christians," "Church Subscriptions for a Fighter
Plane to Oppose America and Aid Korea."

Regarding the compromised "Christians" we need not
depend upon what an outsider may say, nor yet upon what

an enemy may say, but we shall listen to their own testimony. From their own lips we shall hear what kind of "Christianity" is being promoted and what kind of spirit is being gendered in the Church that yields to Communism.

The following articles are taken from the January 26, 1952, issue of the *T'ien Feng Weekly* ("Heavenly Breeze") published in Shanghai. There is enough truth in the accusations to give us a clear picture of the situation. One can see the clever manipulation of the crowds, already cowed by the Land Reform atrocities. Only the few with titanic courage and iron wills dare to stand up against the flood of hatred and wickedness which is masked as the "will of the people."

HOW OUR INDOCTRINATION COURSE DEVELOPED INTO AN ACCUSATION MEETING
by Cheng Chien-yeh

"From the first of January, 1951, our Honan Diocese of the Episcopal Church of China completely severed all relations with the sending society [the "Mother Church" in the West] and at the same time developed the Reform Movement in every congregation. In August we held our first conference after the liberation. Besides passing all kinds of motions dealing with the reform of the diocese we introduced a study course and had an accusation meeting against imperialism by means of which all the delegates and evangelistic workers from all the congregations took a step forward in their thinking. However, that was only a beginning. There were still many thought problems not clearly resolved.

"The work of reform in our diocese had been distinguished by the fact that it had proceeded from the top down. The leaders wanted reform.

"So far the awakening of the rank and file had not been accomplished. A great many people had no understanding of the significance of the reform. Backward portions of the masses even complained against it. Moreover, we had a destructive element which had bored its way in and which was drawing away some of the unenlightened of the masses and trying to injure the cause of reform.

"We had to correct this error, so decided to open a two weeks' study course, using the workers of the Kaifeng churches as leaders (seeing they had already undergone a year's intensive indoctrination and therefore had a level of perception that was comparatively high). The majority of the members from our two Kaifeng churches together with all the workers of the diocese enrolled—over ninety people.

"We had planned two stages for the course, the first of which was aimed at giving an understanding of how 'imperialism had used religion as a means of aggression.' Besides other materials Marcus Cheng's *Accusing Imperialist America of Using Religion for Committing Aggression against China* was adopted as a text book and the history of the local diocese with special reference to the sins of the imperialist missionaries was studied. Thus the brains of all were opened up.

"At the end of this first period of study the assembly petitioned to put on an accusation meeting against imperialism's use of our local diocese for aggression and against the crimes of the individual imperialists. With great enthusiasm such a session was held. Besides accusing, many workers and church members took the first steps in criticizing their own thoughts and confessing how their thinking in the past had been poisoned so that through small kindnesses received they had been blinded as to their own position as Chinese.

"The second stage of the studies concerned the recognizing of the 'teeth and claws' of imperialism—the crimes of the putrid elements of the Church. For study materials the accusations against Yang Shao-t'ang [noted pastor and man of God from the China Inland Mission, who has since knuckled under to Communist pressure and is today participating in accusing other men of God], Hsü Szu-hsüeh [president of Hangchow Theological Seminary deposed by the Reds], Hsü Ch'ao-ch'en [of Nanking], and Ku Jen-en [fiery evangelist of China] were delved into.

"With the completion of these studies the enthusiasm of the people was unbounded and we truly realized that in the beginning we had underestimated the possibilities of the masses. After they had built up a violent hatred of imperialism and of its poisonous influence still remaining in the Church, having recognized the tremendous harm done to the country and to the Church by the crimes of the above four corrupt offenders, the whole group petitioned that they might have a thought examination meeting—that by using criticism and self-criticism as weapons they might thoroughly purge out from every individual's thinking all remaining poison. Thus when the second stage of the course was finished there developed a third stage. It was evident that it had become impossible to just close the meetings with the completion of the second period.

"Accordingly, the assembly was divided into small groups each of which developed ardent thought examination. Following the example of the leaders of the diocese, one by one the members searched themselves. After that they began to criticize and bring out suggestions. Mistakes in living are concrete reflections of mistakes in thinking. Truly the criticisms by the masses are penetrating! Mercilessly fault after fault was brought into the open. One round of examination was not sufficient. The process was repeated twice, three times—until the roots were dug up to the satisfaction of the crowd. This phenomenon was most extraordinary. From being a manifestation of the top ranks, thought examination had truly become a democratic thing and increased the confidence of the masses in their leaders. Very many people were deeply moved. Many who had formerly opposed reform because of the backwardness of their own thinking, this time came forward and laid open their breast. Never again would they harbor an attitude of complaint and slander.

"That rotten thing referred to above which had sneaked into the diocese to destroy and cause trouble is none other than Tung Ling-ku. At first when he saw that the group had zealously developed thought examination and were so earnest about it, he became alarmed. Yet he had no intention of humbling himself before the crowd but instead plotted violent disturbance. He was afraid that as one confessed after another his own turn would soon come, so he tried to sidetrack attention by stirring up the people, making all kinds of false suggestions, and creating a tense atmosphere.

"The group restrained its wrath, but Tung Ling-ku's attitude became progressively worse. When he saw that no one refuted him, he became more brazen than ever, stirred up others to follow him and made it difficult for his co-workers. This exasperated the masses.

"When in his group it came to his turn for self-examination and others criticized him, his attitude was positively evil, for instead of searching out his faults he covered them up. As a result the other discussion groups also began to criticize Tung Ling-ku and his behavior. In the tide of heated discussion that was generated the more the people compared him with Yang Shao-t'ang, Ku Jen-en and the others, the more he resembled them—even surpassed them.

He consistently twisted the Scriptures, using them to oppose Russia, to oppose Communism, to oppose the people and to oppose the Three-self Reform Movement. He ordinarily created rumors to deceive the multitudes. With his incoherent ravings he spoke in favor of imperialism, taking a stand against his own fatherland. He disturbed the Church and tried to instill disharmony between the government and the Church through his rumors and trickery. The objects of his tirades from day to day were the leaders of the reformed Church and their institutions, such as Wu Yao-tsung, the *T'ien Feng Weekly*, the reform committee, as well as the leaders and progressive elements of our local diocese.

"Many were the people who used to respect him, including old women and the youth. Now they stood up and brought out his faults so that everybody recognized him more clearly for what he was. Because each small group had discussed his case they now petitioned for a joint session before which he should be brought for examination.

"The large meeting was held in an atmosphere of solemnity. The chairman reminded the gathering of the importance of speaking with an attitude of responsibility, setting forth one as one and two as two. Though no one should fear to speak, neither should he mix hatred into his attack. Our aim was still to help the culprit to confess his mistakes frankly and correct them.

"Tung Ling-ku got up to speak. He came forth with a long sermon as though he were 'giving a testimony' at an evangelistic meeting. Like an unceasing flood he preached on and on about how step by step he had 'received God's gracious call' and how 'God had given him a special commission.' In no wise could his talk qualify as self-examination. The audience was stunned. As soon as he was done speaking, they struggled for an opportunity to express themselves—old women, pastors, water-carriers, young merchants, and even those who ordinarily are not great at talking. The audience severely rebuked him and once more appealed to him to make a thorough-going, frank confession.

"It was already the twenty-second of December. The following day was the last Sunday before Christmas. Thus it was impossible to close the study course before Christmas. The group decided, therefore, to recess for three days during the festival, then to meet again on the twenty-sixth to hear Tung's case, in this way giving him most ample time for reflection and deep thought in the quiet of his home.

"Mr. Tung's attitude irritated the people more and more. He showed no intention of taking to heart the earnest warning and pleas of the group. The same evening he calmly went with everybody else to eat as though nothing had happened. Hard-hearted, without any sense of shame, he sought to converse with others. The more he acted thus, the more people loathed him and tried not to sit at the same table with him. But he didn't seem even to notice it. Brazenly he attended the entertainment the following day for the workers of the diocese. On the twenty-fourth when everyone was celebrating the Christmas eve program—here he comes again and wants to participate! But the people ignored him.

"Christmas passed quickly, and the following day everyone came to hear Tung's self-examination. But he refused to come, saying that he was not prepared, so the assembly patiently waited for another day. On the twenty-seventh the people again sought to hear him, but again he refused, saying the same thing—that he was not prepared. He had also criticized, saying: 'In these times when we have been called upon to economize they ought not to waste so much money on this indoctrination course. It should have been disbanded long ago.' On hearing this the people were enraged.

"The whole crowd could contain itself no longer. That morning six out of seven discussion groups passed resolutions asking that he be excommunicated from the Church. Some people urged that the government punish him severely according to law. The noon meal was eaten in an atmosphere of tension. Many who used to respect him and who had formerly been deceived by him, especially some old women, rivaled each other at the tables in telling about the many hateful things which he had done. Everyone sensed: 'If we tolerate such a one as this, then it is a proof that our own thinking has not been straightened out. His crimes and his stubborn attitude, his subverting and corrupting activities, all proclaim what his relation is to us. He is no longer our friend but our enemy. A friend we must bear with and help. But an enemy—we may only resolutely fight him.'

"People with great imperfections came to John the Baptist and were welcomed for baptism. But when the wolves in sheep's clothing came, John rejected them for baptism, saying, 'You brood of vipers! Who warned you to flee from the judgment to come?' As for Tung Ling-ku, this 'poisonous viper," it was impossible for us to admit him to the baptism of repentance. We could only deliver him over to the good sense of the people! Their judgment cannot err and their eyes are bright as snow.

"In the afternoon each discussion group met again and the opinion of the seven groups became unanimous and crystallized. They petitioned for the following: (1) that Tung Ling-ku be excommunicated from the Church; (2) that the government be asked to punish him severely according to law; (3) that an accusation meeting be called to reveal and make public his crimes; and (4) that the record of his crimes be printed and published throughout the nation.

"Thereupon a joint session was held in which the members competed with one another to express themselves and they were all filled with tremendous zeal. Against imperialism they had unbounded hatred; against the 'teeth and claws' of imperialism brought to light in every congregation they had unbounded hatred; against Tung Ling-ku, this 'tooth and claw' agent of imperialism so recently sneaked into our midst before our very eyes—against this rotten thing of the Church they whipped up a fiery hatred ten times ten thousand feet high!

"An old pastor said: 'Tung Ling-ku is a ringleader of reactionaries and can't even be considered an evangelist of the Christian Church. Just think, he says whoever opposes him God will destroy before his eyes. This kind of God is not at all the God of Christianity. Tung Ling-ku is a wicked despot. See how he swindles and extorts everywhere he goes and violates women. If he isn't a despot, what is he? Tung Ling-ku is a great spy, the running dog of imperialism, a counterrevolutionary. See, he creates rumors and destroys. When you mention America or Japan or Chiang Kai-shek, he is unwilling to accuse them—but just mention Communism and he wants to accuse it! Everywhere he makes contact with spies and with the corrupt elements of the Church and furthers secret movements. This kind of Tung Ling-ku—if we do not sweep him out of sight, can it ever be countenanced?'

"The assembly decided to adjourn for two days during which they would make propaganda so that those church members who had not attended the course might know why we had to accuse and cut off this rotten thing, Tung Ling-ku. They also had to publicize the accusation meeting to be held on Sunday afternoon, December 30. The collecting of the materials, the writing and re-examining of the accusations, the organizing of the propaganda work, the informing of the churches of other denominations in Kaifeng and the seeking of their advice, the making of arrangements for the place of meeting—all these things had to be tended to during two short days. If the time were put off longer, it would get into the New Year. Few accusation meetings have been prepared in such a hurry, but as the whole affair was the business of the people, it could be accomplished in spite of the pressure of time. The people themselves spread the propaganda, they contributed the accusations, they brought out materials with incontestable proofs and took care of numerous other details. Where there are many people there are many hands.

"Friday and Saturday were tense with activity. On Saturday afternoon the government acted on the petition of the crowd and arrested Tung Ling-ku. The same day there came a great snowstorm which increased the following day, covering the whole city with a precious mantle of purity. With the bitter cold and poor roads, we thought the Sunday audience might be small, but braving the elements one group after another arrived. Every seat in our church was taken and chairs were brought from the primary school. Yet many people had to stand. Never having anticipated such a crowd, we had not arranged for a larger meeting place, nor had we invited all the outside groups as we had only two days in which to work. Still there came between seven and eight hundred people (whereas the total Christian population of Kaifeng is only about two thousand).

"Two comrades from the police station brought Tung Ling-ku to the church. Immediately the mighty sound of slogans rent the skies: 'Strike down Tung Ling-ku, the rotten element of the Church!' 'Strike down the counter-revolutionary Tung Ling-ku!' 'Strike down Tung Ling-ku, the tooth and claw of imperialism!' . . .

"One accuser after another ascended the platform and, pointing at his face, denounced him. During the intervals between the accusations thunderous slogans shook the auditorium: 'If Tung Ling-ku's head remains unbowed, rest from our struggle can not be allowed!' 'If Tung Ling-ku is not overthrown, the Three-self Movement cannot be full-grown!' 'Tung Ling-ku is like rotten eggs—for rumors and havoc he uses his legs!' . . . In harmony with the contents of each accusation the yell leader at the foot of the platform would make up rhymes to be used for slogans. The Church people had learned from the Land Reform how to treat the evil despots.

"This was an exciting and important struggle. When Tung first came to the diocese in the fall of 1950, many people thought he was one of the greatest evangelists of the whole country. They gave him double respect and whenever he preached the people flocked to hear him. And now, some over a year later—confidence in him had been completely destroyed by the revelation of his character and crimes, and everybody came forward in anger to accuse him. One after another those who had formerly loved and respected him, or had even been misled by him, now came weeping and gnashing their teeth to accuse him. When the masses awakened, no longer could this unexcelled spy and saboteur escape from the clutches of the people. Had he been permitted to speak his feelings he would certainly have said: 'Never did I expect that even you and you would accuse me!' Yes, whether you expect it or not, everyone has come to accuse you! When the people were unable to regenerate you all they could do was to spread out the heavenly net and catch you, then accuse and suppress you! When you realized you were caught, perhaps you thought you could take refuge among those you trusted most, those who were most backward and had been deceived by you—but now you see even they take part in arresting you and accusing you! Because each one of us deeply loves his fatherland and deeply loves his Church, we know that it will never do not to purge out completely all such putrid things like you who have thrown away conscience and rebelled against country and Church!

"From the present movement we have learned some supremely important lessons. First, nothing can be properly accomplished unless it truly fosters the democracy of the masses; on the other hand, no difficulty is so tremendous but that it can be overcome by promoting democracy and relying on the people. Second, the solution of any problem depends upon the straightening out of the thinking of the masses. Then only will the solution be thorough. Merely relying on the 'passing of resolutions' is entirely insufficient. Whether it be the democratization of the Church or the unity of workers and fellow believers or even the purging out of corrupt elements in the Church—there is not one thing which does not depend upon the people or upon the clarifying of their thinking."

ACCUSATIONS AGAINST TUNG LING-KU, A CORRUPT ELEMENT OF THE CHURCH
by Wang Shen-yin [a pastor of the Diocese]

"After the workers and Christians of the Kaifeng Episcopal Church had undergone three weeks of indoctrination it became clear that Tung Ling-ku was a corrupt element of the Church who had, under the cloak of religion, furthered the work of spying and sabotage. A large accusation meeting against him was therefore arranged for December 30 at 1:00 p.m. In spite of the heavy snow a large crowd came out consisting of members and workers from the various churches and of the heads of the government departments and institutions. Over 760 people were present. The meeting was presided over by Bishop Tseng Yu-san. After a roll call of the leaders, the criminal Tung Ling-ku was brought under escort to the church. Twelve people came forward with accusations. The chief crimes of Tung Ling-ku are summarized as follows:

"1. Being linked with counterrevolutionaries. Tung Ling-ku's associations in society were almost wholly with spies, reactionaries, and the corrupt elements of the Church. During the war he worked in Peking with Imperialist Japan's great spy, Pastor Ch'ing Shui. When the corrupt element of the Church, Ku Jen-en, a spy of America, was arrested at Tsingtao and made a confession, Tung Ling-ku marked the news item in the paper and said: 'These statements are not the words of Ku Jen-en. . . . The confession is false, it was forced by the government.' He also remarked: 'Ku Jen-en and I are the fruits of Dr. Sung Shang-chieh's ministry' [Dr. John Sung was the Billy Sunday of China] . . . .

"When the news of Yang Shao-t'ang's expulsion from the Church in Nanking reached Kaifeng, Tung Ling-ku was perturbed and exclaimed: 'Evangelists like us are getting fewer and fewer. Yang Shao-t'ang was truly a good pastor. My whole family grieves for him. This is the persecution of the spiritual by those who live after the flesh.'

"He had intimate relations with the corrupt element of the Baptist Church in Chengchow, Tung Tzu-ch'eng [a faithful pastor tried and imprisoned earlier]. In April he went to Chengchow privately to do 'evangelistic work' and he lived in Tung Tzu-ch'eng's home. When the secret police investigated they pretended to be relatives.

"Last spring our diocese organized a cloth factory for the Church workers [as a means of livelihood]. In June he showed intense energy in wanting to go to Hsüchow to sell the cloth. He took the opportunity to travel on to Taian, Tsingtao, Tientsin, Peking, and other places to promote secret activities and to unite and organize from all the churches in the whole nation the corrupt elements which were being accused. He was gone for over five weeks, covering up his steps. He has consistently refused to confess what secret connections he was making or who was financing his activities.

"He has told many people that he joined the Episcopal Church because the times were evil and it was more secure to belong to an organized Church than to travel as an independent evangelist. From this one can see that he was in need of being shielded and that he had unspeakable connections.

"2. Secretly printing counterrevolutionary leaflets. A year ago when the Kaifeng Episcopal Church was being reorganized to oppose America, Tung Ling-ku contacted Ning Shang-te, a spy (already executed), and secretly printed and distributed a reactionary tract titled *An Earnest Warning*, opposing the Three-self Reform of the Church and maliciously slandering the government. In this tract he wrote: 'The Church is headed for a grave crisis. Although not a few Churches are echoing Reform and laying out plans, so that at first sight it may seem as though something wonderful has happened—the New Church has arisen!—yet, if we look closely, we can see that some Churches seem to have gone to an excess, for they are wholly following the trend of the times, seeking the favor of men, and have gradually turned the Church into a tool of society.' Furthermore he directly attacks Reform and looks with hostile eyes upon the government, saying: 'So many leaders of the Church have become entirely engrossed with the things of this world that even the Federation of Churches has changed its character. Aside from transmitting orders from the government it has nothing whatsoever to give the people.'

"3. Destroying the Three-self Reform Movement of the Church. Tung Ling-ku's attack on the Three-self Reform Movement was planned and purposeful, and made to look reasonable. He argued: 'When a child is grown the parents want him to take care of himself.' Who does he mean by 'parents'? He refers to the imperialists [the missionaries]! He has constantly called upon believers to be martyrs for their faith, saying: 'Why has the Church survived these two thousand years? Because the saints and prophets have been willing to die for the Lord.' But whence comes the persecution? It is needless to say that he implies it comes from the Reform Movement. That is to say it would be better to die than to accept the Reform. Because he had these reactionary thoughts, he tried in every way to sabotage the getting of signatures for the Reform Manifesto. He caused trouble on every hand, preventing Christians from signing because he maintained that the Manifesto was contrary to the teachings of Scripture. He also asserted that if the Church were under the leadership of the People's Government, then it was no Church at all. . . .

"On November 12, 1950, when all the Churches of Kaifeng were meeting to decide on their attitude to the Manifesto, Tung Ling-ku arose before the whole assembly and registered his opposition. He especially pointed out two things: first, that the Church should not be under the leadership of the government; second, that the words

'strike down imperialism' should be left out because that
was not the Church's business.

"At the meeting of the Diocese in August . . . Mr. Tung
said, 'I feel as though devils are attacking my body to
destroy me.' From this you can see what kind of fellow
this self-proclaimed 'spiritual' Tung Ling-ku is! He also
despises the others by claiming that the gathering did not
resemble a Church meeting and that the plan for reform
of the diocese was not spiritual.

"4. Trying to cause a split between the government and
the Church. Tung Ling-ku had a most subtle and poisonous way of trying to stir up trouble in order to make
separations between the government and the Church.
To the officers of the diocese he would say, 'No matter
how often we meet we will never get freedom. See how
many people the authorities send to spy on us. He always said, 'The government's freedom of religion is a
farce. Yes, the government is good, but everybody is
afraid of it.'

"5. Twisting the Scriptures and deceiving the believers.
Shortly after Tung Ling-ku's arrival in Kaifeng he used
his sermons for misinterpreting the Scriptures and mis-
leading simple Christians. Once when preaching on Gene-
sis, he set forth the utter deceitfulness of the serpent (the
devil), which travels in a crooked path. He added that
the present People's Government does things in the same
crooked way. He maligned the government for its way of
trying to solve problems. He even said that the government in trying to get the whole nation to learn the *yang
ko* dance was making them move in the twisting motions of
the snake.

"In a sermon to the Ladies' Aid on Esau's selling of his
birthright he said that today also there are those who for
a mess of red pottage sell the Church. The red pottage

was applied to Communism and the progressives. To promote the Three-self Reform was to sell the Church. He confessed, too, that he had formerly taken the red horse of Revelation, whose rider took peace from the earth, to refer to the 'Red Army.' . . .

"6. Rumor-mongering and spreading of counterrevolutionary propaganda. Tung Ling-ku was constantly creating rumors such as: 'Russia is also imperialistic. If we intend to cut off relations with imperialism, then we should cut off relations with Socialism, too.' In this way he made false propaganda against Russia. With regard to the Korean war he said, 'You can't go by what the papers say on this side only. We still do not know what the papers on the other side say.' Truly Tung Ling-ku, without any sense of shame, has completely lost his national consciousness and has willingly become a running dog of American imperialism!

"In April during the joint accusation meeting of all the churches against America, Japan, and Chiang Kai-shek, just as we were gathering materials, he said: 'For accusing America, Japan, and Chiang I have no materials, but for accusing the Communists I have plenty of materials.' America, Japan, and Chiang, whom all hate, he would not accuse, but he thought he would accuse the Communists! His position is altogether that of a traitor. No wonder then that during the August meeting of the diocese when the delegates with thunderous applause passed a resolution to send respectful greetings to Mao Tse-tung and other government officials, he not only did not clap but with angry countenance tried to hinder his co-worker beside him from clapping.

"He descended to the point where he advocated substituting the doctrine of *i pien k'ao* ['trusting one side'—that is, in God] for Chairman Mao's *i pien tao* ['falling to one side'—that is, leaning on Russia]. He explained: '*Falling to one side* means *to tumble down.* Our Church can only say that it is *trusting one side.*'

"Whenever our country celebrated various occasions, some of the leaders of our Kaifeng Churches would write articles for the *Honan Daily* urging the Christians to join the patriotic parades. But Tung Ling-ku always ridiculed and criticized them. One time he saw an article by Pastor Wang Fu-yin in the paper. Immediately he went to see him, but, since he was not home, he said to the man's wife: 'At present some of the leaders of our Church are being used as tools of the Communists to spread their propaganda for them. You ought to urge Pastor Wang not to allow himself to be a tool of the Communists any longer.' Mr. Tung did not permit his children to join the Youth Corps, and if they did he put pressure on them to quit.

"7. Being a hypocrite. As to Tung Ling-ku's private life there is plenty to prove his shameless hypocrisy. His home was used for spinning thread for our workers' cloth factory. For a whole month he kept stealing until he was found out.

"His attitude to indoctrination has been changeless. He once told Bishop Tseng, 'Were we not forced to attend the courses, I would not go.' In September when the workers were studying *The Remarkable Accomplishments of the People's Republic of China in the Past Two Years,* he feigned eye trouble and was excused, but secretly he ran over to see the movies. We also heard that when he was on a preaching mission in the Northwest he went out to peddle paper kitchen gods. You can see that he is altogether an apostate. . . ."

And so this man of God was taken from the church back to prison, there to await the tender mercies of a Communist government!

a hardheaded businessman

ON OUR shopping trips into town from Gospel Breeze Mountain, we would usually stop at the Lutheran Center in Kowloon to transact business or visit friends. On one such occasion, as we were enjoying a cup of coffee, I was introduced to a British couple, perhaps in their fifties, who had just arrived from Shanghai. He was a burly, red-faced business man, born and raised in Shanghai. While he did most of the talking, his wife, who seemed to be of a different national background, added interesting details and side lights.

Coffee and refreshments were finished—but not our conversation. When other guests had left, we talked on, leisurely and in private, about the China of our childhood, of the changes which the years had brought and especially of the *big change* which had come with the arrival of Communism. The circumstances in Shanghai under the Reds were described as follows:

"During the years of the National regime we had found many of the Kuomintang officials to be rascals and I had truly expected that the Chinese Communists would be better. To be sure, I had read reports and books about conditions in Russia, written by people who had escaped, but what they wrote was unbelievable. I didn't think their stories could possibly be representative or that people could act on a large scale as described. I was a fool for not believing those reports. Now I have truly been 're-educated'!

"Though at the beginning of the Red rule I was favorable to the new regime, what first set me straight was the continuous sight of death-trucks driving by our home. From our house we had a grandstand view of the avenue down which the trucks speeded with sirens screaming. Every half hour throughout the day these open trucks passed by loaded with scores of victims, trussed up like pigs and jammed into the conveyances. The victims had their hands tied behind their back and pulled upward with a rope which passed around their neck and down again so that they were constantly on the point of strangling, especially when their wrenched arms pulled downward from fatigue. When they fell on top of each other, as the vehicles jolted along, they were helpless to get up. Day after day for weeks on end this traffic continued. Apparently realizing that their publicity of terrorism had gone too far for the people to stomach, the authorities later covered their deathtrucks, and also used ambulances. Because they knew too much, drivers who had been employed for some time were likewise liquidated.

"When I was interned by the Japanese during the last war, I saw with my own eyes how they beat some of the internees who had infracted the rules—but there you at least had the rules, and you knew what they were! Compared to the Reds the Japanese were gentlemen.

"With regard to the Communists you are never sure of the score. Anyone they are against they accuse as a subversive and anti-revolutionary. Last year [1951] during the round-up beginning in April there was wholesale slaughter throughout the land. In Shanghai the Chinese themselves figured that millions of people must have been executed in the country during those few months. The number of suicides was beyond reckoning. In the city dozens were jumping to their death every day.

"Justice with the Communists is a rough-and-ready sort of affair. Our lawyers would be horrified at such a system. Whereas in the purges many notorious crooks have been executed—and they had it coming to them—yet the great majority of the victims are innocent. There are no definite rules on black and white to go by. Before it is ever brought before the People's Court, the outcome of a case is decided by the authorities.

"I had an experience with a minor case. In the house which I had rented there was a former tenant, an opium-smoking woman, who refused to move out. My Chinese friends told me that there was no use to bring the matter before the courts, that the case would be sure to go against me—there could be no doubt about it whatever. Yet I felt there was nothing like trying.

"The court was an informal sort of thing, with people smoking and lounging about. An ordinary fellow had been drafted to preside over the meeting. It did me no good to argue that I was not the landlord, that the woman had rented her quarters from the previous occupant and was supposed to have vacated them long ago and that I objected strenuously to having an opium smoker in my house. The People's Court decided against me, just as my friends had foretold, and it informed the woman that she could stay as long as she wished. Later my problem was solved in a different way when, for some reason or other, the opium smoker jumped into the river.

"Communists are the biggest liars on earth! Many white Russians in Shanghai were lured by bright promises into returning to their fatherland. But when they arrived there, they were subjected to pitiful conditions. In writing back to friends, they smuggled out their ideas by using statements with concealed meanings. In one letter, for instance, a man wrote that everything was so wonderful that not even Marconi [the name of his friend's dog] could have it so good in Shanghai! As the news spread, large numbers of the remaining White Russians changed their plans, most of them evacuating from China before the travel regulations became too stringent.

"When the Communists first came to Shanghai, they avoided radical actions in order to lull the people into a false sense of security. Later they ordered all connected in any way with the former government to register their names, promising that nothing would happen to those who complied, as it was merely a formality. Nothing did happen for some time—but then, of a sudden, all of those people were arrested and liquidated.

"The 're-education' system of the Communists is a euphemistic name for imprisonment. They take a fellow off for three months or half a year for re-education. He may come back and he may not. Besides, 're-education' is a very elastic term. When the police pick up a beggar from the street and lecture him for a couple hours, telling him that he must never again appear on that street as a beggar, he has been 're-educated.' He will never dare to beg there again, for what the authorities tell you, you do. There is no such thing as disobeying. Everybody is held in line by terrorism.

"In China, the police methods have been taken over completely from the old Russian OGPU and from the related Gestapo. Most arrests are made in the dead of night, between twelve and three. These calls at night strike terror into the populace.

"The authorities announced through the guilds and other organizations that every establishment must hold accusation and self-confession meetings. An employer of only half a dozen men was forced to put on these meetings, too. Reports of accusations, confessions and all that transpired had to be sent in to the authorities. In the various sections throughout the city the government also rigged up containers, like mailboxes, for collecting accusations. At first these could be written anonymously. Later, when the authorities were swamped, they demanded that the accusations be signed. This cut down the number considerably. Leniency was promised to those who were honest and confessed everything they had done wrong in their lives.

"If at a meeting one fellow confesses to having accepted a bribe from so and so ten years ago, the authorities check on the latter to see if he has confessed to having offered the bribe. If he has not, he is punished. Thus everyone who has done misdeeds involving others is petrified with fear, knowing that most likely he will be exposed in the long run, so it is expedient for him to confess all his sins before it is too late.

"Aside from the young folks from eight to sixteen, most of the people hate Communism. Even many of those working for the government detest it. If deliverance from the outside should come, the Communist structure would collapse. Should there be another turnover, the conditions in China would be appalling! There have been so many executions, that the revenge for all the relatives and friends who have been liquidated will be terrific. It is bound to be! Every action has an opposite and equal reaction.

"Shanghai has become a dead city. When I took a walk down to the bridge which formerly teemed with multitudes of vehicles and pedestrians, I found that all was quiet except for three or four people walking by. The busiest thoroughfare has become an unfrequented lane. Though commodities have become very cheap, nobody has the money with which to buy. There are still, to be sure, some rich people living in Shanghai, but they go about in rags and tatters for fear of being thought to possess money. Since it is not yet unlawful to possess gold bars—though it is to use them—many people have hid away their wealth. However, as soon as the government sees fit to get hold of this, it will crack down on the possessors. According to reports received from the Chinese, we realized that Shanghai was a paradise compared to the countryside. There the Reds were pauperizing the people, taking things from them right and left.

"Though we were not confined to our compounds, we seldom ventured out because of the unpleasant atmosphere and the hatred hovering in the air. However, when our Chinese friends, who were horrified at the sacrilege, told us about the vile desecration of the foreign cemeteries, I went for a walk to see for myself. Sure enough!—at one of the oldest cemeteries which contained the graves and monuments of people from the earliest days of Shanghai, there were now only holes where the graves used to be, and the monuments had been removed. The bones were thrown into heaps and disposed of by the rubbish trucks.

"The day before leaving Shanghai I went to the barber shop for a haircut. When I asked that my hair in the back be cut shorter, the barber remarked, 'Oh, I think that can be left till next time!'

" 'There will be no next time,' I replied.

" 'How is that?'

" 'I have an exit permit and I'm leaving tomorrow.'

"The word acted like an electric switch. In a moment all the barbers in the shop and all the clerks in the adjoining store (which comprised the other half of the room) were swarming around me.

" 'Oh, how wonderful!' they exclaimed. 'Be sure to tell the outsiders about conditions in here. Plead with them to come and rescue us!'

"As one has to be very careful, I did not dare to say anything one way or the other. I thought at first that it was a Communist plot to catch me at giving some unwise remark which could be used to prevent me from leaving. Later I realized that the Communists had nothing to do with it. It was a spontaneous expression of the feelings of the people.

"As we were about to leave Shanghai, we were anxious to take as much of our jewelry with us as possible. It is useless trying to smuggle it out, as the inspectors rip up suitcases and look into everything. If you are caught, you are in a precarious situation. Last year when my brother left China, he decided to ship his piano out rather than lose it. When it was to pass customs, however, the security police came around to search and they took the whole piano apart, piece by piece. Though the customs men had tried to screw things together again, when the piano arrived at Hong Kong it was merely a pile of junk.

"To be aboveboard and to make sure, I went to the Bank of China to inquire as to how much I could take out with me.

" 'You may take a half-ounce gold bar,' was the official's reply.

" 'I have no gold bars, but I would like to take some jewelry with me. How much may I take?'

"The official hesitated but, having no regulations to go

by, evaded the issue. 'You will have to inquire at the customhouse about that.'

"This I did—but they were no wiser there. 'The amount you may take out,' they said, 'depends upon your station and position.'

" 'How much will that be in my case?' I inquired, trying to explain as best I could what my station and position were.

"They were nonplused. After much fidgeting the man in charge replied, 'You just wear it all—and if that is too much, they will tell you at the station and you can leave the extra pieces behind with your friends.'

"The time for our departure arrived. We had bought the tickets and were ready to board the train when the police came to make inquiries. For two hours we were searched and interrogated, then we were dragged off to police headquarters where we underwent a thorough grilling from one o'clock in the afternoon until seven in the evening. I was stripped of every single piece of jewelry, including my cuff links, and my wife was stripped of most of hers. We lost a couple of heirlooms which were precious to us beyond words. Not only were we incessantly grilled, but the police officer kept shouting at me: 'Confess your crimes! Confess your crimes!' I said I didn't have any crimes, but he still persisted in his demands.

"When we were finally released, we were in a bad situation. We were hungry and exhausted. We had arranged to have just enough money with us for our trip and now we had lost our train and forfeited half the price of our tickets!

"With the help of friends, however, we survived the ordeal and the next day were on our way. Once on the train we were not permitted to step off at the stations to stretch our limbs. Both at Canton and at the border we experienced provocative incidents as our belongings were again ransacked and half ruined. But being so close to freedom we swallowed our pride.

"At long last we stepped across the international bridge and slipped into an entirely different world—a new existence!"

in a "pressure cooker"

*I know where you dwell, where Satan's
throne is.*

Rev. 2:13

HE WAS a simple, kindly, lovable character—a successful missionary from Germany whom the Chinese
greatly respected. When the Communists came to South
China, he and his wife being optimistic and tenacious, expected to carry on, whoever ruled the country. But the
knock on the door at night—*that* had blasted their hopes,
and almost their lives.

At our Seminary we had an extra connection with these
friends whom I had met some years previously in the
interior. A student who called them "father" and "mother"
—a man of splendid qualities and earnestness of spirit,
who seemed to have imbibed the atmosphere from his
foster parents' home—was deeply concerned for their well-
being and safety, and we often inquired from each other
if there had been further news.

At last the veil of uncertainty began to recede. In May,

1952, though there was still no news with regard to the father, the alert and attractive white-haired mother, seventy-four years of age, arrived in freedom. It is marvelous what the human frame can endure and still remain unconquered!

"For nineteen months," she related, on a visit to our Gospel Breeze Mountain with its scenery of superb beauty and peace, "—for nineteen months I tried to get out of Communist China. During that time I lived under house-arrest. The Communists are tyrants. Everything they do is done in an arbitrary fashion with no explanation given for their actions. They merely say yes or no, and you dare not inquire further. Suddenly they took my husband and have given, even yet, no reason for his detention. For over a year and a half, without telling me why I could not go, they kept me waiting for permission to get out, until on the twelfth of May they abruptly said, 'You must leave by the fifteenth!'

"That very day, in a few hours, the weekly truck was leaving our city—but how could I get ready to catch that? Yet, willing to grab at any straw, I inquired at the office. To my dismay this truck was filled—and I had to be out of our area before the next one was scheduled to leave! The easiest way to travel is by boat, but the authorities refused to let me enjoy that convenience! Instead they marked out for me a longer land route which I had to take. The only thing left for me to do was to walk hundreds of miles or go by bicycle. It was pretty late for me to learn to ride a bicycle! However, our beloved Chinese pastor came to my rescue by obtaining three trusted cyclists to take my baggage and by himself taking me on his own bicycle. We strapped a cushion on to the carrier and on this springless seat I sat, clinging for dear life to the pastor in front of me lest I fall off. From eight in the morning till eight at night he pumped over the bumpy roads till all my muscles ached and I thought certainly I would drop dead. In the downpours of rain we got drenched, in the sultry heat we dried out. For three days we traveled in this fashion until we came to a town where I was able to transfer to a bus. For a stretch I was able to go by boat also. On the seventh day I arrived in Hong Kong. As for my husband, I have no idea what fate awaits him, though I have heard that he is still alive."

Some months later the scene again is Gospel Breeze Mountain, but this time I am seated with "father." The date is October 25, 1952. His wife, unable to do anything for her husband, has already left for the homeland. It is over a month since his "expulsion" from China, but he is still recuperating, still trying to find himself. From the Communist "pressure cooker" he came out a human wreck, physically undernourished, mentally unbalanced—but gradually, with the pressure removed, he has almost straightened out. His old bouncing faith is returning. In some respects, because the man himself is without guile, his naive optimism does not seem to fathom the tricks and cunning of the Reds, and his report, at times, is self-contradictory. We listen to his story with amazement:

"It was God who put me in prison—not the government. I was dissatisfied with myself. I was too proud, too superficial. I had been praying that, if there were no other way, God would crush me, that I might become nothing and He might become all. God heard that prayer and I was thrown into prison and have been crushed.

"What I saw regarding the government was only good. I did not see any bad things. Of course, being isolated in prison, I don't know what happened at large. However, they told me they never killed anyone unless he was hopeless and wouldn't change. How could they kill people, they said, and thus antagonize the masses? That would only lead to uprisings.

"The Communist spy system is all-pervading. I have no doubt but that they know that I am having coffee with you up here. They told me that they know everything about us, and I believe it.

"One night, about two years ago, there was a knock at the door. When I opened up, in came a group of police agents who said I must go with them to headquarters. My wife came out in her nightgown and kissed me goodby as the men stood about the room. I told her not to worry, I would be back in the morning. As I had a perfectly clear conscience I fully expected to clear myself when I got to headquarters—but to this day I have not seen my wife again!

"I was put into confinement and told that I was a spy and had a radio. Though I said I had no radio, they would not believe me. So day after day passed and I sat in prison. The Communists torture their victims during the first part of their imprisonment to make them confess and submit. They take for granted that, to begin with, every prisoner tells lies, so they must break down his resistance and make him come out with everything. I had read considerably about Nazi forms of torture, so now I thought for sure that I was in for Gestapo-type of treatment— with gas, operations, and all the rest. I was deathly scared.

"I had made up my mind from the beginning that I would tell only the truth. Because of this I was at a disadvantage and I complained to God: 'If I were a spy and confessed it, then I would get out; but now I am not a spy and so cannot confess it, and here I must sit!'

"They accused me of leading an international spy ring with six other fellows, including spies from South Korea, Vietnam, Thailand, Formosa, and the United States. I said I had never heard of such a thing! I think they must have really believed that I belonged to such an organization. And indeed there must have been such an organization, because they said China was filled with its activities. Yet how could I tell a lie, when I knew nothing about it? They said that if I would hand in only one name connected with the spy ring, I could go free. But how could I involve the safety and perhaps the life of some one else in order to save myself? Since I could not do this I had to stay in prison. They threatened me, saying: 'If you don't confess, you will be executed,' and they demonstrated on me with a sword how it would work. Expecting that I would surely be killed, I prayed the good Lord that I might be shot rather than die by the sword, which the guards were time and again poking at me.

"The Communists asked the people to accuse me, but no one did. They then forced my adopted Chinese daughter to accuse me. Finding she had nothing to say, they coached her in making an accusation. They kept on with her for days. I could not see her, but I could hear her crying in another part of the building. One morning I heard a loud sob, 'Papa, help me! Papa, help me! Papa, help me!'—but what could I do? I thought I would go crazy.

"Finally, they forced my daughter to say that indeed I had adopted her and had raised her—but I had done it with money squeezed out of the Chinese. I was accused of not having paid my servant enough salary, though, actually, I paid him more than others were paying their servants. I was told that I should have paid him three times as much! What I had squeezed out of him, they said, I had used for nurturing my daughter.

"I became so upset, so nervous, so tense from all the pressure and from the distress of my daughter, that I felt my mind slipping. I came to the conclusion that suicide was the only way out. To save my friends from becoming involved because of me—to keep myself from accusing them—I felt that I must kill myself. I philosophized about Christians in Germany who had committed suicide to escape the tortures of Hitler. Three times I prepared for the final act, but each time I was hindered. The last time I rigged up a heavy beam with my towel. I attached it so that—one jerk, and the beam would fall down and crush my head. Everything was in readiness. I lay my head in position. I seized the end of the towel with a firm grasp. Just as I was going to pull, I lost courage and became paralyzed with fear. That moment of indecision saved my life. While I was struggling with myself, a guard broke into the room, dragged me away with curses and notified those in charge. After that they gave the dirty room a thorough cleaning which it certainly needed, removed all objects that might be used for suicide and put me back in. It was the good hand of the Lord that kept me from this desperate end!

"When I was thrown in prison I had come empty-handed. I did not get to take my Bible with me nor would they permit me to have one. Then, unexpectedly, on a burning rubbish heap just outside my window I caught sight of a Gospel portion. A girl happened by and I asked her to pick it up for me. This she did. Rolling it up she stuck it through the bars and wire netting of my window. It was a Gospel by Luke and only the corner had been scorched. Another time during a housecleaning in one of the adjoining rooms I caught sight of more portions. When I asked the guard if he could get one of them for me, he said, 'All right.' These happened to be the Gospel of John. I hid these portions, more precious than gold, and from this time on I memorized dozens of chapters. In the winter, when it was so cold, I walked back and forth studying. I expected that sooner or later these portions would be taken from me but I knew that what I memorized they would not be able to take away.

"After eight months of solitary confinement I was moved to another place of imprisonment. Here the authorities treated me better, that is, they did what they could to make me comfortable according to their standards, and they were always polite. Now I decided that I must do all possible to make myself persevere until I should gain my liberty. Day after day for three months we had spinach and rice. We prisoners were allowed to have all the rice we wanted. Though I longed for a change of diet, I continually forced myself to eat as much as I could. Thus I had not suffered too much physically when I came out.

"When the pumpkin season arrived and we got pumpkin with our fare instead of spinach, I thought I was in heaven! Now I know what a relative thing is the enjoyment of food! By the time I was released I had practically lost my sense of taste except for sweets.

"During this stretch of my imprisonment, which lasted over a year, I suffered much from one of my fellow inmates. I call him the *angel-devil*, because he did so much good to me and so much evil. He was a well-educated, clever man, a former Nationalist, whom the Communists put in charge of me. My eyes were going blind and he treated me according to their instructions. When I could not see to eat, he fed me with a spoon.

"He seemed very friendly when I first arrived. We sang hymns together and were pals. When we were rebuked for singing loudly, we continued by singing softly. He knew more Christian songs in Chinese than I did. He even asked me to pray with him in our cell. I felt I had someone to confide in and I told him everything about myself, both good and bad.

"After some time of this he turned on me and said, 'You have fallen into my power! You have been trapped! Now I have the dope on you and I am going to report everything to the government.'

"His high hopes were deflated when I told him, 'I have already written out a completely frank confession and account of myself and handed it in to the government.'

"This man wanted to curry favor with the authorities. Whenever officials or guards were looking, or walked by our cell, he would take to beating me up mercilessly. When they left he would desist. He was a strong man and knocked me black and blue on my arm, beat me in the head, hit me anywhere. I did not dare to complain to the authorities, as he said I would go blind in three days if he stopped treating my eyes.

"The officials saw what was going on, but they did not hinder him. One time, however, they took him out and asked him in my hearing why he beat me up like that.

" 'I hate that man!' he answered. 'I hate imperialists!'

" 'But,' they said, 'you are not allowed to beat him up like that.'

"He promised to do so no more, yet continued to beat me as usual—and they did nothing about it. Once he grabbed me by the throat with his iron claws and strangled me. I could not breathe. I could not struggle free. I was finished—almost—when he picked me up and threw me on to my bed. All this he did to prove to the authorities that he was 101 per cent Communist.

"One day I was called out and an officer told me, 'You've got to get clear on one thing. You must either choose

Communism or you must choose America. There is no third way.' After this followed a lengthy lecture for me to absorb.

"During my confinement the Communists kept arguing with me about religion. 'You don't know,' they said, 'whether you believe or not. You were taught by your mother to pray. You were taught religion in school. Through your religion you get your salary. Sweep all these away—then will you believe?'

"On one occasion as I was kneeling in prayer, a Communist officer in charge of the guards saw me. He took up a handful of sand and threw it on me through the window.

"Under this pressure I got to the point where I practically lost my faith. For three months I stopped praying. In the end I gave up everything, but I could not give up Jesus and the Cross. I could not forget God in my heart. He graciously granted me a vision of the cross of Christ and of my sins forgiven, and my faith was revived.

"I want to write a book, but not just now. I need to wait a while so I can get a better perspective. My mind, at present, is still muddled from my experiences."

woman with a bald spot

I T WAS an elaborate Chinese feast introduced with appetizers spread on the table—pickled garlic, watermelon seeds, peanuts, pealed orange sections, sweets. A bewildering succession of dishes followed, course upon course—cauliflower, sweetsour pork, beef fried in fat, steamed buns, eels, fish fried to a crisp, shrimp with peas, whole chicken in soup and other foods prepared in southern style.

The weather was hot that August day in 1952 and our Chinese fans were in constant motion. Attending the feast were some of our Cantonese friends, professors from a prominent school in Hong Kong together with some of their acquaintances recently escaped from Red China. Though the latter lived only twenty miles from the border, they had had a rugged time getting out. I became interested in knowing how they had fared. There were especially two of them with whom I visited through an interpreter. Living in different villages they had made their escape independently within a few weeks of each other. One was a man, the other a woman—but I noticed

288

especially the woman because she had a peculiar bald spot on her head which her hair-do failed to cover. However, let us first hear what the man had to say about his experiences.

He was a husky-looking lad of twenty-two, a hard-working, straightforward peasant—one who would be considered an asset by any normal government, not a person to be shot! But the Red government of China was out to get him—and all those who fell into his class. He was a "rich farmer."

"I owned fourteen *mu* of land [two and one-third acres]," he related, "which we worked ourselves. For a time I had been a resident of Hong Kong where I received a modest education, returning to my home less than two years ago. We were a happy family until the Communists came. My father was a Christian and my grandparents before him, members of the Church in our village established by the Rhenish Mission. When the Communists came, they classified the pastor as a vagabond, turned him out and told him to get to work. They prohibited the people from supporting him, so he had to return to his home where he has been keeping bees for a living. Services were discontinued and the Communists used the church for a school and for a marriage bureau.

"When the Communists started their program they classified the peasants into many categories. At first they designated me as a well-to-do farmer. However, they are constantly reclassifying people and when before long they changed my status to that of a rich farmer, I knew that my position had become untenable. Even a farmer who owns little land but has lived frugally and saved some money is classified as a rich farmer and marked for liquidation, whereas a shiftless fellow who has squandered his means is awarded rank and authority.

"The Party workers organized the poor farmers and landless peasants into a Union or Farmers' Association which they used for accusing and judging the upper classes. Special privileges were doled out to individuals who were specially proficient at accusing others.

"To begin with the landlords were taxed 120 per cent of their crops and the poor farmers 80 per cent of theirs. Not only the former became desperate, but the latter also, as they couldn't live from the balance of their income. However, the Communists operate on the 'dog eat dog' principle. The bitter struggle for survival which is imposed upon the people brings out the depths of beastliness in every man. With only one door left open the poor peasants are forced to accuse their fellow farmers who have been more fortunate or industrious or clever than they, and to torture the rich in order to get their wealth to divide among themselves. This type of criminal behavior is their privilege and glory under the new regime. This being their only recourse, they use it to get out of their own predicament.

"The government was collecting and storing grain to send northward, extorting huge quotas from the wealthy and at the same time bringing about their ruin. If a person could pay one hundred piculs of rice they deliberately taxed him two hundred piculs. If he didn't pay within six days, they made him sign a confession written according to their dictation that he was against the laws and the system of Land Reform and that he was subject to be shot or otherwise punished. I myself was forced to sign such a confession.

"Having been reclassified as a 'rich farmer,' I was assessed six hundred piculs of rice. Besides that, the government slapped on back taxes from 1946—several years before they came into power! When I could pay only a part of the assessment, they tied my hands behind my back, strung me up to the rafters and beat me. This I suffered at their hands three different times, but still I could not pay the assessment. All the rich farmers and landlords suffered the same fate. When I continued unable to pay, they took my pregnant wife and beat her as well as the other members of my family, and forced me to sign a confession making me liable to the death penalty.

"It was heart-rending to leave my family, but we all knew it had to be done. The next time might mean my torture to death. During those six months twenty landlords and rich farmers in our village of 800 inhabitants had been executed. They were always tortured beforehand. Because of the tense situation a still larger number of people committed suicide. In a neighboring village less than three miles away, of 1,300 people about twenty were executed and eighty committed self-destruction. In one night alone there were ten suicides. Everywhere the conditions were the same.

"Since it was either to escape or die, I wagered on the possibility of getting away. As it was necessary to have a travel pass, I had to make one myself. I could not trust another soul to help me. Fortunately, I was able to write, so I made out on a slip of paper a statement giving me permission to go to Shumchun, the border town, 'to borrow grain in order to pay my taxes.' Then I cut a sweet potato in half and carved a seal with the name of the chairman of the Farmers' Association on it. Actually, it makes little difference whose name you use, because most of the Communist guards can't read. The Communists put more faith in these illiterates than in the intellectuals. Having completed the chop [seal], I pressed it on a red ink pad and stamped it on the bottom of the paper slip, making the latter an 'official' pass.

"Armed with this forgery, I disguised myself as a coolie and set out on my venture of life or death. I walked all the way from my home, avoiding the main roads and taking side paths. After I had gone for some time the path converged with a more traveled road where Communist guards were on duty. My first impulse was to turn aside and run, but it was too late. Such action would immediately give rise to suspicion. With a brazen front—but with my heart in my throat—I walked to the intersection and showed my pass to one of the guards. He was a boy of about eighteen and apparently illiterate. He let me by.

"Before long I was confronted by other guards whom I could not avoid. Though I had already experienced success, it was impossible to banish my nervousness; but I managed to cover it up with an attitude of unconcern—and once more it worked. When nearing Shumchun I went through my worst ordeal, as the inspectors examined the pass carefully, mumbled under their breath and handed it from one to the other, while I forced myself to remain calm and cool! Most of the guards and inspectors were young fellows between eighteen and twenty-five. Evidently reaching satisfaction, they waved me on. Having passed this check point I could see the village ahead but I knew that by all means I must avoid it or my luck might run out. The Communists in charge there would certainly be more suspicious and clever.

"As the day was waning I skirted the village and whiled away my time in the country until night cast its veil over the hills and fields. Then in the dark I hiked to some mountains which I figured were close to the border. The going was rough but I stumbled onward as this was the chance of a lifetime—only a few miles from Hong Kong and freedom! I kept my directions straight by watching the searchlights playing at the border. The closer I came, the more precarious my situation! Each time the beams of light shot out in my direction I fell to the ground. Each time they returned I inched my way forward. It was a nerve-racking experience, with death packed in each beam of light, but I received one final break when I stumbled on to the pathway made by smugglers and could use the hole which they had cut through the maze of barbed wire separating the British from the Chinese. Presently I was on Hong Kong soil—out of danger, back in freedom! Having been a resident here before, I easily found my way to friends and relatives—and to a new lease on life."

The lady with whom I talked—a lady of slight proportions—was dressed in simple garments made of the blue cloth used throughout China. She had the dignified bearing of one who had made good in life, one who had learned self-control and poise. She was trim and neat-looking. The bald spot on her head seemed out of place on such a personage. And, indeed, I learned that she was a woman of some renown! Widowed at twenty-three she had lived for ten years in purity of life without remarrying. For this type of widows the Chinese bestow great honors during life and are accustomed to raise monuments of glory after their death for the inspiration and admonishment of posterity.

This was her experience in the New China as told to me:

"My home is not far from here, only twenty miles on the other side of the border. Ten years ago my husband died, leaving about four acres of land for me and my son. By renting out the fields we have been able to get along —until the Communists came.

"According to their policy I was classified as a landlord and, besides taxes, was fined for having received rent since 1946. I was ordered to refund the whole amount. The total came to the utterly unreasonable sum of 2360 piculs of rice. I was only able to pay 80 piculs, having used up the rent money over the years. This gave the Communists the opportunity they were seeking of doing me to death. Through the poor farmers' militia they applied their regimen of torture until I despaired of life.

"My eleven-year-old son and I were tied, suspended and beaten half dead. When that failed to yield any funds, for a period of two months they kept me kneeling a large part of the time—now in the hot sun for a whole day, now for a stretch of two hours. At such times they reviled me, spat on me, picked out my hairs, took me by my braid and swung me in a circle until I could not kneel without falling. When I fainted they kicked me black and blue to make sure I was not pretending, then revived me for more torture.

"They set me in the middle of a yard and forced me to balance an eighty pound tree trunk on my left shoulder and hold a twelve pound brick above my head with my right hand. When I became so fatigued that I could not hold up my hand any longer, they subjected me to severe beatings. In the case of a lady friend of mine, the Communists rigged up steel pins so that when she became fatigued from holding weights aloft, her elbows came down on the sharp pins which pierced her flesh and stuck into the bone. It was fortunate that they did not think of this in punishing me.

"At times the Communists would make me stand on a stool in the ancestral hall while they fastened my hair to the beams overhead. Then they would suddenly remove the stool; with a jerk my braid would become taut and they would leave me hanging by my hair for an hour or more. This seemed to be a favorite pastime of theirs and they repeated the game often. Do you see this bald spot on my head? That came from having a piece of my scalp pulled out by the hair during one of these performances. When, suspended this way between heaven and earth, I fainted, they would throw urine and human dung into my face or burn me to see if I were pretending.

"I could endure the treatment no longer. My mind was ready to snap. If only they would kill me it would be easy —but there was no end to their tortures. I decided to take matters into my own hands. On being released after a series of tortures, I found a rope which I attached to the rafters with great difficulty because of my sore muscles and bruises—but determination did it. No one was around.

"Some minutes later my son chanced by. Horrified at what he saw, he raised the alarm among the neighbors and soon a swarm of people were around me. They cut down the rope, found that life was still in me, though I was unconscious, and proceeded to revive me.

"Later when we were alone, my son said, 'Mother! whatever you do, don't kill yourself!'

" 'Son,' I replied, 'I simply cannot bear this torture any longer.'

" 'Why don't you try to escape? Even if you die in the process, that is better than killing yourself!'

"With his encouragement I grasped at the desperate idea—not a new one, to be sure—but an impossible one.

"To leave my son behind to beg for a living and perhaps to experience the wrath of the Communists—how could I bear the thought! Yet it was his desire that I make the attempt—and there *was* the possibility that some day we might meet again!

"Next time the authorities came to torture me, I pretended that I was going to yield to their demands. Because I promised that if they gave me a chance I would go to some of my relatives and borrow the necessary funds, they released me and I got an opportunity to leave my village. Once out of the hands of the local militia I had greater freedom of action, but still danger lurked on every side.

"I slipped into the home of a friend, disguised myself as a poor peasant woman and started out in the direction of Hong Kong. I had traveled there before, so knew my bearings well. Not having a pass, I ran into trouble each time I came to a Communist check point, but I told the guards I was going to market. When they saw I was a poor peasant woman speaking the local dialect, their suspicions were allayed and they let me pass, except for one place where the lady comrades stripped and searched me.

"I thought my time had come—the impossible moment which I had dreaded! What if they should ask me about the black and blue bruises on my body? What explanation would be plausible enough to satisfy their probings? Miraculously, finding no money or secret articles on me, they asked no questions, simply let me pass—or was it a spark of humanity not yet stamped out by Communism which moved them to act in my favor? Whatever the reason, I was on my way again, still moving in the direction of freedom!

"Arriving at Shumchun I went around the village, took a good look at the lay of the mountains and waited for dark. From my vantage point I could even see the bus depot on the British side.

"I was all alone in the dead of night. I had impressed on my mind the exact course I was to take in my break for freedom—so many steps straight ahead—a swerve to the right—forward again—a lunge over or under or through the wires—a dash down the river bank and across the shallow waters—again a struggle over the barbed wire entanglements on the British side—then a jump into freedom!

Could I make it—with searchlights playing and patrols marching? This was my supreme moment.

"Though the night seemed like an eternity, yet it was passing. Two o'clock arrived and I had not dared to venture forth. The moment of decision was pressing upon me. Would the guards hear the pounding of my heart? There they were with their powerful flashlights. They had passed. Action must be squeezed into the space of a few minutes. Since it was now or never, I decided to move. That in itself calmed my nerves and renewed my strength. Without throwing caution to the winds, I worked along the pathway marked out in my mind—stealthily, efficiently. All came off as planned. I reached the river, waded across, started to climb over the barbed wire on the farther side, by which time reason was leaving me and I clawed frantically at the nasty entanglements. Nothing could stop me now. My clothes were torn in shreds; my hands and flesh were lacerated and bleeding—but I jumped on to free soil! As I lay there exhausted, I saw the flashlights on the other side piercing the night in search of me—but I was not there! Another refugee had escaped from the talons of Communism!

"On the main road to Hong Kong I lay and rested till morning. As the Communists had not discovered a dollar bill which I had sewed into my clothes, I was able to use it for buying a bus ticket into the city where my relatives received me, bought a new outfit for me to wear and gave me shelter.

"My son was right. Freedom *is* worth risking one's life for!"

in mao's terrestrial paradise

NOT only the Christians but also the pagans—not only the Americans but also all Westerners—not only the missionaries but still more the Chinese Christians —not only Protestants but also the Catholics have been deluged with the wrath of atheistic Communism. In fact, the Catholics suffered more widely at the hands of the new government in China than perhaps any other religious group. Of their five thousand foreign missionaries in China "over three thousand were subjected to arrest, trumped-up charges, kangaroo courts or fixed public 'trials by the people,' and then expelled" (*Mission Bulletin*, March, 1955, p. 184). Sixty of their missionaries died from the prison tortures or were executed, while the remaining nearly two thousand came out with minor tribulations. I have spoken with Catholic Fathers, some of whom evacuated from the districts where we had formerly worked, and their reports have depicted the same ugly persecution of the faithful as we have already noted.

At their headquarters in Hong Kong in the offices of the *Mission Bulletin*, each time a Catholic missionary expelled from China arrives, an account is taken of his experiences and—even more telling—a photographic record of his condition is kept, revealing the agony etched on his face, the fear burned into his eyes, the scars and deformities stamped upon his body. "Glib statements like 'there is no torture' in Communist China, do not carry much weight against such damning evidence."

In Peking, the headquarters of Mao Tse-tung and Chou En-lai's Communist Paradise—at the very time that Atlee, Bevan, et al were touring the country, singing praises to the Reds because they could see no flies in the market places—the innocent, thick, silent prison walls, which even Nehru's eyes could not penetrate, were hiding from view an essential feature of the Communist ideal and way of life, such as is revealed in the following story written by a Belgian missionary, Father Albert Sohier, in the 1955 March issue of *Mission Bulletin:*

"On July 25, 1951, I was arrested and put in jail in Peking. The prison interrogators started their work on me at ten o'clock that evening. One of them stated first, 'Of course you know why you were arrested.' My answer was, 'Either because there is some misunderstanding about my conduct or I am in prison for religious reasons.' The judge corrected me saying, 'The Communist program allows freedom of worship and therefore it is not a question of religion. But you have opposed the interests of the People's Government.'

"They questioned me that night on the date of my arrival and on my various activities in China. After the interrogation I was put in a cell with six Chinese prisoners. The cell chief said he was in prison for burying people alive. The prospects under such a man were not very bright. He rebuked me severely the next morning when I made the Sign of the Cross at meal time. A little later he advised me to be frank and confess everything during the interrogations. If I did so, he said, I would be rewarded with generous treatment and soon be released . . . .

"The second night in prison I was brought up again for interrogation. The subject of the questioning was, for the most part, my relations with Father De Jaegher, a Belgian priest whose anti-Communist activity was notorious. I admitted having known him personally after my arrival in Peking but not before. . . . The same questions were asked in a thousand different ways, but I always gave the same truthful answers. The magistrate lost patience and angrily threatened me because I was not frank and honest in my answers. After a long threatening lecture he suggested that I go back and carefully think over my crimes. But I was left alone for only two hours and then called back again for more questions. . . . I too became impatient and protested vehemently when they questioned my honesty. As punishment for the protest my hands were handcuffed behind my back and iron fetters weighing about twenty pounds were fixed to my ankles. With that they sent me back to my cell for more reflection.

"The cell chief, following instructions no doubt, decided that I should not be permitted to sleep. He appointed fellow prisoners to watch in turn and keep me awake. During the four weeks following I slept only sixteen hours altogether. . . .

"During the third night of interrogation the magistrate asked me again if I had known Father De Jaegher before coming to China. When I persisted truthfully that I had never seen him before coming to China, I was ordered to sit on the ground, stretch out my legs and lie back on my shackled wrists in a way that made the handcuffs dig into the wrists until they bled. The pain finally made me falsely confess that I had met him in Rome in 1939. As a matter of fact, Father De Jaegher had been in China continuously since 1931. I was asked to sign and thumb-print questions and answers after each period. When I protested that the answers were not correct, the inter-rogators promised to make rectifications at the next period which of course was never done.

"The interrogations went on night and day for three months. Two to six sessions were held every twenty-four hours, most of them at night. I was bold enough to ex-press great indignation at the methods of the Communists in forcing confessions of crime. But this seemed to make no impression. Lies had been circulated which said that I had a radio transmitter. They said a young lad at a public trial had confessed that I had directed him to write re-actionary slogans and to paste them on the city walls. I was accused also of sabotage, espionage, of having con-cealed guns and of preparing an army for insurrection.

"When I related these accusations to the prisoners in my cell, they said it was simply a matter of confessing all these crimes to clear the record and they urged me to confess. I half believed them. Then when the suf-fering, sleeplessness, and fatigue of repeated interrogation became unbearable, I accepted the proposal of cell mates and gave out a fantastic confession of the following crimes: (1) at the time of the Red army liberation of Peking I had concealed a radio sending set. Later I had set it up and collaborated with Tiao Hwa-jen in organ-izing an information net to cover the city of Peking. I said that in the summer of 1950 Tiao Hwa-jen had left for Hong Kong and that I had communicated with him through secret or code messages, assisted by a certain Sung Wei-ly. (2) I had organized a group of twenty or thirty children to paste anti-Government slogans on the city walls, to throw stones at the windows of schools, public buildings, and street lamps.

"The magistrate warned that I should reflect on the gravity of these confessed crimes and so I began to retract the lies with great relief. He then said, 'Weigh your words well, for if your first confession was false you have deceived the Government and that in itself deserves punishment.' Caught in a web of lies I felt discouraged and said, 'I have not been permitted to sleep for many days and I have been beaten repeatedly. My exhausted mind now wanders like a man dreaming and I can no longer distinguish between imagination and fact.'

"The cell chief had kept me from sleeping now for 110 successive days because he asserted that I needed the time to reflect on my crimes and make a good confession. I was forced to stand continuously day and night. When the prison doctor saw my swollen legs he gave orders to let me rest. The cell chief then permitted me to sit down but not to lie down except for brief periods, and they still kept me from any sleep. If I nooded they slapped or pinched me or jabbed chopsticks into my ribs. This treatment could have been the idea of the cell chief, but it was not stopped by the police who frequently looked into the cell.

"After each interrogation I had to repeat to the cell mates what had been asked and what I had answered. The cell mates under the direction of the chief, criticized my answers and then proceeded to 'help' me confess sincerely. All this pressure was according to the prison regulations, but it is supposed to have been stopped since 1953 except under official instructions for some cases. The help was frequently punctuated by punches on the nape of the neck and in the ribs or jabs in the stomach with stiffened fingers. Sometimes I was ordered to stand up with my arms overhead or was ordered to sit on my wrists which were held tightly in shackles. The cell chief repeatedly forbade me to moan or to cry out from pain under the threat of more severe beating. In spite of it all I was unable to keep from crying out many times. I am sure that the guard outside could hear me but he did nothing to stop it. Once I complained to the interrogating judge but this also did no good. It drew a severe reprimand for my attitude and refusal to confess. This convinced me that the authorities after all did approve of the torture and coercion directed by the cell chief, so there was nothing to do but put up with it.

"My strong protest against their imputation and absurd lies they wanted me to tell was considered rebellious. As a result they applied feet shackles which I wore for four weeks until my ankles bled and my legs became dangerously swollen. When I denied that I knew a certain fourteen-year-old boy or had told him to paste up anti-Communist slogans, he was brought in to confront and accuse me. I tried to remember if I had ever seen him but could not. Again the judge declared that I was not frank and honest. He then ordered me to sit on my handcuffed wrists until the torture made me admit that I had told this lad to write the slogans and that I had paid him to do so. They also brought another accuser who said he had sent secret messages to Hong Kong for me. His accusation did not hold water since I was in the hospital recovering from an operation on the day he mentioned. A few hours later the judge told me that although the date might not be correct the other details of his accusations were true. I denied the whole trumped-up case with firmness and self-assurance. As a result I was again submitted to the shackle torture.

"In the afternoon of August 23, 1951, a light chain,

without the twenty-pound weight this time, was fastened on my ankles. When the interrogation started that evening, only a few words were exchanged. The judge declared, 'I see that you cannot be frank and honest in your answers.' I replied, 'I want only to give honest and satisfactory answers; I hope I can find some way to answer properly.' The judge then added, 'I'll find a way for you.' He then gave an order to the guard who went out immediately. A few minutes later he returned with five other gendarmes who ordered me to squat on my haunches. Since I was weak and unable to stay in that position, they had me sit on a brick. Two men seized my knees and pulled them outward while the chains pressed into the ankle flesh; another held my feet down; the fourth tied a string to the wrists chained behind my back, then pulled my arms upward; the fifth gendarme applied a towel gag over my mouth to stifle the screams; the last one, the biggest, jumped on my back for ten to fifteen minutes at a time to force me to confess. This same torture was repeated seven times during that night. The last period of torment was at dawn August 24. Suddenly my head dropped and struck the floor between my feet. The back was broken and I was doubled over in agony. They left me lying on the floor. My legs were numb and powerless. I could not sit up even when braced against the wall. The torturers came back and tried to make me sit up but it was impossible.

"An hour later a man came to me who spoke French. As I lay helpless on the floor, he questioned me about Father De Jaegher's activities. When the pain allowed me to talk I slowly told him what I knew. The awful agony would let me speak no more, so I begged him to wait until some later time for further questioning. I felt that my mental and physical condition made me incapable of answering anything rationally, and besides I knew nothing more than I had already told.

"Under torture in the past I had made up several stories on the subject and I dreaded repeating them now since death seemed only a short way off.

"They decided to take me back to my cell. I was supposed to walk resting on the arms of two gendarmes but it proved impossible; my useless legs refused to respond so they dropped me to the floor. An hour later the prison doctor came to examine me. He found that the back was broken so I was finally loaded on a stretcher, carried back and left on the cement floor of the cell unable to get up. The unbearable suffering kept me twitching on the cement floor for relief. Ulcer sores soon formed in many places on my back. No medical help was given except to smear iodine on the sores. The cell chief forced me to sit up as exercise, resting on my arms propped against the wall. Since I could not bear this position for more than a few minutes I was showered with insults from the cell chief. After some weeks the guard ordered the cell mates to place me on a board bed. Another fifteen days went by. Three large festering wounds had now formed; one was at the base of my spine, the other two on the hips. When the stench got so bad that the prisoners complained, the doctor made up his mind to do something about it. Bandages were now applied to the ankles, wrists, knees, and elbows, and renewed regularly. The back sores were dressed daily and shots of penicillin were also given.

"For many months I had to lie on my stomach with my toes pressing into the boards. My toes and ankles were gradually being twisted out of shape. The doctor took note of it and ordered the cell chief to keep a bundle of clothes under my shins so as to let the feet hang free. But the cell chief refused to carry out the instructions after his departure. I dared not complain, for complaint would only bring me more torture. As a result of lying in this position for the greater part of the year, one of my ankles is still badly twisted and the big toe of each foot is bent under the other toes. A partial paralysis and pain still continues to be felt in the toes and feet, but this is probably an effect of the broken spine.

"The cell chief decided he was going to cure me, and he and the fellow prisoners started shaking my legs to give them exercise. Their intentions may have been good, but their handling was so rough that I could not refrain from screaming. The warden heard the noise, came to our cell, and personally forbade them to continue their 'help.' Communism does not leave its followers much room for charity. Many times I had to go full days without a drink of water since the cell mates would not take the trouble to bring me a drink.

"On November 21, two months after my back had been broken, the judge came to my cell and said, 'The confessions you have written up to now are useless. You have exaggerated many facts and you have omitted others. Hence nobody can make anything out of them. You are to start from the beginning and write another confession and you must make it sincere and honest this time.'

"They moved me to another cell. Since I could not write I was told to dictate my confession. The cell chief who was to take it down said, 'You must revoke everything which was incorrect in your former confession.' I began by saying that I was hereby contradicting three main points that I confessed before—'I have no radio sending set; I have had no connection with Tiao Hwa-jen or any other spy-net; I did not direct any children to sabotage and did not organize them or any one else for that purpose.' The surprised cell chief put down his pen and said, 'I see that you are not yet prepared to be honest. We shall write a confession when you are better disposed.'

"Although the punishment was less brutal than in the first cell, I was still subjected to 'help' stunts by cell mates to make my confession properly. They struck my biceps, slid chopsticks between my fingers and squeezed them, twisted my ears until they tore and bled, and jabbed chopsticks into my neck just under the jawbone. I was completely helpless against it all since the broken back would not allow me to move.

Several times I was severely beaten because I was noticed praying. Although the Government professes freedom of religion, the facts do not bear this out. The only way I could pray was in secret and unnoticed. . . . But a man under the conditions that I was under could not pray very much.

"On the twenty-fifth of July, the first anniversary of my arrest, the judge came in to my cell and asked, 'What do the cell mates think of you?' I answered, 'They are evidently not pleased because they say I have made little progress toward making a good confession of crimes. They are also displeased because I have dysentery most of the time, cannot take care of myself, and dirty the cell.' He replied, 'Who else makes such a mess? It is not a man who dirties his clothes and his bedding. It is an ass. Your whole conduct is that of an ass.' And after ten more minutes of continued insults he concluded, 'After a full year it is now high time that you clear your conscience and confess your crimes properly.'

"For several days after that the acting cell chief beat and tortured me thoroughly. He was sent to another cell after severe criticism for his excesses. About the first of August, 1952, all my cell mates were changed and after that I suffered no more physical torture. But I was still the object of jibes, painful criticism, and insults. . . .

"It was a year now since my back had been broken and I thought I might be able to use my legs again. I started to stand on them for a few moments resting against the wall or a small table. Some weeks later I could even take a few steps from the wall to the bed. By November, after three months' exercise and trial, I could walk as far as the toilet but with difficulty. The officials thought I was well enough to start writing again so they pressed me to write confessions about all the people I had known in China and they told me I should also write all my own personal activities. I made up my mind to write fully all the details of my deeds and actions since coming to China whether they seemed criminal or not. First I submitted an outline and then I wrote little by little, day by day, handing in the finished document a month later in December.

"Now that I was able to walk a bit, they started a series of weekly or bi-weekly interrogations in January, 1953. I retracted the former declarations about having a radio sending set and about directing children's sabotage. The cell chief still urged me with threats to admit these false accusations again but this time I refused. When April came around I was required to write whatever I knew about the Legion of Mary members. When that was finished I was told to do the same about all the priests, Brothers, and nuns of the Peking Archdiocese. The dictated material was written by a scribe but many suggestions and interpolations were written into it, suggested by fellow prisoners. They no longer used violent methods but my terror experience of the past prevented me from objecting. In July, I was again taken daily for questioning by another judge. Everything I said was written down. And then I was asked to sign. . . .

"In May, 1954, I was called into the office of a Government official whom I had never met. First he asked about my physical condition. Then he produced the general confession which I had written under four points in 1953, saying, 'You are going to rewrite this but leave out the lengthy passages. . . .' Immediately I went back to my cell to start writing the new French text, which was finished the next morning. . . . In the evening I was brought to another office to make a Chinese translation with the assistance of an interpreter. We worked through the night and the next day, when the work was finished rather late. I was then brought before the interrogator who studied the text. He ordered me to make many changes in the French text to correspond with the Chinese translation he had made. The changes distorted many of the facts and added guilt in more damning terms. Though it was supposed to be my own confession, the finished product was far from it.

"When this task was finished, they gave me a short recess and then I was led into a large hall. On the desk was a microphone wired to a recording machine on a side table. The agent who had forced me to write the changes into the text now ordered me to sit down at the desk and read clearly. He was standing with a secretary (who knew French) close by, in order to watch me read every word. When the recording was over they took a picture of me reading the text into the microphone. I don't know whether or not the confession was broadcast over the radio, but I presume it was.

"I'll skip the intervening episodes down to November 4, 1954, when I was once again brought before an interrogator. The interrogating judge asked me, 'What do you think of your crimes?' In substance I gave him just about the same views that were expressed in my recorded confession. It was useless to say anything else although I knew many of the statements were untrue. One gives up protesting when it does no good. Thirty months of Communist prison ordeal had taught me that much.

"During the conversation the judge said to me, 'You must realize that the gravity of your crimes deserves at least a ten year sentence in prison. Concerning your relations with De Jaegher it is quite possible that as a newcomer to China you did not realize exactly what you were doing. But you have certainly helped De Jaegher who is an enemy of the Chinese people.' On November 5, 1954, at 9:30 in the forenoon the judge did notify me that a decision had been made to expel me instead of sentencing me to a long prison term. . . .

"And so after almost three and a half years in prison they had given me a sentence. I was asked if I had anything to say about the verdict. Any words were useless now so I answered, 'Nothing to say.' Then I was led to an automobile and immediately taken to the railroad station at T'ien Men (Heaven's Gate). It had a special meaning for one just released from Hell, so to speak. Escorted by two gendarmes I reached Tientsin about midnight and was taken to the prison of the fifth police division. The following afternoon I was led through the Customs to the steamer *Hupeh* to leave China 'forever' with much grief in my heart.

"This brief account of the long years in prison was written during my first week of freedom, as the ship sailed from Tientsin to Hong Kong. No 'help' or torture was applied to make this 'frank and honest.' I am not a writer and can only be simple, frank and honest and, I hope, objective—as my friends, the Communists, ordered. They are my friends, fellow creatures created by God and I bear them no malice, though they call me an enemy. . . .

"My account shows how weak and useless I was, when I should have been a hero or perhaps a martyr. . . . I am really guilty of many sins, but not the ones the Communists accused me of. . . . The perjury, lies, and cowardly acts as a Communist prisoner weigh heavily on me. I hope that the world will understand and that God will forgive His poor servant. Under torture 'the spirit is willing, but the flesh is weak.'"

cross versus hammer and sickle

Thou hast given a banner to them that fear thee, That it may be displayed because of the truth. PSALM 60:4

In the name of our God we will set up our banners. PSALM 20:5

THERE is a titanic struggle going on in the world today, a mortal combat between the forces of light and darkness, liberty and slavery, truth and falsehood, love and hatred, Christianity and Communism—the banner of the Cross and the ensign of the Hammer and Sickle. The battle line is drawn, and whether we realize it or not, it is a fight to the finish. Not to accept the challenge of Communism is to go down to ignominious defeat. There is no middle way. There is no backing out.

Communism's plan of world conquest is, without doubt, to subvert and gain control of individual countries one by one without a world war, if possible, until whole continents fall into its grasp and the United States, the main bulwark of freedom, is isolated. Russia is willing to wait a generation or two for this to happen—and then, surrounded, America will fall into her lap like an overripe apple.

We can see the broad outlines of World Communism's strategy—the conquest of Formosa, which would shake and demoralize the neighboring areas; then the gradual take-over of Indonesia, Malaya, Thailand, Burma and also India (or perhaps the process may be reversed); the subversion of Japan through trade necessity and population pressure, and the overrunning of South Korea; the overturning of Africa whose condition of race hatred and poverty offers an open opportunity for Red activity (I was told by a prominent missionary on the continent, the Reverend Gustav O. R. Reusch, S.T.D., D.D., who had originally fled from Russia, that in Ethiopia, which he visited, there were three hundred Russian agents who had entered under the guise of a medical mission. How is the Christian Church matching that situation with foreign missionaries? Another worker from Central Africa reported that Communists were distributing pamphlets leading off with Bible passages to trap young Christians); the fishing in troubled waters of the Near East; the bullying of Europe into submission and the infiltration of South America. In a special dispatch from Washington of January 22, 1956, we are told that in Prague, Czechoslovakia, Russia is training "1,000 Latin Americans as Communist agents." This is not a matter to sneeze at. Such procedure was the first step in the fall of China. In the path of this world program, blocking the way, lies the United States, chief defender of the free world.

And do people think that this nation can escape feeling the pressure of the hidden hand of Communism? Or that the danger is not so great as some of us try to make out?

Let us not forget how the supersecret of the atom bomb was stolen from us or how the Reds got into the high councils of our State. Their agents and fellow travelers— I have met some of them—are working overtime infiltrating our institutions of learning (not to mention our social structure) and seducing our youth and intellectuals into their way of thinking. Thank God that many in our country are awake to the danger; but as long as so surprisingly many still continue blind, the danger remains.

In the Far East the pressure is on to an alarming degree. The great Red Dragon—the creation of the Hammer and Sickle—is breathing fire down the back of Southeast Asia. In the same way that Mao Tse-tung conquered China, he is now trying to infiltrate the countries of Southeast Asia with his secret agents. Thousands of persons from these regions are being trained in China for subversive activities in their respective countries. Moreover, Mao Tse-tung has a made-to-order potential fifth column in the millions of overseas Chinese scattered throughout the islands and peninsulas of that vast area. He is making use of the opportunity by infiltrating the schools and the results may be seen from the thousands of Chinese youth who flock through Hong Kong each year on their way to Communist China for intensive indoctrination and training.

How may this onward march of Communism be stayed? Military might and preparedness alone can never overcome it. An idea cannot be slain by the sword. A spiritual foe must be met with spiritual weapons. When that foe takes to material weapons a material defense is required by the nations. But primarily the battle will be won on other fields.

First of all we must know our enemy. That victim who does not understand his peril is in the gravest danger. If the free nations or Democracy or the Christian Church do not comprehend the nature of Communism their situation becomes desperate. A most disturbing factor in this country is the great number of intellectuals and liberals who have only a hazy idea about Communism and are out in front in wanting to co-operate with it or to compromise. Many Church people fall into this group.

From a study of the development of Communism in China and of the case histories cited one can get a glimpse of the *spirit* of Communism. These cases are merely a sampling of happenings from all over China, a little drop from a large pool of facts. There are literally millions of cases which will never become known to the world—some because they are shrouded in Sheol and others because there is no one to pass them on. The recording of these facts is not an attempt at sensationalism; it is Communism and its methods which are sensational. These facts have not made pleasant reading—but consider how much more unpleasant the facts have been for those who have had to experience them! By facing these facts of the Twentieth Century, we shall learn to know the nature of our enemy and beware lest some day these very facts overtake us and become our own experience.

As a nation we must not weaken in our stand against the recognition of Communist China and her admittance into the United Nations. Whatever the pressure may be from the outside we need to stand on principle and not follow a course of expediency. Communist China is an outlaw, an international gangster that has defied the United Nations and gotten by with it—and now many quarters are proposing that we embrace this outlaw and give him a respectable seat among the mighty! Recognizing that the charter of the United Nations, noble as it may be, is more or less a series of empty pronouncements—with Russia, a charter member, ruling with an iron hand over satellite nations and her economy being geared to the exploitation of from twelve to sixteen million slave laborers (most of them political prisoners)—we ought not to add to the confusion by admitting another bandit to the assembly.

Even certain Christian groups have strayed so far from the principles of Christ that they seek fellowship and representation from the puppet Church of false prophets, the hands of whose leaders are stained with the blood of evangelical martyrs! They do not recognize that the real Church is the persecuted Church—the underground Church—not the compromised Church which believes in the "Gospel according to St. Marx" and goes forward under the leadership of Mao Tse-tung.

Some people say they love freedom—and yet they do all they can to bring another slave state into the United Nations so the voice of free nations may be diminished! Some people say they love justice—yet they strive to bring into the United Nations a bandit nation which has been branded for aggression against the Free World yet has never repented but, on the contrary, has railed upon its victims as being the aggressors!

In our national economy we would not think of such a thing! Would any of our city administrations ever negotiate with a vicious murderer and kidnaper—Public Enemy No. 2—to join its councils? Do not say that the villain is a brilliant man, that he treats his wife with respect and loves to play with his children, that he attends social functions and enjoys reading. Do not even mention that he gives sizeable sums of money to public projects. The one-sided fact that he has killed half a dozen policemen and terrorizes society in order to support his family and social activities is sufficient to condemn him in the eyes of all right-thinking people.

Is time expected to heal all wounds? Let enough time elapse until the crimes are forgotten; then admit the unregenerate outlaw! In our country the FBI will not forget the crimes of gangsters even after fifty or sixty years, but in the international field we are expected to forget crimson sins against humanity and to embrace the murderers in our arms. It is a common axiom that it is harder to reform a suitor after he is married than before.

The Free Nations of the world ought to stand united. The saying is trite that if we don't hang together we shall he hanged separately. Were there unity here, Communism could make no further headway; but there is no unity, and for that reason as many as can should work together in harmony and understanding, determined to prevent wedges from being driven in between by the enemy.

We need to recognize that Communism is not apt to change its objective of world conquest in the foreseeable future. This concept of universal domination is basic to its philosophy of history. How can Communists give it up? Only through world conquest can they bring in their Utopia, and this Utopia is the basis of their religion and fanatical zeal. Without it their whole system is apt to collapse. To give it up would be for International Communism to commit suicide.

Speaking before the Communist Party Congress in February, 1956, Krushchev boasted that Communism could conquer the world without war. Earlier he had said: "We are in favor of a relaxation of tension, but if anybody thinks that for this reason we shall forget about Marx, Engels and Lenin, he is mistaken. This will happen when shrimps learn to whistle."

We must not be so naive as to believe periodically that the Kremlin's reformation is around the corner. Can the leopard change his spots? When frustrated, Communists may slow up for a while, put on a false front of peace, or turn their course on a detour—but *their primary goal they will not give up*. They will scheme and plot and carry on until they think they can blot out the opposition, even if half the world must perish in the process. Lenin said: "It does not matter if three-fourths of the world is killed off—just so the remaining one-fourth is Communist."

Dimitry Z. Manuilsky, Presiding Officer of the United Nations Security Council in 1949, said in a speech some years ago at the Lenin School of Political Warfare:

"War to the hilt between Communism and Capitalism is inevitable. Today, of course, we are not strong enough to attack. Our time will come in twenty or thirty years. To win, we shall need the element of surprise. The Bourgeoisie will have to be put to sleep, so we shall begin by launching the most spectacular peace movement on record. There will be electrifying overtures and unheard-of concessions. The Capitalist countries, stupid and decadent, will rejoice to co-operate in their own destruction. They will leap at another chance to be friends. As soon as their guard is down, we shall smash them with our clenched fists."

Eternal vigilance is the price of liberty. We must not be deceived by a system which preys upon the good faith of its victims. Since our recognition of Russia she has brazenly violated at least forty solemnly signed agreements. Deeds, not words or promises, will constitute the proof of a change. No change is genuine which does not embrace *a lifting of the iron curtain, the forsaking of vicious, lying propaganda, the abandoning of subversive activities in foreign countries and a willingness to negotiate honestly for atomic energy control and general disarmament*. Meanwhile, through vigilance and strength the free nations can make it unprofitable for the Kremlin to indulge in swallowing new territories by force and can perhaps cast doubt in her mind as to the value of ruling over an atomic rubbish heap, should she contemplate provoking another world war.

Faced with a vigorous, aggressive, politico-religious movement like Communism, we need to re-examine our own stand, our own faith, our own convictions. Are we willing to pay the price for continued freedom? Are we losing the spirit which gave birth to our republic—"give me liberty or give me death"? Are we willing to discipline ourselves with regard to lesser freedoms in order that we may preserve the possibility of freedom at all? Many do not understand the nature of Communist infiltration and the infinite care needed in rooting it out. These people would prefer to keep intact their personal inviolability even if it should mean the crashing of Liberty above their heads. These Fifth Amendment Americans are like people who would refuse to submit to an examination to find out if they might be carriers of the black plague. No red-blooded American should be afraid to stand up and tell the world that he has no taint of Communism! In World War II we curtailed many of our liberties in order to preserve *Liberty*. In some ways our present cold war is even more dangerous than a shooting conflict.

The long arm of Communism stretches far beyond its own borders. It reaches out across the oceans to foreign lands. I have been asked a number of times: "Do you dare to write a book against Communism?" If those who know about Communism don't dare to expose it, then who is going to do it? The time to speak up is while you are still free—whatever retribution the future may have in store. Else how are we to preserve our freedoms?

We must not fear. Two of Communism's most powerful weapons are fear and ignorance—fear of the enemy and ignorance of the true situation. Why should free people be cowed by the threats of Communism? Fear is at the root of appeasement and fear and blindness at the root of neutralism. Both evils need to be swept away by a love of the truth. I believe that we should not be fearful about proclaiming the facts. As President Eisenhower has aptly said: "When you are fighting something evil, you are not going to beat it by keeping quiet about it."

As Christian workers we should not hesitate to oppose Communism openly—in the pulpit and out of it. We need to watch and pray and work that this diabolical teaching may make no headway in our own country. We need make no apologies for our stand. Some Christians have feared to preach against Communism supposing the latter to be a political issue on which preachers and missionaries had better not touch—at least in public. My observation has been that the farther one has strayed from the evangelical standpoint the more tolerant he may become toward the Communist system. Christian leaders, like the prophets of old, need to sound the alarm, warning people of the threatening catastrophe. "America, repent or perish!" Much has been made of the dangers of the atom and hydrogen bombs, but the threat of Communism is far greater. What would it profit the world to be saved from the "atom" but to lose its soul? There would be little to live for with all of life's true values destroyed by Communism!

Communism is not a political system; it is much more. It is a *religion* spawned in hell. It collides head-on with the Christian Faith. It is the system and spirit of the Anti-Christ. Nothing could be worse than that which denies God and works on an anti-Christ basis!

On almost all fundamental issues we find that Communism and Christianity are diametrically opposed. Christianity is a spiritual system, Communism the acme of materialism; Christianity is founded upon faith in God, Communism upon atheism; Christianity holds the Will of God to be supreme, Communism the will of the Party; Christianity exalts love, Communism hate; Christianity lives by Truth, Communism by falsehood; Christianity brings freedom, Communism bondage; Christianity relies upon persuasion, Communism upon force; Christianity proclaims the individual's worth, Communism his insignificance; Christianity holds to the sacredness of human life, Communism preaches murder; Christianity teaches the brotherhood of man, Communism vicious class distinction; Christianity builds a wall about the family, Communism tears it down; Christianity nurtures democracy, Communism totalitarianism and dictatorship; Christianity fosters human decency and honor, Communism despises both; Christianity looks forward to life eternal, Communism to death in the grave.

The Communists have recognized Christianity as their mortal enemy—why should we not recognize them as ours? According to Harold E. Fey of *The Christian Century*, the Communists killed "nearly five hundred pastors and priests" alone in the small country of Korea because they considered Christianity incompatible with their materialistic creed. They are out to annihilate the true Church—and if we keep still, we will be helping to lull people to sleep so the Communists can the sooner gain control.

The Christian Church throughout the Free World, including the mission fields, should, while it is still in freedom, set itself squarely and publicly against this system which is the archenemy of Christ. We must not be bound by the paralyzing fear of lining up against Communism as it marches along, or of being liquidated under their hands should they gain control. Every Christian must determine *beforehand* to be willing to suffer rather than yield, to refuse to compromise or stifle one's conscience, to die rather than bow to the new Baal. In facing Communism we need the spirit of the early martyrs. Communists are willing to die for a counterfeit religion—why should we be unwilling to die for the real thing?

A half-hearted Christianity, a people without conviction, will never be able to withstand Communism; but a Church that is really on fire will never be stamped out by it. The blood of the martyrs is the seed of the Church. Christianity is stronger than Communism.

As a nation and as a Church we need to be more aware of the power of propaganda. Do we believe indeed that "the pen is mightier than the sword"? The Communists spend fifty times as much on propaganda as we do on getting out the truth. We are told that 90 per cent of what the Indonesians read about the outside world is Russian and Chinese propaganda. For the last decade or two the Communists have had the whole field to themselves; it is about time for the democracies to get out the truth to counteract the barrage of lies and perversions. People who hear falsehoods a thousand times believe them rather than the truth they hear but once.

The lengths to which the Communists will go to spread their story may be seen from a personal incident. In 1954 I paid $3.50 for a year's subscription to *People's China,* a semimonthly magazine in English, from Peking. For *air post alone* from Hong Kong (excluding the production cost of the magazine and postage from Peking to the British colony) the Communists put out Hk$175.00 or about US$30.00—almost ten times as much as I paid for the subscription! Their magazines have been found in the libraries of our Church schools—showing pictures of smil-

ing people and unprecedented progress! It is all intended
to soften us up to the superiority of the Communist
system.

Unless the democracies spend more effort in spreading
the truth and disseminating their side of the picture, their
battle for the hearts of men will be lost. We must also
show the people that we are interested in *them*—in their
freedom, equality and prosperity—in their willing partner-
ship. Instead of curtailing our appropriations for the Voice
of America and Information Services, as we have been
doing during critical periods in the past, we should mul-
tiply our efforts many times. The dread with which the
Soviet Union meets the possibility of having its people
exposed to the truth may be seen from the fact that she
uses more men just to jam the Western broadcasts than
we use in our entire world-wide radio operations!

Not only must the Free Nations meet lies with facts and
propaganda with "truth, the whole truth and nothing but
the truth," setting forth the actual conditions behind the
iron and bamboo curtains as well as explaining the life
and aspirations of free people, but above all we who are
Christians must proclaim the ultimate Truth—the Gospel
of Jesus Christ. In the areas still free we need to redouble
our missionary efforts and meet the forces of Satan head-
on, using our spiritual weapons.

As St. Paul says: "Put on God's complete armor so that
you can successfully resist all the devil's methods of attack. For our fight is not against any physical enemy: it is
against organizations and powers that are spiritual. We
are up against the unseen power that controls this dark
world, and spiritual agents from the very headquarters of
evil. For though we live in the world, the battle we are
fighting is on the spiritual level. The very weapons we
use are not those of human warfare but have divine power

for the destruction of strongholds. Our battle is to bring down every deceptive fantasy and every imposing defense that men erect against the true knowledge of God. We even fight to capture every thought until it acknowledges the authority of Christ."*

Finally, the Lord has given us a key to power which we use altogether too little. By prayer we can intercede for the suffering saints. By prayer we can plead for the conversion of the deluded souls in Communism's clutches. Though we hate the system, we must love and pity those who have fallen into Satan's net. By prayer we can rely on Him who can say to the Great Red Dragon: "Thus far and no farther!" Though it looks like

> "Truth forever on the scaffold,
> Wrong forever on the throne—
> Yet that scaffold sways the Future,
> And, behind the dim unknown,
> Standeth God within the shadow,
> Keeping watch above His own."**

By prayer we look for the triumph of Faith and Truth in the end.

----

*Eph. 6:11-12, II Cor. 10:3-5 (a combination of phrases from the Revised Standard Version of the Bible, copyright 1946 and 1952, and Phillips' *Letters to Young Churches,* copyright 1947, used by permission of The Macmillan Company.

**From *The Present Crisis* by James Russell Lowell.

bibliography

Books

Bell, Montague, H. T. and Woodhead, H. G. W., Editors, *The China Year Book 1919*, George Routledge & Sons (London)

Bosshardt, R. A., *The Restraining Hand*, Hodder and Stoughton (London, 1936)

Brandt, Schwartz and Fairbank, *A Documentary History of Chinese Communism*, Harvard University Press (Cambridge, Mass., 1952)

Chapman, H. Owen, *The Chinese Revolution 1926-27*, Constable & Co., Ltd. (London, 1928)

Ch'en Han-po, *Chin Er Pei P'ing* (Peiping Today), Freedom Press (Hong Kong, 1951)

Ch'en Han-po, *Wo Tzen Yang Tang Cho Mao Tse-Tung Ti T'e Wu* (How I Was a Spy for Mao Tse-tung), Freedom Press (Hong Kong, 1952)

Chiang Kai-shek, General and Madame, *General Chiang Kai-shek, The Account of the Fortnight in Sian*, Doubleday, Doran & Co., Inc. (Garden City, N. Y., 1937)

China Continuation Committee, Lobenstine, E. C., Editor, *The China Mission Year Book 1917*, The Christian Literature Society for China (Shanghai, 1917)

China Continuation Committee, Lobenstine, E. C., and Warnshuis, A. L., Editors, *The China Mission Year Book* (two volumes covering the years 1918 and 1919), Kwang Hsüeh Publishing House (Shanghai)

China Handbook Editorial Board, *China Handbook 1952-53*, China Publishing Co., (Taipei, Taiwan, 1952)

Crow, Carl, *China Takes Her Place*, Harper & Brothers (New York, 1944)

Communist Indoctrination Text Books in Chinese

Fischer, Louis, *The Soviets in World Affairs,* Jonathan Cape (London, 1930)

Fitzgerald, C. P., *Revolution in China,* The Cresset Press (London, 1952)

Forster, Lancelot, *The New Culture in China,* George Allen & Unwin, Ltd. (London, 1936)

Gamble, Sidney D., *Peking, a Social Survey,* George H. Doran Co. (New York, 1921)

Hu Shih, *The Chinese Renaissance,* The University of Chicago Press (Chicago, 1933)

Huang, Quentin K. Y., *Now I Can Tell,* Morehouse-Gorham Co. (New York, 1954)

Hughes, E. R., *The Invasion of China by the Western World,* The Macmillan Co. (New York, 1938)

International Relations Committee, *The Sino-Russian Crisis,* The International Relations Committee (Nanking, 1929)

Jaegher, Raymond J. de, and Kuhn, Irene Corbally, *The Enemy Within,* Doubleday & Co., Inc. (Garden City, N. Y., 1955)

King-Hall, Stephen, *The China of Today,* Leonard and Virginia Woolf (London, 1927)

Latourette, Kenneth Scott, *The Chinese, Their History and Culture,* The Macmillan Co. (New York, 1942)

Latourette, Kenneth Scott, *The Development of China,* Houghton Mifflin Co. (New York, 1928)

Latourette, Kenneth Scott, *A History of Christian Missions in China,* The Macmillan Co. (New York, 1929)

Lattimore, Owen and Eleanor, *The Making of Modern China,* W. W. Norton & Co., Inc. (New York, 1944)

Lin Yutang, *A History of the Press and Public Opinion in China,* The University of Chicago Press (Chicago, 1936)

Liu Shaw-tong, *Out of Red China,* Duell, Sloan and Pearce, Inc. (New York, 1953)

MacNair, Harley F., *China in Revolution,* The University of Chicago Press (Chicago, 1931)

MacNair, Harley F., *China's International Relations and Other Essays,* The Commercial Press (Shanghai, 1926)

Mac Nair, Harley F., *China's New Nationalism and Other Essays,* The Commercial Press (Shanghai, 1926)

Mao Tse-tung, *New Democracy,* Rapid Current Publishing Co. (Shanghai, 1949)

Mao Tse-tung, *On People's Democratic Dictatorship,* New China News Agency (Peiping, 1949)

Millard, Thomas F., *China Where It Is Today and Why,* Harcourt, Brace & Co. (New York, 1928)

Morse, Hosea B., and MacNair, Harley F., *Far Eastern International Relations*, Houghton Mifflin Co. (Boston and New York, 1931)

Nelson, Daniel, *The Apostle to the Chinese Communists*, Augsburg Publishing House (Minneapolis, 1935)

Nourse, Mary A., *The Four Hundred Million*, The Bobbs-Merrill Co. (New York, 1935)

Park, No Yong, *Making a New China*, The Stratford Co. (Boston, 1929)

Payne, Robert, *Mao Tse-tung*, Henry Schuman Inc. (New York, 1950)

Peake, Cyrus H., *Nationalism and Education in Modern China*, Columbia University Press (New York, 1932)

Pott, F. L. Hawks, *A Sketch of Chinese History*, Kelly and Walsh, Ltd. (Shanghai, 1936)

Quigley, Harold S., *Chinese Politics Today*, The University of Minnesota Press (Minneapolis, 1934)

Rawlinson, Frank, *The China Christian Year Book* (two volumes for years 1926 and 1928), The Christian Literature Society for China (Shanghai)

Richter, D. Julius, *Das Werden der christlichen Kirche in China*, C. Bertelsmawn (Gütersloh, Germany, 1928)

Schwartz, Benjamin I., *Chinese Communism and the Rise of Mao*, Harvard University Press (Cambridge, Mass., 1951)

Sharman, Lyon, *Sun Yat-sen His Life and Its Meaning*, The John Day Co. (New York, 1934)

Sheridan, W. J., *Watching the Chinese Curtain Fall*, Mitchell Printing & Publishing Co., Ltd. (Vancouver, 1954)

Smedley, Agnes, *Battle Hymn of China*, Alfred A. Knopf (New York, 1943)

Snow, Edgar, *Red Star Over China*, Random House (New York, 1938)

Stauffer, Milton T., *The Christian Occupation of China* (Shanghai, 1922)

Steiger, G. Nye, *A History of the Far East*, Ginn and Co. (New York, 1936)

Stuart, John Leighton, *Fifty Years in China*, Random House, Inc. (New York, 1954)

T'ang Leang-li, *The Foundations of Modern China*, Noel Douglas (London, 1928)

Tvedt, Kristofer N., *In Captivity*, The Lund Press, Inc. (Minneapolis, 1937)

Vinacke, Harold M., *A History of the Far East in Modern Times*, F. S. Crofts & Co. (New York, 1938)

Wan Yah-kang, *The Rise of Communism in China (1920-1950)*, The Chung Shu Publishing Co. (Hong Kong, 1952)

Wang, Tsi C., *The Youth Movement in China*, New Republic, Inc. (New York, 1927)

Woodhead, H. G. W., Editor, *The China Year Book* (eight volumes covering the years from 1921 to 1928), Tientsin Press (Tientsin)

Woodhead, H. G. W., *Occidental Interpretations of the Far Eastern Problem*, The University of Chicago Press (Chicago, 1926)

Wu Chao-kwang, *The International Aspect of the Missionary Movement in China*, The Johns Hopkins Press (London, 1930)

Yakhontoff, Victor A., *The Chinese Soviets*, Coward-McCann, Inc. (New York, 1934)

Yakhontoff, Victor A., *Russia and the Soviet Union in the Far East*, Coward-McCann (New York, 1931)

Periodicals and Papers

China Pictorial, a Communist publication in English, scattered issues (Peking)

China Reconstructs, a Communist publication in English, scattered issues (Peking)

Foreign Policy Association, *Foreign Policy Reports*, scattered issues (New York)

Foreign Policy Association, *News Bulletin*, vols. 5-7 (New York)

Foreign Policy Association, Research Department, *Foreign Policy Association Information Service*, scattered issues (New York)

Hongkong Tiger Standard, vols. 1-5, March 1, 1949 to Nov. 21, 1953 (Hong Kong)

Hsin Chiao Hui (The New Church), formerly *Hsin I Pao* (The Lutheran Weekly), now an organ of the puppet Church, scattered issues (Hankow)

Jen Min Er Pao (People's Daily), scattered issues (Peking)

Lee, Thomas I., *Circular Letters*, 74 issues, sent out from 1948 to 1953 (Hong Kong)

Lee, Thomas I., *Release*, Nos. 1-10, 1954 to 1956, regarding the Church situation in Red China (Minneapolis)

Letters from Chinese in the interior sent to Hong Kong

Mission Bulletin, published by Catholic missioners (Hong Kong)

North China Herald, the weekly edition of the *North China Daily News*, 22 vols. for 1917-20, 1922, 1924 and 1927 (Shanghai)

People's China, May, 1954 to April, 1955 (Peking)

Powell, J. B., Editor, *The China Weekly Review*, formerly *Millard's Review*, 40 vols., 1917 to 1927 (Shanghai)

Rawlinson, Frank, Editor, *Chinese Recorder*, 12 vols., 1917 to 1928 (Shanghai)

Ta Kung Pao, Communist daily in Hong Kong, scattered issues (Hong Kong)

T'ien Feng (Heavenly Breeze), a religious periodical of the puppet Church, scattered issues (Shanghai)

Time, 1942 to 1956 (New York)

U.S. News and World Report, scattered issues (Washington, D.C.)